Content

Acknowledgements

The author would like to thank all those heads, chairs of governing bodies and governors who kindly assisted the research project by giving up their valuable time to complete questionnaires and provide information. Particular thanks are due to the case study heads and governing bodies for allowing themselves to be interviewed and their deliberations observed. It is hoped that the report is seen as doing justice to both the range of their responses and the insights offered.

Thanks are also due to Lawrie Baker for assistance with the fieldwork, and Margaret Hitchcock for the coding of the questionnaire data. Within the NFER, Dr Judy Bradley and Lesley Saunders provided helpful comments on the report, Dr Wendy Keys had general oversight of the project, whilst Dr Ian Schagen offered guidance and assistance with the statistical analyses. Finally, I would like to thank Alison Bannerman who produced the report, Mary Hargreaves for preparing the manuscript for printing, Tim Wright for the cover design and Enver Carim for overseeing publication.

Executive Summary

Background

- This NFER research, funded by its Membership Programme and lasting 12 months, investigated the operation of school governing bodies since the *Education Reform Act, 1988*, with particular emphasis on notions of effectiveness.

- The project, undertaken in the autumn and spring terms, 1993-94, made use of both survey and case study research methods. Survey data were collected from a stratified sample of nearly 500 schools throughout England and Wales. Response rates were high from headteachers (63 per cent) but low from chairs of governors (35 per cent) and governors (36 per cent). In addition, case studies were undertaken in six LEAs.

The Main Findings

The Composition and Function of Governing Bodies (Chapter 2)

- One-third of the governing bodies surveyed had one or more governor vacancies.

- Seven out of ten governing bodies had not experienced difficulties in governor recruitment.

- Governing bodies experiencing recruitment difficulties were more likely to be found in inner-city schools and those with a high percentage of pupils entitled to free school meals.

- Difficulties in recruitment and retention were often attributed to governor workload.

- Just under eight out of ten heads had decided to become governors.

- Governing bodies typically met five times over the school year with most meetings lasting about three hours.

- Attendance levels were generally high.

- Governors were generally satisfied with the conduct of full governing body meetings.

- The vast majority of governing bodies made use of a committee structure.

- About 90 per cent of governors were committee members.
- Over a quarter of heads and nearly a fifth of chairs were responsible for taking notes or minutes at subcommittee meetings.
- Chairs attended six subcommittee meetings per annum and governors four, with each meeting lasting about two hours.
- The main topics discussed at length by governing bodies were: resources (LMS), building maintenance, annual parents' meetings, staff appointments and structures, the school development plan, the National Curriculum, school aims and objectives, and provision for pupils with special educational needs.
- In term time, chairs reported spending an average of nearly five hours per week on governing body matters compared with about three-and-a-half hours per week for headteachers and 40 minutes per week for governors.
- About seven out of ten governors were in paid employment, of which about two-thirds had taken time off work to fulfil governor duties.
- The average amount of time taken off work was nearly five hours per term. Fifty eight per cent of employed governors received payment for such absences.
- Over 80 per cent of working governors reported the attitude of their employer to requests for time off work to be generally supportive.
- More than half of respondents thought their governing body had the correct balance of skills and expertise, although more chairs than heads responded in the positive.
- Areas of expertise and experience most likely to be missing were identified as general managerial, financial and legal.
- Governing bodies of inner-city schools and those with a high proportion of children entitled to free school meals were significantly less likely to report having the correct balance of expertise.
- The commitment, involvement and willingness of governors were said to be as important as specific skills. It was noted that governing bodies could no longer afford to take on any 'passengers'.
- Although nearly seven out of ten chairs stated that discussions were always held with heads prior to full governing body meetings, this was reported to be the case by just under half of the headteachers.

- The vast majority of heads and chairs communicated regularly, on average about once a week.
- Respondents saw the main contribution of the governing body as providing support, encouragement and guidance.

The Operation of Governing Bodies (Chapter 3)

- About two-thirds of heads, one-half of chairs and one-third of governors felt that the extent of governing body responsibilities under recent legislation was too wide-ranging.
- Primary school governing body chairs and heads were more likely than their secondary colleagues to perceive the extent of responsibilities as being 'too much'.
- There was no significant difference in headteachers' responses to this issue and the number of years they had been in post.
- Personnel issues, finance and budgetary matters were commonly mentioned as areas in which governing bodies had too much responsibility, with headteachers also often making reference to the curriculum and policy-making.
- A significant proportion of respondents expressed the view that the amount of responsibility given to part-time volunteers was unreasonable and that a group of amateurs would most likely lack the requisite skills and expertise needed to cope with such wide-ranging responsibilities.
- Primary heads were more likely than their secondary school counterparts to refer to the unreasonable demands made on a group of part-time volunteers.
- When presented with a series of statements about the operation of the governing body (e.g. 'the governing body is challenging in its role as critical friend') headteachers were found generally to agree less strongly with the statements than were other respondents.
- Opportunities for governors to visit the school at work was mentioned most frequently as an area where heads felt **more** involvement of the governing body would be beneficial.
- Inner-city school heads often made reference to budgeting, finance and LMS as areas where greater involvement of the governing body would be welcomed.

- In several of the case studies the success of the governing body was said to centre around a small number of governors who took on many responsibilities. All reported having one or more inactive members.
- The case studies recognised the need to spread the workload and involve all members of the governing body. This was something that had to be 'worked at' and induction of new governors was important.
- The case study governing bodies demonstrated the importance of effective chairing, the role of subcommittees and clerking.

The Training and Support of Governors (Chapter 4)

- The vast majority of chairs (86 per cent) and governors (76 per cent) had received some formal training for their role as school governors. Eight out of ten had found it helpful.
- The amount of funds devolved to governing bodies for training and development (1993-94) was, on average, £450 for secondary and £300 for primary schools. These devolved funds were mainly spent on LEA-provided training and services.
- The main areas or topics where training had been received were LMS, roles and functions of governors, recruitment and selection, other personnel management issues and the national curriculum.
- Further training needs were said to include the above topics and the necessity to keep abreast of recent developments in education; for example, the governors' role in OFSTED inspections.
- Eight out of ten governing bodies currently made use of LEA-provided training.
- Very few governors claimed reimbursement for expenses incurred in attending training sessions or in carrying out their duties. Most were unaware whether such reimbursement could be made or whether the LEA provided childminding facilities during training sessions.
- A comparison with the findings of an NFER study carried out in 1990 showed that governors were now making greater use of the information and support services offered by LEAs.

- Newsletters, bulletins, handbooks and guidance notes were found to be especially valuable, though less use was made of videos, telephone hotlines and reference collections in libraries.

- The vast majority of respondents regarded the information provided for school governors by the LEA to be 'about right'. The role of the LEA was seen as providing advice, information, support, help and guidance to governing bodies, as and when requested.

- Data from the case study governing bodies demonstrated that the support and training provided by LEAs was generally viewed favourably. However, the overall take-up of training was patchy and some governors, especially the more experienced, did not always see the need for further training or updating.

- Governor training coordinators reported spending a growing proportion of their time on school-based training for the whole governing body, tailored specifically to their needs.

- Governing bodies, partly because of the OFSTED inspection process, were beginning to want to evaluate their effectiveness. Concern was expressed, however, that LEAs and governor training coordinators were unable to be more proactive in monitoring governing body effectiveness.

Who Becomes a Governor and Why? (Chapter 5)

- About one-half of governors but only 29 per cent of chairs of governing bodies were female.

- Sixty per cent of secondary school governors and 46 per cent of primary school governors were male.

- In primary school governing bodies two-thirds of chairs were male compared with 80 per cent in the secondary sector.

- Chairs of governing bodies tended to be older than other governors (a quarter were over 60, compared with 15 per cent of governors).

- Very few governors were from ethnic minority backgrounds.

- For chairs, the median length of service as **governors** was eight years and, as **chair of governors**, four years. Governors had generally served for a shorter period — a median of four years.

- One quarter of governors had been a governor at their current school for one year or less.

- Chair and governors were found to be well-educated and highly-qualified. (Nearly half of chairs and 44 per cent of governors held first or higher degrees.)

- About a quarter of chairs and governors were in possession of a teaching qualification.

- Representation of governors from skilled manual workers was extremely low (less than five per cent) and non-existent from semi-skilled or unskilled occupations.

- The main reasons for becoming a governor were reported as having a child (currently or formerly) at the school, having a sense of public service or being invited to serve.

- The most rewarding aspect of the role was in seeing the school improve and in developing good relations with staff and students.

- The most time-consuming tasks were dealing with paperwork and attending meetings of the full governing body and its committees.

- The areas or topics mentioned as the most difficult aspect of being a governor were personnel issues, particularly redundancy, incompetence proceedings and salary determination.

Effective Governing Bodies (Chapter 6)

- Respondents made reference to a large number of features of an effective governing body.

- The features of an effective governing body most commonly mentioned by chairs and governors included its members' willingness to share tasks and responsibilities as part of a working team; its commitment, along with a balance of skills, expertise and local community representation.

- Other important factors mentioned were the development of excellent working relations with the head and staff, knowledge of educational issues, involvement in key functions and being able to see the school 'at work'.

- Headteachers, significantly more so than governors or chairs, regarded the notion of a 'critical friend' to be an important feature of an effective governing body.

- Just over two-thirds of heads believed there were factors preventing the governing body from being as effective as it might be.

- The predominant factors in preventing greater effectiveness were said to be the shortage of time available to fulfil governing body responsibilities, and members' insufficient knowledge and understanding of educational matters.

- LEA advisers and inspectors were mentioned by chairs as an important source of advice and guidance to whom they would turn if they were experiencing problems with the head or the governing body.

- Although the view was expressed that the effectiveness of governing bodies was largely a matter of good fortune, the attitude of the head towards the governing body was seen as the crucial factor in determining its overall effectiveness.

The Case Studies (Chapter 7)

- Notions of effectiveness were explored further in the six case study governing bodies and LEAs. Views were also sought on model guidelines recently produced by AGIT.

- The relations between heads and governors, particularly chairs, were seen as crucial to the success of any partnership. The headteacher-chair relationship should not become 'cosy' and both parties should ensure the governing body plays a full part in decision-making.

- Notions of partnership and links with the school were identified in the case studies as key factors.

- An attempt to explore the specific role of governors in school improvement elicited a range of views. Many governors pointed instead to the crucial role of high-quality staff, others made reference to improvements in the learning environment and their role in the appointment of teachers.

- Heads and others spoke positively of the benefits of an effective governing body. This, it was said, had to be defined in terms of the difference it was able to make to the **quality of teaching and learning**.

Chapter 1
School Governance in the 1990s

Recent legislation has led to major changes in the management and governance of schools. As a result of the *Education (No. 2) Act 1986, the Education Reform Act 1988* and *the Education Act 1993,* there have been a number of far-reaching changes in the ways in which schools in England and Wales are governed. Important changes brought about by the new legislation include the reconstitution of school governing bodies (for example, so that elected parent governors form a larger proportion of each governing body) and the introduction of local management of schools (LMS). Fundamental changes have occurred in the way schools are financed, organised and operate. LMS delegates the overall control of school budgets to governing bodies who have been given responsibility for resource allocation and financial management. Most LEAs have now had LMS schemes (for some or all of their schools) in operation since April 1990. Many school governing bodies therefore have had several years' experience of managing their own budgets, whilst others have decided to opt out of LEA control altogether and become grant-maintained or 'self-managing'. School governing bodies have also had varying experiences of the related key functions of development planning, priority setting, policy making and monitoring. (Useful accounts of legislative changes affecting school governing bodies between 1944 and 1992 are found in Deem, 1993, and Tomlinson, 1993.)

Although there is a growing body of research into governorship and school governing bodies, it is still the case that little is known about the structure and functioning of governing bodies since the 1988 *Education Reform Act*. At the moment there is much confusion, uncertainty and concern about governing bodies and their roles and responsibilities. Despite the fact that there is a considerable amount of material produced for governors outlining how, in principle, they should fulfil their role, there is still little practical guidance on such matters as effective partnerships or successful models of operation which are based on the actual practices of governing bodies. Relationships between headteachers and governing bodies are said to vary considerably and there are no blueprints for partnership.

Partly as a result of such concerns and unanswered questions, the National Foundation for Educational Research (NFER) wished to build on two of its earlier studies of school governance – namely the case-study based research into effective governance (Baginsky, Baker and Cleave, 1991) and the questionnaire survey of school governing bodies (Keys & Fernandes, 1990) – to investigate how governors nationally were coping with their new responsibilities. How are governing bodies currently operating and what progress, if any, has been made? The research also wanted to clarify notions of effectiveness and to describe the effective governing body in operation. More specifically, the aims of the 12-month study, funded by the NFER's Membership Programme, were to:

- ascertain how effectively school governing bodies were fulfilling the responsibilities devolved to them as a result of the *Education Reform Act;*
- seek information on governors' own perceptions of their roles and responsibilities;
- identify the most important training needs of governors;
- seek information on ways in which LEAs and others could help school governing bodies to fulfil their roles more effectively.

The issues and areas addressed by the research were varied but the major ones included: the composition and function of governing bodies; governor workloads; arrangements and support for governors; the training governors had received to date and their perceived training needs for the future; perceptions of their statutory responsibilities and other aspects of their roles; and factors which prevented governors from fulfilling their roles effectively. Notions of effectiveness and the nature of effective governing bodies has been a central theme of the research and views on this issue sought from headteachers, governors and chairs of governing bodies.

The project employed both survey and case study research methods. It commenced with a series of exploratory interviews with relevant personnel to explore issues of current concern. The material collected from these interviews, complemented by an analysis of recent research studies, was used to develop three questionnaires. In fact, many of the questions were taken from the earlier NFER research on governors to enable some comparisons to be made. The questionnaires, after piloting, were sent to a sample of nearly 700 schools and were completed by headteachers, chairs of governing bodies and individual governors. The sample of schools involved approximately equal numbers of primary and secondary schools and was stratified according to such variables as the *type of school* (e.g. infants, first, junior, comprehensive 11-16, comprehensive 11-18), *area* (e.g. metropolitan, non-metropolitan) and *region* (e.g. North, South, Midlands and Wales). Each school was sent a set of three questionnaires, one each to be completed by the headteacher, the chair of governors and one other governor (to be selected according to the initial letter of their name). Although there was a considerable degree of overlap between the three questionnaires there were some questions that were asked of one category of governor but not others. (The headteacher was provided with stamps in order to forward the governors' questionnaires by post.) The survey was undertaken in the autumn term, 1993 and over **900** questionnaires were received from a total of **499** school governing bodies. About equal numbers of returns were obtained from primary and secondary school governing bodies but the response rates varied considerably from category to category. Only 118 schools (23 per cent) completed all three questionnaires, although sub-sample response rates were much higher. Sixty three per cent of headteachers (n = 428) provided returns, whilst a lower response was received from both chairs of governors (n = 233 or 35 per cent response) and governors (n = 241 or 36 per cent response). Further details of the sample of schools, headteachers, governors and chairs of governors are found in Appendix 1.

In the second phase of the research, a small number of school governing bodies were selected for more detailed study. Case study investigations were undertaken of six school governing bodies in six LEAs and involved a researcher visiting each school on several occasions. During this time interviews were conducted with heads, governors, teacher governors and LEA training coordinators, and documentation and other materials collected. Governing body meetings were also attended along with meetings of the various subcommittees. The fieldwork took place towards the end of the autumn term (1993) and throughout the spring term (1994). The six case study school governing bodies – three primary and three secondary (including one grant-maintained) schools – were selected by the researchers using a number of criteria but generally because their survey returns indicated varying levels of effectiveness. (Further details of the case study schools and their governing bodies are provided in Appendix 2.) The LEA governor training coordinators were not involved in the selection of the case study schools. Lengthy interviews with the

LEA governor training coordinators in the six LEAs where the case studies were located, explored notions of governing body effectiveness and details of the current provision of training and support offered to school governors in each authority were provided.

The results of the research – drawing on both the questionnaire surveys and the case studies – are presented in the following sequence. The next chapter attempts to provide a national picture of the composition and function of school governing bodies, whilst Chapter 3 focuses more specifically on how governing bodies operate, as perceived by governors and heads themselves. It also examines views on the extent of governing body responsibilities and the areas in which it was felt governing body involvement was beneficial to the school's work or decision-making. The following chapter deals with the key areas of training and support, particularly the services offered by LEAs. It also documents governors' views on their future training needs and discusses how helpful the information and support services had proved to be. Chapter 5 uses the survey data to build up a picture of the sort of people who become governors and the reasons for so doing, whilst the following chapter explores notions of governing body effectiveness and considers the main factors preventing them from being as effective as they might. Chapter 7 focuses more specifically on the case study element of the research. The final chapter then draws upon the research findings to suggest ways of moving forward so as to enhance the possibility of governing bodies operating in a more effective manner and to the benefit of all parties.

Chapter 2
The Composition and Functioning of School Governing Bodies

This chapter draws predominantly on the data from the questionnaire surveys of governors, headteachers and chairs of governors to provide a national picture of the composition and functioning of school governing bodies. It commences with an analysis of the current membership of governing bodies before giving details of the length and content of governing body meetings, both its full sessions and various subcommittees. It also gives consideration to the constitution of governing bodies, governor workload, communications between heads and chairs, and documents views on the main contribution of governors to their schools.

Governing body membership

Details of the membership of the school governing body (as at the beginning of the summer term 1993) were sought from the chair of governors, in particular the current number of vacancies for each type or category of governor. As specified in *School Governors: A Guide to the Law* (DFE, 1993) a school governing body is a mixture of elected, appointed and co-opted governors, and its combination is set out in the school's Instrument of Government. The precise membership of the governing body varies slightly depending upon such factors as the type of school (e.g. voluntary aided, grant-maintained) and the number of pupils registered. For example an LEA-maintained school with 300 - 599 pupils on roll should have a governing body with the following membership:

- four parent governors (elected)
- four governors appointed by the LEA
- two teacher governors (elected)
- five co-opted governors
- one headteacher.

The current membership of school governing bodies in the survey was found to range from a minimum of three members (in only one school) to a maximum of 22 members (in three schools). The average (or mean) number of governors per governing body was just over 14. A total of 232 governor vacancies were reported by the 233 chairs of governors completing the NFER questionnaire but only about one-third of school governing bodies (37 per cent) had **one or more** current vacancies on the governing body at the start of the summer term, 1993 (see Table 2.1). This figure compares favourably with the earlier NFER research which found that almost half of the chairs surveyed had at least one vacancy on the governing body (Keys & Fernandes, 1990). In the current survey, for the 86 governing bodies with vacancies the average number of vacancies was just under three, with LEA appointed, Foundation and co-opted governors being the categories most likely to be unfilled. The percentage of school governing bodies with vacancies for each type of governor is shown in Table 2.2. Data were available from only 17 grant-maintained schools but **all** reported having one or more First governor vacancies on their governing bodies.

Table 2.1: Total number of governor vacancies (at start of summer term 1993)

No. of vacancies*	% of sample
0	63
1	18
2	11
3	1
4 plus	7
	100
	(n=233)

(No. of governing bodies with vacancies = 86 or 37% of total sample. For governing bodies with vacancies, Mean = 2.7, Median = 2.0.*

NB The mean refers to the average number in a distribution, whilst the median is the mid-point or the middle number in a given distribution or sequence.)

Table 2.2: School governing body: vacancies and resignations

	%* of governing bodies with:	
Type of governor	**current vacancies**	**resignations over last year**
Head	1	6
LEA Appointed	13	32
Teacher	0.5	9
Parent	9	23
Co-opted	12	22
Minor Authority	4	17
Foundation	13	31
First (GM)	100**	18
	(n=233)	(n=233)

(The percentage figures have been calculated from the number of schools relevant to the category (e.g. voluntary aided) and not always from the total sample of schools.)*

*(** Data were only available from 17 GM schools of which all had one or more vacancies.)*

Headteacher governors

Headteachers are able to choose whether or not to become a member of the school governing body. In the current NFER survey just under eight out of ten heads reported that they had opted to become a governor of their school. This figure is slightly higher than in the earlier NFER survey which found about three-quarters of headteachers had opted to become governors of their schools (Keys & Fernandes, 1990) but about the same as reported in the most recent DFE survey (P.E. International, 1993). Those heads who had chosen not to become a member of the governing body (21 per cent) were asked to give their reasons for such a decision. The majority made reference to such notions as independence, impartiality, flexibility and detachment with others showing preference for an advisory, representative or consultative role that non-membership was said to bring. As one secondary head noted:

> *I would like to be viewed as a professional adviser to the school. I like to feel that the governors do feel part of the school and do not have the headteacher dominating decision making at governor level.*

Another commented:

> *I feel I can best represent the staff and pupils for the governors if I remain as their employee. As a non-governor I am fully involved in the*

preparation of all committee and full governing body meetings. I play a major part at the meetings and usually implement all decisions.

For other heads, not being a member of the governing body helped to clear the lines between managing and directing or made more apparent the separate role of governors and school managers, whilst emphasising the part that governing bodies played in the decision-making process. The earlier NFER survey reported similar views and noted that 'the main reason given by headteacher governors for becoming a member of the governing body was a desire to be involved in the decision-making process' (Keys & Fernandes, 1990).

All six of the case study heads had decided to become members of the governing body, although one admitted she did not at the time realise there was an option (for non-GM schools). The reasons given were similar and centred around notions of partnership, decision-making and ensuring that *'the voice of the school was heard as loudly as it ought'*. Two of the heads – one secondary and one primary – gave their reasons in some detail:

For many years I wasn't a governor. I thought the role of the headteacher was to be the executive arm of the governors but in the last few years there have been one or two issues where the voting was rather close, and I thought I ought to have a chance to put my vote in. My professional association doesn't give any particular advice. In general they advise headteachers to bear in mind they have to carry out the governors' wishes but they also stress that headteachers are responsible for the general management of the school. The exploration of boundaries is something my professional association is very interested in. There are some schools where the governors are trying to take too much of an interfering role, particularly in primary schools. The professional association advises headteachers to be very clear that they are managing the school and the governors are governing it.

Yes, I decided to be a governor because I chose to be all in together with the governors, in partnership. I did not want to be an adviser on the side. The reason heads do not want to be governors is because they want to distance themselves from decisions with which they do not agree. Also with the current pay policy, the governing body determines the head's salary and heads feel they should be apart from that. The professional associations list a number of factors that heads should consider when making the decision but do not advise 'yes' or 'no'.

Resignations and recruitment

Chairs of governing bodies were also asked to indicate the number of governors of all types who had resigned from the governing body during the three term period before the NFER survey (i.e. autumn 1992 to summer 1993). Just over 80 per cent reported having had one or more resignations over the specified time period with most being received from LEA appointed and Foundation governors (see Table 2.2). During the specified one year period each governing body had, on average, received resignations from 1.75 governors.

Nearly seven out of ten chairs (69 per cent) reported that their school governing body had **not** experienced difficulties in recruiting governors. (No significant differences were found to exist between primary and secondary schools in relation to governor recruitment.) Schools experiencing difficulties were more likely to be found in the inner cities and where a higher percentage of pupils were entitled to free school meals. The types or category of governor where vacancies were most difficult to fill were reported to be parent, co-opted and LEA-appointed governors. This finding compares with the earlier NFER survey which found the proportion of vacancies was highest for co-opted, LEA-appointed, Foundation and minor authority governors and lowest for teacher, headteacher and parent governors (Keys & Fernandes, 1990). According to the chairs of governing bodies in the current survey, the main reasons for difficulties in the recruitment of governors were because very few individuals were prepared to make such a commitment, there was a shortage of those willing or able to devote the time to governance or there was a dearth of suitable candidates for the vacancies. A chair of a primary school governing body, who noted that most responsibility seemed to fall on one or two governors the remainder being 'passengers', remarked that the role of the governor: *'needs to be more clearly explained, as does the amount of time required to be an effective governor. This information should be given to all those intending to stand for governship'*.

Indeed, in one of the case studies the LEA governor training coordinator described how governors were given a clear indication of what was expected of them from the outset. For a number of years they had run a potential governors evening:

> *It's been very successful. The meetings are always packed and there is enormous enthusiasm. We do hear that in certain areas it's quite*

difficult to recruit, and in certain villages the same people do all the jobs, as once they're coopted there's no-one else to do it. The new responsibilities of governing bodies far from putting off potential governors seems to have attracted more interest. Some people seem to want to put something back into the community by being a governor, whereas in former years, they might have stood for the local district council. It's possible to see something developing in the school.

(LEA: GTC.)

One secondary head explained in detail why he thought governors were becoming more difficult to recruit:

The dramatic increase in governors' responsibilities in recent years has not met with the approval of those to whom power has been given and has made recruitment more difficult. For example, our chairman, a governor with 20 years' experience and a supporter of this government, resigned as a governor four years ago when it became clear to her what extra responsibilities the government was giving to governors. At the time of parent-governor elections 12 months ago we received only one nomination for the three seats available. When a (co-opted) parent-governor resigned at the beginning of this term we did not receive a single volunteer or nomination.

The head added:

These points need to be set in context. We receive marvellous parental support (P.T.A committee of 15, parents volunteering to supervise the library, accompany visits, assist at functions, etc. over 90 per cent attendance at parents' evenings). Despite their commitment and support they emphatically do not want to undertake the duties expected of a governor in the 90s.

Another secondary head expressed the view that:

If present conditions remain and current trends are not reversed, either governors will typically be O.A.P's or those who are affluent/privileged, or those who seek the role for questionable purposes.

Others spoke of failed attempts to recruit governors from the world of business:

Despite strenuous efforts we have failed to attract closer links between the governing body and local business/industry. This, in my view, hinders our effectiveness.

In one of the case study governing bodies the head referred to a changing situation: in the past the number of candidates had exceeded places by 3:1. This was no longer the case with the number of vacancies and candidates about equal. In the head's view this was entirely due to workload and increased responsibilities. However, some heads referred to an abundance of volunteers:

Three of my parent governors are now 'out of time' – but all three have asked to be co-opted as First governors – even though we have no vacancies. The governing body have decided to co-opt them.

The head of this GM secondary school asked:

Is this not rather against the national trend i.e. governor shortages everywhere? We have too many!

Governing body meetings

By law the full governing body of every school must hold a meeting at least once in every term and may meet more often if necessary. Data from the 499 schools involved in the research indicate that the full governing body met, on average, just over five times during the academic year preceding the survey (autumn 1992 - summer 1993) with the number of meetings varying from a minimum of two per annum (found in one school) to a maximum of 25 (again found in only one school). The median number of meetings of full governing bodies during the specified three-term period was five (which is one meeting more than found in the earlier NFER survey).[1] The length of these full governing body meetings varied from between one hour to over six hours, with the most typical or average meeting being of three hours duration. Over 75 per cent of respondents reported that meetings of the full governing body lasted between two and three hours. (In the earlier NFER survey 90 per cent of governors indicated that meetings were of two to three hours duration.)

Both governors and chairs of governors were asked to indicate their levels of attendance at these full governing body meetings. As can be seen from Table 2.3 over eight out of ten chairs and two-thirds of governors reported a 100 per cent attendance level. (It should be recalled, however, that the response rates for these two categories of governor were low. It could be, of course, that those governors most likely to return completed

---

1 The *mean* refers to the average number in a distribution, whilst the *median* is the mid-point or the middle number in a given distribution or sequence.

questionnaires were also more predisposed to attending governing body meetings.) However, with a larger response rate Keys & Fernandes (1990) found nearly 70 per cent of governors had attended *all* the full meetings of the governing body, whilst the more recent P.E. survey states that governors missed hardly any meetings (one in every four years of the full governing body (P.E. International, 1993)). Headteachers were not asked about their attendance levels as it was assumed they would normally attend all meetings of the full governing body.

Committees and working groups

Information was also sought (from heads and chairs) on whether the governing body had divided up its work by the creation of formal (sub) committees and working groups. As can be seen from Table 2.4 just over 90 per cent of governing bodies made use of a committee structure with about half also setting up working groups of governors to investigate particular issues. About the same number of governing bodies had assigned issues to particular governors. (P.E. International found that 87 per cent of governing bodies had established sub-groups or committees to consider matters of finance, whilst Keys & Fernandes found just over three-quarters had divided up their work by establishing committees with, as in the current survey, about half setting up working groups assigning issues to particular governors.)

Table 2.3: Attendance at meetings of the full governing body

	%	
% attendance	Chairs	Governors
25 - 49	0.5	2
50-75	6	11
over 75	10.5	20
100	83	67
Total	100	100
	(n = 225)	(n = 237)

Table 2.4: Governing body subgroups and committees

	%*	
The governing body has:	**Heads**	**Chairs**
Created formal (sub) committees	92	93
Set up working groups to look at particular issues	49	51
Assigned issues to particular governors	50	52
Used other approaches	4	7
	(n = 366)	(n = 232)

*(*Percentages do not total 100 as more than one response could be made.)*

Although specific information of the various committees of the governing body was not sought as part of the national survey, such details were obtained from the case study school governing bodies. An outline of one has been reproduced in Appendix 3 and gives an indication of how a governing body has divided its responsibilities and workload. Within the law, governing bodies are able to delegate some of their functions and powers to the head, individual governors or committees. In some cases, committees make recommendation to the full governing body for it to make a decision, in others the committees are accorded delegated powers and report to the full meeting on decisions made. Some key decisions, however, cannot be delegated and must be taken by the full governing body (DFE, 1993).

Committee membership is determined by the governing body and the head has the right to attend all committee meetings. Table 2.5 shows the membership of the committees and working groups of the governing body as well as the percentage of heads, chairs and governors who were assigned particular responsibilities or took minutes and notes of the various meetings attended. It is interesting to note that whilst 90 per cent or more of respondents were members of committees, over a quarter of heads and nearly a fifth of chairs of governors stated that they were responsible for note or minute taking at the various meetings. Indeed, such a situation had occurred in one of the case studies where the head explained that as nobody had offered or volunteered she had to take the notes. Understandably this limited the contribution that she could make.

Table 2.5: Membership of various subgroups and committees

The governing body has:	%		
	Heads	**Chairs**	**Governors**
Member of any formal (sub)committee(s) of the governing body	90	90	93
Member of any working group(s) looking at particular issues	47	47	40
Assigned responsiblity for any particular issue(s)	41	36	39
Taking minutes/notes for meetings/subcommittees,etc.	26	18	21
(n =	354	228	229)

The average length of these committee/working group meetings was reported to be two hours. Chairs of governors attended, on average, nine meetings over the academic year (1992 - 1993), whilst the average number attended by governors, as might be expected, was lower (about six meetings per annum). Members of committees and/or working groups from six school governing bodies reported having attended no meetings over the specified time period, whilst one governor and one chair of governors stated they had attended over 50 committee meetings in the year! (For chairs the median was six meetings and for governors four meetings per annum.) The earlier NFER survey also found the length of meetings to be about two hours, whilst the median number of committee/working groups attended by governors who were members thereof was about three (Keys and Fernandes, 1990).

The conduct of meetings

Governors and chairs of governing bodies were also asked if they were generally satisfied with the conduct of the meetings of the full governing body and a very high percentage (89 per cent and 96 per cent respectively) responded positively. (The earlier NFER survey found a virtually identical figure – 88 per cent – of governors reporting satisfaction with the conduct of meetings.) Perhaps unsurprisingly, chairs of governors reported being satisfied with the conduct of meetings to a greater extent than did governors. In fact, these differences were statistically significant although no significant differences were identified when the data were analysed from those governing bodies where **both** chairs and governors had returned questionnaires (n = 128).[2] Positive comments on the meetings – such as that they were reasonably short, well-attended and with all governors contributing – were frequently offered. Where negative comments were raised – by both governors **and** chairs – they tended to focus on the fact that the meetings were too long, unstructured, dominated by a minority of governors familiar with procedures, unnecessarily discursive and inadequately prepared. The importance of such matters was also commented upon by the case study interviewees.

Main topics considered

In order to ascertain the main issues or areas considered by the governing body, either in full session or in formal/informal sub-groups, heads and chairs were presented with a list of topics and asked to indicate which had been discussed at length (i.e. for more than **one hour** in total during the academic year 1992-93). As can be seen from Table 2.6, certain themes dominated governing body discussions. Resources (including LMS) was the most common topic but building maintenance, annual parents' meetings, staff appointments, the school development plan, arrangements for the national curriculum, staffing structures, school aims and objectives and special needs provision were discussed (for more than one hour during the year) by over half of the school governing bodies involved in the survey. Certain topics will no doubt remain permanently on governing body agendas (e.g. LMS, buildings, staffing) whereas others are more likely to reflect particular concerns at the time (e.g. national curriculum assessment). If the survey was undertaken again it may well be that issues of current concern to governing bodies (such as sex education, special needs and OFSTED inspections) would be given greater prominence. Interestingly, the earlier NFER survey found a similar order of frequency of topics discussed at length (Keys and Fernandes, 1990).

---

2 A statistically significant difference exists between two groups in some quantity if the probability of that difference arising by chance is less than a pre-set value (in this case 5 per cent).

Table 2.6: Main topics discussed at length by governing bodies during 1992-93

Main topics:	% of sample*
Resources (including Local Management of School)	91
Building maintenance	81
Annual Parents' Meetings	78
The appointment of teaching staff, interviewing, etc	73
The school development plan	73
Arrangements for the National Curriculum/assessment/ other curriculum issues	69
Staffing structure	67
Aims and objectives of the school	53
Special needs provision	51
School discipline, exclusions, etc	45
Governor training	44
School prospectus	38
The respective managerial roles of the Head, other staff, governors, etc	37
Other relations with parents/Community links	35
GM status	34
Sex education	33
OFSTED inspection	28
Collective worship and religious education	24
In-service training	22
Extra-curricular activities (e.g. school trips)/charging for school activities	21
	(n = 432)
	(No response = 67)

(Percentages do not total 100 as more than one response could be given. The sample consists of the combined responses of heads and chairs.)*

Workload and composition of governing body

An attempt was made to gauge the amount of time headteachers and chairs of governors were spending on *all* their activities as members of the school governing body. They were asked to indicate the average number of *hours per week* (in term time over the academic year 1992 - 93) that they were devoting to governor duties. The results indicate that chairs of governors were spending longer on gubernatorial matters than were headteachers. The mean or average was 4.7 hours per week for chairs and 3.4 hours per week for heads. The median for chairs was four hours and, for heads, two hours. For some heads it was impossible to make the distinction between their roles as governors and school leaders, although most were able to answer the question. Interestingly, the earlier NFER survey found that chairs reported spending a median of 30 hours per term and heads 20 hours, which suggests although the figure for headteachers is similar, that for chairs is not. Assuming a 12-13 week term, the current survey gives a median of 50 hours for chairs and 25 hours for heads. For chairs in particular this represents a substantial increase.

Governors too were asked to indicate their respective workloads. On average, nearly eight *hours per term* (or about 40 minutes *per week*), was spent preparing for meetings of the full governing body, its sub-groups and their resultant workload. The median number of hours *per term* was five which is exactly half the number of hours reported by governors in the earlier NFER survey (Keys & Fernandes, 1990). These statistics suggest a shift over the last few years, with chairs and headteachers taking on an even greater workload.

The sample of governors who were in paid employment were also asked if it had been necessary for them to take time off work in order to fulfil their responsibilities as governors. About seven out of ten governors were in paid employment which suggests that the remainder were either retired, unemployed or engaged in home duties. Two thirds of those governors in paid employment had taken time off work to attend meetings, training sessions or to fulfil other responsibilities, such as visiting the school.

The amount of time off work governors were able to take was, on average, approaching five hours per term, with one quarter of employed governors reporting that they took over eight hours per term. Fifty-eight per cent of governors were paid for any time taken off work to fulfil their responsibilities as governors, whilst the remainder were either unpaid or used part of their annual leave. Views were also sought on the attitude of employers towards governors' requests for time away from work and over 80 per cent of working governors reported this to be generally supportive. Seven per cent of governors noted that their employers were reluctant to meet any such requests, whilst just over one in ten stated that agreement was given but only if time off was taken as leave.

An effective governing body – as further described in Chapter 6 – is often said to be one whose composition has the correct balance of people, skills and interests. Both headteachers and chairs of governors were asked if they thought their governing body, as currently constituted, had the appropriate balance of people and expertise. More than half of respondents (55 per cent of heads and 70 per cent of chairs) thought their governing body had the needed expertise, although more chairs than heads responded in the positive. Further statistical analysis did not find a greater degree of consistency of views between heads and chairs from the *same* school governing bodies. Although no statistically significant differences were found between school phase or types (e.g. voluntary aided, LEA controlled, grant-maintained), governing bodies in inner-city areas and where there was a high proportion of pupils entitled to free school meals were significantly *less likely* to report having the correct balance of expertise on their governing body. The type of people/skills/interests mentioned as currently lacking in governing bodies – which were very similar to those recorded in the earlier NFER survey – were, in order of frequency: general management experience (e.g. governors from industry and commerce); finance, accountancy and budgetary skills; and legal expertise. Heads also made reference to a knowledge or understanding of education as often lacking from the governing body. Some, however, saw *willingness* as a more important factor than specific expertise. One secondary head commented:

> *I do not believe that there is a correct balance of people/skills/interests as such. I should like to have some people more willing to come in to school to associate with specific faculties. Some of my governors do this – but not all.*

The issue of governing body composition was further explored in the case studies. The case study governing bodies had worked hard to ensure that they had the right balance of interests and an appropriate range of skills, abilities and expertise. In some cases a conscious effort had been made to achieve balance by using the cooptions to recruit people from different fields of experience – an option that was not available to schools with

Foundation governors. Interestingly, two of the case studies with such governors spoke of the varying degrees to which they had been able to exert an influence on the choice of individual governors. In one case, the head and chair would have liked a greater say in the selection to ensure there was the necessary **commitment** as governing bodies *'could no longer afford to take on any passengers'*. It was important to have a mix of skills which, in the view of many, was more important than having, say, a bank manager, a solicitor, an architect, an accountant, etc. As a governor remarked:

> *We have been fortunate. We've had a variety of people involved, some of whom have brought professional skills and others who are laymen bringing in interests, such as parents. I'm rather suspicious of the approach that recruits all the skills you need. There's something to be said for having people with a wide background and knowledge and there are experts whom the school should consult because not to do so could be rendering us liable should professional advice be given which turns out not to be so prudent after all. Hitherto we've had a bank of experts at the LEA, but that is beginning to wither away. It is perhaps now a question of having to buy the services.*
>
> (Foundation governor: Primary.)

Commitment and involvement were the key criteria rather than a particular expertise:

> *I used to think the governing body had to have specific skills represented (e.g. accountant) but now I think they should have people who have the best interests of the school at heart and are prepared to do the jobs. It's important to recognise that many of the people who are candidates for the governing body do not have a particular professional expertise.*
>
> (Headteacher: Secondary.)

But management experience generally was also something sought in governing bodies although not always available:

> *I should like to see people with more management experience - people who are used to meetings, used to getting through business, seeing the point without being rude, stopping the waffle, giving advice and making recommendations. Someone who has the foresight to be able to draw it all together, focus it in to avoid us going off at tangents. It is difficult because people with those skills haven't time to come to governing body meetings. We had a lawyer who came with everything colour-coded and arranged by his secretary but he didn't have time to*

come into school, to go on training. It didn't matter in a way because he saw the point and was able to get things through but he only came to 1 meeting in 4. Perhaps it needs someone who is retired, who has these skills, who can get to the root of things, talk to us, the children, the staff. (Headteacher: Infants.)

A governor from the same school commented:

No, we haven't got the balance right. It's very difficult now with LMS, the budget. We haven't anybody with financial experience. Also with clerking it tends to be anyone. People are asked beforehand. The LEA used to provide a clerk. That was much easier. They also knew who to contact and where to get papers. There is a lot more burden now on chairs and headteachers. It's very difficult if you're taking minutes to have full participation in the meeting. I don't think this is a balanced governing body. (Coopted governor: Primary.)

LEA governor training coordinators also made reference to notions of commitment and the involvement of stakeholders:

I think the Government should look again at the constitution of governing bodies: where is the commitment to school development coming from? There is a need for partnership and a big role for the governing body to play, but it has to be people who are committed. Usually this is provided by parent governors and cooptees, not LEA governors or teacher governors, who don't really understand their role. (LEA: GTC.)

Governing bodies have (some) control over the make up of the governing body, but I do worry if individuals are lined up by the headteacher, who can easily suggest clones of himself (sic) to fill vacancies. I know a governing body where 12 of the 16 governors are parents. Where there is a lot of parental involvement, there is commitment to the school. I come across most criticisms from Church and Aided schools, where the Church appoints governors who have no connection with the school: they often never turn up to meetings or visit the school, but are taking decisions about the development of the school. We must consider how we involve ***stake-holders****, rather than how we involve* ***title-holders****. Commitment should be the prime consideration. GM schools have a much more open ended power to coopt, but I find it worrying how that is carried out. I think there's evidence in this authority that self-interested groups have coopted (certain people with appropriate skills) in a way that will perpetuate* *the interest group. There is no evidence that political appointments exercise undue influence in terms of dominating the governing body, but particularly in secondary schools in the cities there tend to be political machinations.* (LEA: GTC.)

The GM case study head – in another LEA – commented on the composition of the governing body and the selection criteria they had used:

There can be problems if any of the First governors represent a pressure group. From the governing body before GM status, we have lost the LEA nominees, who did nothing anyway – they represented their party, not the school. The governors will debate how to fill a vacancy. Our policy is to appoint people who have the interests of the school at heart, so many of the First governors are parents. We have toyed with the idea of bringing in specific expertise, and this has happened a lot, but there has been difficulty if the people are unknown. Therefore if we were looking for a particular skill, we would want to appoint someone we had worked with in the past. There is specific expertise on the governing body (e.g. an architect) and this has been an advantage.

The deputy head, who as part of his job description clerked governing body meetings, made a similar point:

The governing body could have more input from industry, but whilst they have a different perspective, they may not have an affection for the school: there is no substitute for commitment.

He also added:

People are beginning to realise the full responsibility and commitment of being a governor, and this means not so many now wish to volunteer. The governing body is responsible for many things that the LEA would normally do. (Clerk: Secondary.)

Communications between heads and chairs of governors

Although it is generally recognised that relations between heads and chairs of governors are crucial to the effective functioning of governing bodies, little is known about the level or degree of communication between them. Both chairs and heads were asked whether or not they discussed business in preparation for meetings of the full governing body, whether they communicated on a regular basis and, if so, how frequent was that communication.

The data show that nearly seven out of ten chairs of governors but just under a half of headteachers stated that discussions were **always** held prior to meetings of the full governing body, whilst only 11 respondents (three per cent of heads and 0.5 per cent of chairs) remarked that such discussions **never** took place (Table 2.7). No statistically significant differences were found in the responses to this question when it was analysed further according to type or status of the school. The vast majority of both headteachers (96 per cent) and chairs (98 per cent) said they communicated regularly with each other over the course of the year, with most communicating, on average, about once a week.

Table 2.7: Discussions held between heads and chairs in preparation for full governing body meetings

		%	
		Headteachers	Chairs of governors
Discussion held:	Always	47	69
	Usually	32	21
	Occasionally	18	9.5
	Never	3	0.5
		(n = 362)	(n = 231)

The issue of relations between heads and chairs of governing bodies and their frequency of communication was pursued further in the case studies (see Chapter 7).

The contribution of the governing body

In an attempt to gain insights into what was seen as the governing body's **main** contribution to the school, all three categories of respondent – heads, governors and chairs – were given the opportunity to give their views on this matter. They were not presented with any suggestions or a pre-determined checklist to tick but rather had to respond to an open-ended question. It was possible, however, to categorise their responses and although a large number of suggestions were made only the most frequently mentioned have been tabulated (Table 2.8). *Providing support,* *encouragement and guidance* for the head, the school and its staff was the governing body's most significant contribution mentioned most frequently by all three categories of respondent. There was less agreement, however, on the other suggestions proffered; in fact there were found to be statistically significant differences between the groups in relation to *decision-making and budget control*, and *partnership*. For both suggestions, governors, to a greater extent than headteachers or chairs of governors, perceived these as constituting the main contribution that the governing body could make to the school. Interestingly, there were hardly any references to policy-making.

Although the contribution of the governing body to the school is discussed in more detail at a later stage, the following comments give an indication of the kinds of comments and suggestions that were made:

> *The governing body provides a lay person's overview that supports the school in a practical way - week by week involvement that puts parents' criticism into perspective and helps the management to stay realistic!* (Headteacher: Primary.)

> *The governing body is useful in removing the isolation of the head and creating a team to share the responsibility and load in a way that cannot be shared between head and deputies.* (Headteacher: Secondary.)

> *The governors are a great source of expertise and enthusiasm, bringing an outside perspective to school life. Plus they come free of charge!* (Chair of governors: Secondary.)

> *The commitment to use its skills and expertise to benefit the education of the children attending the school, in partnership with the head and staff.* (Chair of governors: Secondary.)

> *The governing body provides a strong, supportive, informed and responsive contribution to the high level running of the school, and does not interfere unnecessarily with the day-to-day management which is properly the job of the head and his senior staff. As 'employer', the governing body is fair and believes in the school and its ethos, and the staff know this absolutely.* (Governor: Secondary.)

Governing bodies can make a major contribution to the work and life of the school and its staff, including senior management. Factors preventing governing bodies from effectively making this contribution are considered in more detail in Chapter 6.

Table 2.8: The governing body's main contribution to the school

Main contributions:	%* Heads	Chairs	Governors
• Support, encouragement & guidance	64	56	49
• Practical and professional expertise	33	26	24
• Decision-making and budget control	19	27	42
• Critical friend/objective oversight	13	14	8
• Monitoring and accountability	10	10	10
• Partnership/shared responsibility	6	12	14
(n =	354	228	229)

*(*Percentages do not add up to 100 as more than one response could be made.)*

Summary

Successive Education Acts have given increasing responsibilities to governing bodies and frequent reports in the press have noted the consequent increase in workload. This was confirmed by heads and chairs participating in this study. One third of the governing bodies surveyed had one or more vacancies. Difficulties in recruiting and retaining members were often attributed to the size of their workload. A comparison of the findings of this study with an earlier NFER investigation undertaken in 1990 indicated that the bulk of this additional workload may be falling on the shoulders of the chairs. In 1993 chairs were putting in a substantially greater number of hours than was reported in the 1990 survey, whilst this did not appear to be the case for other members.

Given the important role of governing bodies in determining school policy and procedures in a wide range of areas, it is not surprising that most heads had chosen to become members in order to be fully involved in the decision-making process. The majority reported having frequent communication with the chairs of their governing bodies and holding specific meetings with their chair prior to full governing body meetings. Once having made the necessary commitment, most governors attended all full meetings. The vast majority of governing bodies had also set up subcommittees and working groups of members to investigate specific issues. For members currently in employment their governing body duties usually involved taking some time off work and, in general, employers were found to be supportive to requests for time off.

The role of the governing body was most commonly described as providing support, encouragement and guidance to the school. In practice, the issues allotted most time on the agenda for meetings related to resourcing and resource management. The areas of expertise and experience most likely to be lacking among governing body members were identified as general managerial, financial and legal skills.

Chapter 3
The Operation of Governing Bodies

The previous chapter concluded by examining respondents' views of the governing body's main contribution to the school. This chapter continues this theme by analysing further the various views held by heads and governors about a) their roles and responsibilities and b) the actual operation of their school governing bodies. In so doing it is intended to draw upon data from the case studies as well as the questionnaire surveys.

The extent of governing body responsibilities

All three categories of participants in the survey – headteachers, governors and chairs of governors – were asked about the degree and nature of the responsibilities given to school governing bodies under recent legislation. As earlier indicated, these responsibilities have increased considerably as a result of the *Education Reform Act* and subsequent legislation. It was, of course, difficult to know the degree to which governors were actually aware of all of their responsibilities and duties. Nevertheless, did governors think that the extent of the responsibilities currently given to governing bodies was *too little, about right* or *too much?* Table 3.1a shows the range of views on this question for the heads, chairs and governors. Further analysis showed that there were statistically significant differences between the respondents with headteachers more likely to perceive the extent of responsibilities given to governing bodies as being *'too much'*. Approximately two-thirds of heads, for example, responded in this way, whilst approximately one-half of chairs and only one-third of governors regarded the extent of governing body responsibilities as too wide-ranging under recent legislation. The earlier NFER survey (which only asked heads and governors this question) found virtually identical figures for heads, although more governors (42 per cent) perceived governing bodies as having *too much* responsibility (Keys & Fernandes, 1990). Interestingly, whilst statistically significant differences were found between primary and secondary headteachers and chairs of governors on this issue – primary heads and chairs were more likely to perceive the extent of responsibilities as being *'too much'* compared with their secondary colleagues (see Table 3.1b) – no significant differences were found for governors. There was no statistically significant relationship between headteachers' responses to this question and the number of years they had been in post. Several heads found it difficult to answer this question as they were aware that although the situation was, in their view, satisfactory, it could nevertheless easily change for the worse. As a primary head noted:

> *The governing body delegate to me most of what they're able to delegate and we have a good working relationship and my role is clear. However, I am aware that the balance could change and governors could take a lot of responsibility from me making my job 'hell', leading me to not knowing what was happening and spending so much time with governors I had little time for children, parents and staff.*

Table 3.1a: The extent of governing body responsibility under recent legislation

The extent of the responsibilities given to governing bodies is:

	%		
	Heads	Chairs	Governors
Too little	*	2	3
About right	37	47	65
Too much	63	51	32
	100	100	100
	(n=421)	(n=226)	(n=238)

*(*Only 1 headteacher reported the extent of responsibilities to be 'too little'.)*

Table 3.1b: The extent of governing body responsibility under recent legislation: phase differences

The extent of the responsibilities given to governing bodies is:

	%					
	Heads		Chairs		Governors	
	Primary	Secondary	Primary	Secondary	Primary	Secondary
Too little	-	0.5	1	3.5	3	3
About right	30	43	37	56.5	58	71
Too much	70	56.5	62	40	39	25
	100	100	100	100	100	99*
(n=	214	207	111	115	119	119)

*(*Due to rounding errors percentages may not total 100.)*

Respondents were also asked to indicate the specific areas in which they felt governing bodies had too much or too little responsibility. The open-ended responses to this question were categorised and as can be seen from Table 3.2, the areas most commonly referred to where governing bodies had too much responsibility were quite similar between the three categories of respondent. As in the earlier NFER survey, personnel issues, finance and budgetary matters (LMS) were often mentioned but headteachers, to a greater extent than chairs or governors, more frequently made reference to the curriculum and decision-making/policy-making as areas where governing bodies had *too much* responsibility. (No differences were found between primary and secondary heads in relation to levels of responsibility with the one exception mentioned below.) There was, however, a similar proportion of respondents agreeing that the amount of responsibility conferred on part-time volunteers was unfair and/or unreasonable, and that a group of amateurs would most likely lack the requisite skills and expertise required to cope with the wide-ranging responsibilities given to governing bodies. The following comments encapsulate some of these latter views:

> *Too much responsibility but too little accountability – we have discipline procedures for teachers – why not governors? Many areas of responsibility are too difficult for governors, let alone teachers, to understand fully.* (Head: Secondary.)

> *Generally the overall responsibilities, I believe, are extreme for a group of people who give their time voluntarily. This would be scoffed at in industry, a board of managers working for nothing alongside another manager's job!* (Head: Primary.)

> *The type of person who is often approached for this role normally has a full work/personal schedule already. The increasing demands on governors both in terms of sheer workload and importance of decisions are making this position untenable. I feel that a large burden has been placed on a group of people who have volunteered to serve on a governing body. I believe that saturation point has been reached (or passed!). It is not clear what future role the LEA will fulfil and what economic benefits have accrued from devolving decision making to governing bodies.* (Governor: Primary.)

Primary headteachers were more likely than their secondary school counterparts to make reference to – in their view – the unreasonable demands made on a group of part-time volunteers. As one remarked:

> *It is unrealistic to expect amateurs to make the detailed decisions needed to run a school. In the end governors tend to 'rubber stamp'.*

Table 3.2: Areas in which governing bodies have too much responsibility

Main areas mentioned:	%*		
	Heads	Chairs	Governors
• Personnel issues	41	38	32
• Finance/budget/LMS	25	42	36
• Curriculum	23	9	5
• General lack of expertise/skills to cope with responsibilities	22	16	15
• Unfair on volunteers/part-timers	18	22	26
• Policy & decision-making	18	5	8
• Health & safety	6	7	2
• Buildings/premises	4	5	2
(n=	228	96	66)

(The percentages are calculated from only those respondents who answered 'too much' and not from the total samples. Percentages do not total 100 as more than one area could be suggested.)*

The operation of governing bodies

In an attempt to ascertain how governing bodies were operating in the light of their newly-acquired responsibilities, respondents were asked to indicate their level of agreement with a number of statements. These statements focused on the areas of policy-making; information about management decisions; roles and duties of heads, governors and the LEA; school support; critical friendship and mediation between the school and the community. The levels of agreement on each of the statements for headteachers, governors and chairs of governing bodies are shown in Table 3.3.

As can be seen from the table, there were considerable degrees of agreement amongst the three groups of respondent. Over eight out of ten heads, chairs and governors *'agreed'* or *'strongly agreed'* that their school governing bodies were *'well informed about internal management decision and events'*, *'clear about the heads' role and duties'*, and *'very supportive of the work of the school'*. There was also a high level of agreement by all three parties that the governing body was *'fully involved in discussing policy'*. It is worth noting that there was not a single statement with which over half of the respondents *'disagreed'* or *'strongly disagreed'*. In fact, at least seven out of ten of both chairs and governors *'agreed'* or *'strongly agreed'* with **all** of the statements. The statement that the governing body was *'clear about the LEA's role and duties'* attracted the overall lowest level of agreement. The general picture of the operation of governing bodies which emerges from responses to this question was therefore generally positive with far fewer respondents disagreeing than agreeing with the nine statements offered. However, further analyses identified some interesting differences between the groups.

Additional statistical tests were undertaken in an attempt to clarify the nature of the differences between the three groups of respondent. There were found to be statistically significant differences between the groups on **all** of the statements. Headteachers were *less likely* to agree to the statements than were governors and chairs of governing bodies. (These statistically significant differences were confirmed when the data were analysed from the 117 school governing bodies where returns had been received from **all three** categories of respondent. Clear differences emerged between headteachers and the other respondents: heads, in general, were less likely to strongly agree with the statements about the school's governing body.)

The responses from the headteachers were subject to further analyses in an attempt to identify any important differences existing by *phase* (primary/secondary), *type of school* (voluntary aided, GM, LEA-controlled, etc) or *number of years in headship*. No statistically significant relationships were found when the nine statements about the school's governing body were cross-tabulated with the above mentioned variables. There was, however, one exception. The levels of agreement by heads on the statement that the governing body was 'fully involved in determining policy' differed according to the status or type of school. Grant-maintained school heads were more polarised in their views regarding this statement, whilst heads of voluntary-aided and voluntary-controlled schools, as might be expected, generally expressed higher levels of agreement than did those of LEA-maintained schools.

Table 3.3: Levels of agreement about the operation of the school's governing body

The school's governing body is:	% responses											
	Strongly agree			Agree			Disagree			Strongly disagree		
	H	C	G*	H	C	G	H	C	G	H	C	G
a) Fully involved in discussing policy	18	47	39	61	48	50	19	6	10	2	-	1
b) Fully involved in determining policy	12	39	34	54	52	46	30	8	20	4	1	-
c) Well informed about internal management decisions and events	23	32	31	61	52	53	13	15.5	16	3	0.5	-
d) Clear about the Head's role and duties	24	47	46	57	47	46	16	5	7	3	1	1
e) Clear about the Governors' role and duties	15	34	38	49	54	47	32	12	12	4	1	3
f) Clear about the LEA's roles and duties	13	20	15	46	59	56	38	20	27	3	1	2
g) Very supportive of the work of the school	69	74	68	27	26	30	3	-	2	0.5	-	-
h) Challenging in its role as a 'critical friend'	15	22	19	50	57	53	31	21	24	4	-	4
i) A useful mediator between the school, its community and other bodies	18	27	25	53	54	56	26	18	18	3	1	1
(n=366 heads) (n=231 chairs) (n=241 governors)												

(H = headteachers, C = chairs of governors, G = governors)*

Levels of involvement of governing bodies

Respondents were asked to indicate if there were any areas of the school's work or decision-making where they felt that *less* or *more* involvement of the governing body would be beneficial. The responses to this open-ended question were analysed and the majority of comments offered concerned those areas where *more* involvement of the governing body was perceived to be beneficial. Many areas were suggested by respondents but the main ones are shown in Table 3.4. As can be seen from the table, there was a reasonable degree of agreement between heads, governors and chairs of governing bodies about the main areas where more involvement of the governing body would be beneficial. Opportunities for governors to visit the school at work to increase their awareness of how it operates was mentioned most frequently by heads and chairs. For example, a primary head remarked that more involvement would be beneficial in all areas, and added:

> *I feel that the governors have no awareness of the life of the school or of the responsibilities carried by the headteacher and yet they decide my salary! We would welcome their involvement in school policies.*
> (Head: Primary.)

Similarly, a secondary head pointed to:

> *More involvement via staff-shadowing and pupil-shadowing schemes: these have been established for some years but few governors can spare the daytime hours for this valuable contact.*

Over one-fifth of respondents who offered suggestions made reference to greater governing body involvement in development planning and strategic policy making. Interestingly, the curriculum (or what is taught in schools) was also commonly mentioned as an area in which *more* involvement of the governing body would be beneficial. Headteachers – to a greater extent than chairs or governors – made reference to the area of budgeting, finance and LMS. Governors, however, were more likely than heads or chairs to refer to personnel and staffing matters, and the improvement of the morale and motivation (of staff and students) as areas where greater governing body involvement would be beneficial.

Further analyses were undertaken to discover if there were any statistically significant relationships between heads' views on the areas where *more* involvement of the governing body would be beneficial and other factors, such as number of years in post, school type, phase and catchment areas. No statistically significant differences were recorded on any of the above variables and the various areas put forward by headteachers, except for one. There was found to be a statistically significant relationship between school *location* and the area of *budgeting, finance and LMS*: headteachers of schools in inner urban/inner city catchment areas had a greater tendency than heads of suburban or country town/rural schools to make reference to the latter as an area where greater involvement of the governing body would be beneficial.

Table 3.4: Areas in which *more* involvement of the governing body would be beneficial

	%*		
Main areas suggested:	Heads	Chairs	Governors
• School visits/seeing school 'at work'	26	27	19
• Curriculum	24	22	16
• School development plan and strategic planning	23	22	21
• Budgeting, finance, LMS	20	11	12
• Improving morale and motivation (of staff and students)	11	8	15
• Personnel/staffing	9	7	15
(n=	231	90	99)

*(*Percentages do not total 100 as more than one area could be suggested.)*

Far fewer suggestions were offered concerning areas in which *less* involvement of governing bodies would be beneficial. Of the 74 heads who responded to the first part of this question about one-third made reference to distinctions between 'management and governance' and/or governor's involvement in the day-to-day running of the school. As noted by a governor:

> *Some governors need to be more aware of their particular duties and responsibilities - some involve themselves in issues which are not strictly their domain.*

A secondary head felt that issues such as staffing and finance were management responsibilities and that *'there is a "muddying of the waters" between management and governship'*. Another commented on the current lack of clarity regarding roles and responsibilities:

> *(The legislation has) created confusion between the role of management and of governing thereby limiting and occasionally working against the proper professional guidance and decision-making of the head and senior staff. There is a dichotomy between improving the 'managerial' approach of schools with greater lay involvement. There is again the difficulty of power without responsibility. Functions of the governing body can only be exercised through the headteacher.*
>
> (Headteacher: Secondary.)

Finance, staffing and personnel, and the curriculum were also mentioned, but not so frequently, as areas where it was felt less involvement of the governing body would be beneficial. (The number of responses to this part of the question from chairs and governors were too few to enable meaningful comparisons with heads to be made.)

The operation of the case study governing bodies

During the interviews with governors details were sought on how their governing body operated. In several of the case studies it was suggested that the success of the governing body centred around a small number of governors – five or six – who took on many responsibilities and were most active. All the case study governing bodies were reported to have one or more 'passengers'. This situation was generally considered to be no longer tenable as responsibilities had grown and there was a greater need for *'the sharing of the ever-increasing load'*. In relation to this, the necessity to involve **all** members of the governing body was acknowledged and for the need for people to put themselves forward for consideration as governors only if they were prepared to make the necessary commitment. Spread throughout the governing body the workload was not onerous: concentrated on a small number of individuals it could be too demanding and unreasonable. There was a recognition of the need to involve all governors but that this had to be 'worked at' as new governors could easily be 'put off' by their more experienced colleagues. As a case study headteacher explained there was a need for induction:

> *There is a danger, which governors are aware of, that you have a nucleus of very experienced governors, and this makes it difficult for new governors to join in: induction of new governors, therefore, has to be given a lot of attention. There will inevitably be a difference of contribution at first, simply because of lack of experience. The contribution of new governors, however, is sought, valued and seen to be valued.* (Headteacher: Secondary.)

The conduct of the case study governing bodies and the handling of meetings by the respective chairs was generally considered in a positive light with some interesting comparisons being made with other governing bodies or previous chairs. The following interview extracts give an indication of how the case study governing bodies conducted their business:

It's a very happy band - always has been. No violent disagreements but enjoyable discussions. Everyone has the opportunity to speak and all are listened to - it's an amicable and cheerful occasion. The chair keeps good time, if we're not finished then we have an extra meeting.

(LEA-appointed governor: Primary.)

The meetings are well-chaired and good humoured. They're kept on as informal a basis as possible given that there is work to be transacted. We've been fairly realistic in delegating to subcommittees and working parties where all the major topics are given the required time, attention and detail. The full governing body have the opportunity to discuss things. There is no problem about that. The chair particularly brings in the parents.

(Foundation governor and clerk: Primary.)

There are various ways you can conduct a committee - you can have it in a fairly formal, disciplined way as in District/Parish council or in a relaxed atmosphere.... I think we have a nice pitch between the two. My only criticism would be that the governors of this school are no different from others, they don't always read the paperwork before they come! Therefore you don't get the depth of discussion you ought to on certain points. On the other hand, you get more explanation from the headteacher or the deputy heads so it takes longer and there are more questions. But that's a problem with most committees. The trouble is we pick busy people for governors and often people become governors and find they are over-loaded. We receive the paperwork in time - I reckon we always need a week. The worst thing is having papers tabled and then being asked to vote. I usually suggest we don't do it but leave it to the next meeting. Inevitably if you have a good chair you have a better meeting and a lot of people have not been trained. He does involve the meeting. I think it's useful if the chair has been chair of one of the subcommittees first.

(LEA-appointed governor: Secondary.)

They go very well, there's open, frank discussion and there are no frictions. All have the opportunity to speak but because they feel insecure in education they don't always voice opinions when they should. They haven't always read the information but it's a problem as there are mountains of paper. Agendas, etc. are in good time.

(Teacher governor: Primary.)

With our new chair the meetings are better organised, more professionally geared. Most certainly, we home in on things much quicker. We tended to muddle through. We covered the ground but we talked round and round for hours. The new chair has a lot of experience of running meetings and she has brought that expertise to the governing body. Meetings went on for three hours or more. They tended to peter out in confusion - is there a decision? Are we going to implement the policies? That's how it was. This chair is more focused. All have the opportunity to speak but don't always take it. We have a fairly quiet foundation governor (a parent). The vicar is not a frequent attender. The new members are finding their feet. But generally we have a good attendance. (Headteacher: Primary.)

However, not all comments about the conduct of governing body meetings were favourable:

The agenda's too long and time keeping's poor. Part of the problem is not giving participants enough information to base decisions on. We've not enough briefing papers. Perhaps headteachers and admin. staff give it a low priority. Governing bodies are administratively poorly served. There is a tiny budget for photocopying and paperwork which sometime gets reflected in reports being hurriedly written on the computer at home. However, all have the opportunity to contribute and most do. (Coopted governor: Primary.)

The majority of meetings are very poorly conducted. The agenda is too long; there's no time allocation. There is no axe. Someone has said subcommittees should not last more then one-and-a-half hours but they have this habit of just going on and on. I agree with the 6.30 pm. finish as long as time is properly allocated to each item. People are allowed to spend time reading documents they have already received. (Teacher governor: Secondary.)

The roles and functions of **subcommittees** were said to be important and should be made clear to all:

On the subcommittees we do have some full powers. It's always a fine line between how much you delegate to committees and how much the full governing body should make decisions. As the full governing body is responsible, things should be passed in front of them even if it is only a matter of reporting. (LEA-appointed governor: Secondary.)

The committees have devolved power; they take decisions, provide guidelines, etc. Large numbers of governors attend the committee meetings (as many as 12 out of the governing body of 17) even if only five are members of that committee. Committees work very well, and because of this the role of the full governing body is not really clear. Occasionally a committee will refer a matter to the full governing body for fuller discussion, but the full governing body is demonstrably less important in terms of the way it operates now compared with what it used to be. (Headteacher: Secondary.)

We have an intelligent, well-informed group of people. They are fully briefed. I think we could prepare them more for the subcommittees and I'm aiming to improve the production of pre-meeting papers. Because they are well-informed relationships are good. There is no sense of confrontation between the governing body and the headteacher. There is sometimes a difference of opinion between the governors. (Headteacher: Secondary.)

The **clerking** of governing bodies was also recognised to be of fundamental importance to its effective functioning but it too was becoming a more demanding task:

When I was asked to be the clerk it was one set of meetings and one set of minutes per term. Now it's three per term and subcommittees so it has developed significantly. (Foundation governor and clerk: Primary.)

The major problem at the moment is the clerk who has no idea what we're talking about, mainly through her lack of educational knowledge. Training is therefore needed. There is a one day course available but she's not keen to devote lots of time to clerking. At the moment when she produces minutes, they go to the chair who has to go through them before they are finally produced. (Chair: Primary.)

(The practices of the case study governing bodies are further explored in Chapter 7.)

Summary

Chairs, governing body members and, to a lesser extent, headteachers generally agreed that their governing bodies were very supportive of the school, clear about their roles and responsibilities and about internal management decisions, and fully involved in policy-related decision making. Concern was however expressed, especially on the part of heads, that the responsibilities now being given to governing bodies were excessively wide-ranging. It was felt that most governors simply did not have the necessary depth of expertise and experience to deal with personnel and financial matters or to make critical decisions in relation to the school curriculum. Increased opportunities for governors to visit the school at work in order to increase their awareness of how it operates was regarded as a possible strategy for overcoming at least part of this problem.

Extracts from the case studies gave an indication of the generally well-received conduct and operation of governing bodies, whilst pointing to the important role of subcommittees and the clerk.

Chapter 4
The Training and Support of Governors

If governors are to function effectively they need to be trained. The importance of training for school governors was recognised by the *1986 Education Act* which gave the LEA a statutory duty to provide the training it thinks necessary for governors to carry out their duties effectively. Every LEA has provided some governor training and most have appointed governor training coordinators and/or support officers. Over the last few years governor training and support has been funded centrally by direct training grants under GEST (Grants for Education Support and Training). At the time of the research, funds were provided by two separate grants: either specifically for governor training, which was paid to the LEA (who in turn used the funds to provide governor training and support or devolved it to schools) or for school management generally. The latter GEST category was devolved entirely to schools and a certain proportion (27 per cent in 1992-93) specified for governor training, although schools were permitted to spend funds on other aspects of school management if they so wished.

The trend towards the greater devolution of training funds to schools has continued however and the GEST circular for the financial year 1995-96 indicates that **all** funds for governor training and support are to be included under the new category of 'School Effectiveness'. Eighty per cent of the grant for 'School Effectiveness' will be devolved to school level and focus on three areas: management (through the training of governors, heads and other staff); support for the basic curriculum and assessment; and information technology. The weighting of expenditure on these different categories will, according to the circular, depend on the specific needs of individual schools and LEAs. Schools will be free to spend devolved funds according to their own priorities. How much will be allocated to meet the training and support needs of governors is, of course, not known at this time.

The significance of training for governors has increased as the extent of governing body responsibilities has grown. As AGIT (Action for Governors' Information and Training) has recently argued:

> *Legislation over the last seven years has piled onto governing bodies an increasing number of vital responsibilities affecting the quality of*

education provision for young people. Many governors are still not clear what their roles and responsibilities consist of, still less how to carry them out effectively, how to plan and make decisions, how to monitor, how to take control of their own agenda and focus on the issues that will bring the greatest benefit to pupils in their school, how to build relationships with their headteacher, the staff and parents. Training is there to help. (Pounce, 1993).

An important part of the research was therefore to gather data on the training and support of school governors and these areas were explored in both the questionnaire surveys and the case studies.

Governor training

Table 4.1 shows the percentage of governors who had received formal training at some stage for their role as school governor. As might be expected the figure was lower for headteachers – just under half stated that they had received formal training – than it was for governors (76 per cent) and chairs of governing bodies (86 per cent). (The earlier NFER survey found that over 90 per cent of the chairs compared with just under 70 per cent of governors had attended training at some time. Data were not collected for heads.) Of those who had received formal training for their role as governors, more than eight out of ten (86 per cent) stated that they had found the training helpful. The proportion of governors who had received formal training for their role did not differ significantly according to school *type* or *status*, although chairs of governing bodies of GM schools generally had received less training than chairs of other school governing bodies. (As the number of GM chairs providing information was very small, not too much importance should be attached to this particular finding.)

Table 4.1: The training of school governors

Have you received any formal training for your role as school governor?	% respondents		
	Heads	**Chairs**	**Governors**
Yes	48	86	76
No	32	13	23
(No response/missing data)	20	1	1
	100	100	100
	(n=428)	(n=233)	(n=241)

Both headteachers and chairs of governing bodies were asked to state the approximate amount of devolved funds which had been received by the governing body (for the financial year 1993/94) to organise its own training and development. Figures from the headteachers and chairs show that the amount devolved to school governing bodies ranged from nothing to over £3,000. The average amount received was about £370 (the median figure was £250) with the larger secondary schools obviously receiving more on average (£446) than the smaller primaries (£298). These devolved funds were being spent mainly on individual training courses and LEA services (including training) or to purchase relevant literature, governor manuals or videos on school governance. Of those heads and chairs who provided information on how the funds were being spent, just over one-tenth made reference to meeting the costs of in-house trainers and speakers who came into the school to work with the whole governing body. About one-in-twenty specifically mentioned that the funds were not being entirely utilised for training and development purposes. Annual parents' meetings, refreshments, photocopying and clerking were mentioned by some as legitimate ways to use these devolved funds.

Heads, governors and chairs of governing bodies were presented with a list of topics and asked to indicate in which ones they had received training for their role as school governor. The results from the survey of the three groups of respondent are presented in Table 4.2 and show the main topics or areas where training had been received. (Interestingly, the four topics mentioned most frequently by governors in the current survey were the same as reported in the earlier NFER study (Keys & Fernandes, 1990), although their ranking was not quite identical.) The main topics were: local management; roles and functions of school governors; staff recruitment and selection; the National Curriculum; and other personnel management issues (the writing of a pay policy was also mentioned by several heads and chairs under 'other topics'). School development planning was also a commonly-mentioned topic. About a tenth of the heads answering this question noted that some or all of the training they had received to date on the various topics had been as a result of being a head rather than specifically a governor. It is interesting to note the relatively low percentage of chairs of governing bodies who had received training in 'taking an effective part in meetings' (35 per cent) and 'chairing meetings' (39 per cent). Also, bearing in mind the importance that was attached to seeing the school in operation (see Chapter 3), it is noteworthy that just over a quarter of chairs and about a third of governors

Table 4.2: Topics included during training for role as school governor

Areas/topics:	%*		
	Heads	Chairs	Governors
The roles and functions of school governors	63	79	86
Local Management of Schools	82	90	75
Recruitment and selection of teaching and non-teaching staff	59	62	47
Other personnel management issues	49	39	25
Taking an effective part in meetings	17	35	25
Chairing meetings	12	39	11
Visiting the school	11	27	32
Writing the Annual Report(s)	13	20	19
Running Annual Parent's Meetings	7	9	13
School Development Planning	44	40	38
Implications of the National Curriculum/ school curriculum	34	50	46
Special educational needs	34	39	28
Equal opportunities for boys and girls	13	17	13
Multicultural education	9	9	7
Sex education	16	23	17
Collective Worship and Religious Education	13	18	16
Preparation for an inspection	33	31	21
The advantages/disadvantages of GM status	29	34	25
School/Community links	13	15	15
Dealing with parents	8	8	11
Other topics	4	4	7
(n=	228	211	189)

(Percentages add up to more than 100% because respondents could select more than one option.)*

had received training in 'visiting the school'. The relatively small proportion of governors having had training in 'equal opportunities for boys and girls' and 'multicultural education' lends general support to the findings of an earlier NFER research report (Bagley, 1992). The other main topics mentioned but not included on the list were behaviour, discipline and exclusion panels, health and safety, premises and teacher appraisal. It is probably not unreasonable to assume that the topics of 'sex education', 'collective worship and religious education', 'preparation for an inspection', 'special educational needs', and 'the advantages/disadvantages of GM status' are likely to become more popular as school governing bodies are increasingly asked to consider such issues and/or embrace new responsibilities. LEA governor training coordinators, for example, made reference to the need for a training programme to have regard for governing body's new legal responsibilities and whatever happened to be the 'topical issues of concern'.

Governors and chairs of governing bodies were also asked to specify which of the training sessions attended they had found to be most useful. Analysis of the responses from 335 chairs and governors revealed that exactly one-quarter made reference to local management of schools, just over one-fifth mentioned recruitment, selection and other personnel management issues, and one-sixth referred to the roles and functions of school governors. About one-in-eight chairs and governors remarked that 'all' or 'most' of the training sessions attended had been helpful, whilst a much smaller number (about one-in-twenty) stated that 'none' or 'not many' had been of use. About one in eight chairs and governors also made reference to the training provided by the LEA as being of most use, whilst the importance of contact with other governors – which attendance at training sessions provided – was often commented upon. Several respondents remarked that every governors' meeting constituted 'on the job' training.

Local authorities currently provide training for school governors, in many cases for governors of grant-maintained as well as LEA-maintained schools. The headteacher survey revealed that just over eight out of ten governing bodies currently made use of the training provided by LEAs. The nature of this provision was further explored in the case study schools and LEAs. In all six authorities an extensive and, in general, highly regarded menu of courses was available.

To a certain extent training for the role of governor is never ending. As issues and new developments come to the fore there is a need, at a minimum, for awareness-raising and an understanding of the possible implications of such developments for the governing body. Governors' and governing bodies' most important training needs for the future was an issue explored with all those involved in the research. The survey of heads, governors and chairs of governing bodies gave respondents the opportunity to specify the nature of these future training needs both for governors and governing bodies. On this occasion they were not given a list of possible topics or areas. The suggestions given in this open-ended question on future training needs were coded and the 10 areas or needs most commonly mentioned have been presented in Table 4.3.

The relative importance of the main areas suggested as governors' most pressing future training needs did not differ significantly from one category of respondent to another. The three areas of finance, budget and LMS; personnel management; and the roles and functions of governors were most commonly mentioned, although chairs and governors referred more frequently to budgetary or LMS concerns than did headteachers. Conversely, curriculum issues were seen as important future training needs far more by heads, whilst governors mentioned legal responsibilities more often than did other respondents. Keeping abreast of recent educational developments and increasing knowledge and understanding of educational issues was mentioned as important by a similar proportion of all respondents. For one primary head, governors needed a real (and not superficial) understanding of the school as *'too many of them approach the role from a "when I was at school" standpoint'*.

Respondents were also asked to comment on governing bodies' – as opposed to individual governors' – most important future training needs. About a quarter of respondents noted that there were no real differences between the two and a further analysis of responses showed that the same areas and topics were commonly mentioned. Table 4.4 shows the ten main areas or topics suggested as governing bodies most important training needs. However, an interesting difference was found in that all three categories of respondent – heads, chairs and governors – mentioned OFSTED inspections more frequently as a training need for governing bodies than they did as a training need for governors (see Tables 4.3 and 4.4). The OFSTED inspection process and the role of the governing body in producing an action plan was, for example, mentioned by just under a quarter of the heads responding to this question. The most commonly mentioned training need of governing bodies – again referred to by about a quarter of heads – was general training in the roles and functions of governors but particularly in teasing out the differences between governance and management. The training need of governing bodies mentioned most commonly by chairs and governors was in relation to finance and LMS, followed by governor training in general, which included aspects of team work and working together (see Table 4.4).

Table 4.3: Governors' most important future training needs

	%*		
Main areas suggested for training:	Heads	Chairs	Governors
Personnel management	24	19	21
Finance, budget, LMS	24	30	34
Roles and functions of governors	23	23	14
Curriculum issues	21	15	7
Keeping abreast of recent developments	17	16	14
OFSTED inspections	15	7	5
All aspects of governance	9	12	14
Legal responsibilities	8	8	13
School development planning	8	6	6
Effective meetings/subcommittees	8	5	9
(n=	296	178	192)

(Percentages do not total 100 as more than one area could be suggested. The percentage figures have been calculated from the numbers providing information and not from the total sample.)*

Table 4.4: Governing bodies' most important future training needs

	%*		
Main areas suggested for training:	Heads	Chairs	Governors
Roles and functions of governors	24	12	9
OFSTED inspections	24	13	13
Personnel management	14	13	12
Finance, budget, LMS	14	28	28
All aspects of governance	13	23	15
Curriculum issues	12	9	9
School development planning	11	13	8
Effective meetings/subcommittees	10	6	9
Keeping abreast of recent developments	9	13	3
Legal responsibilities	8	8	11
(n=	273	588	181)

(Percentages do not total 100 as more than one area could be suggested. The percentage figures have been calculated from the numbers providing information and not from the total sample.)*

Finally, governors were asked if their expenses had been reimbursed for any activities undertaken in the course of governor duties or for the attendance of training sessions. Positive responses were made by only five and 18 per cent respectively. More than half did not know whether such expenses could be claimed. They were also asked whether or not the LEA provided childminding facilities during training sessions. A significant proportion (65 per cent) of governors did not know what the situation was regarding reimbursement or the provision of childminding facilities. Only four per cent of governors stated that the LEA *did* provide childminding facilities during training sessions.

Support for governors

The research was interested in exploring the role of the LEA and other bodies in the provision of information and support to both individual governors and governing bodies. LEAs have traditionally provided a range of information and support services to governors but little is known about how much use is made of the various services or how helpful they are. The survey of heads, governors and chairs of governing bodies therefore specifically sought views on these issues and presented respondents with a list of services provided for governors by LEAs. The percentages of respondents who had made use of the services are shown in Table 4.5. Interestingly, the percentages for each service used were found to be considerably higher for governors in the present survey compared with the earlier one (Keys & Fernandes, 1990). For example, the 1990 survey found only 60 per cent of governors making use of 'newsletters'. Headteachers too, with the exception of policy papers and 'curriculum guidelines' reported using LEA support services to a greater extent than hitherto.

Several observations can be made from the data in Table 4.5. Firstly, of the information and support services provided by LEAs, most use was made of governor bulletins and newsletters. This may have been partly due to the direct mailing to governors of these newsletters and bulletins which appeared to be common practice. (All six LEA governor training coordinators, for example, commented on this.) Instruments and articles of government were also reported to have been used by a high percentage of respondents, as were handbooks and guidance notes, particularly by chairs and governors. The information and support services provided by LEAs that governors made least use of were videos, telephone hotlines and reference collections in libraries. The second observation to be made is that of the LEA information and support services used by chairs and governors – and approximately 90 per cent had made use of one or more – a very high proportion found them to be helpful. As shown in Table 4.6, on each and every service provided by LEAs, three-quarters or more of chairs and governors (who had used them) found them to be helpful. (Headteachers were not asked this question.) For four services – curriculum guidelines, information packs, handbooks/guidance notes and briefing sessions – over 90 per cent of both governors and chairs reported them to be helpful. An analysis of the earlier NFER survey shows a very similar pattern of responses to the current survey i.e. a generally very high proportion reporting the service(s) to be helpful. (Keys & Fernandes, 1990).

Table 4.5: Use of information/support services provided for school governors by LEAs

	% reporting use*		
Type of information/support service used:	**Heads**	**Chairs**	**Governors**
Newsletter(s)/bulletins for governors	81	82	85
Curriculum Guidelines	50	51	48
Information packs	58	50	54
Handbooks/Guidance Notes	59	65	66
Policy papers	59	63	51
Instruments and Articles of Government	75	79	65
Videos	30	19	23
Link governors	45	36	31
Briefing sessions on specific topics	55	59	41
Telephone hotlines	16	19	11
Reference collections in libraries	16	10	10
(n=	339	209	207)

(Percentages do not total 100 as more than one response could be made.)*

Table 4.6: How helpful were the information/support services that were used?

Type of information/support service used:	% finding service helpful*	
	Chairs	**Governors**
Newsletter(s)/bulletins for governors	91	86
Curriculum Guidelines	95	94
Information packs	96	96
Handbooks/Guidance Notes	99	95
Policy papers	92	88
Instruments and Articles of Government	89	84
Videos	75	76
Link governors	78	81
Briefing sessions on specific topics	96	95
Telephone Hotline(s)	85	92
Reference collections in libraries	79	83
	(n=205)	(n=221)

(The percentages have been calculated from those who have made use of the various services. The total number (n) refers to those who have used one or more of the services.)*

Recent developments, including the devolution of in-service training (INSET) funds to schools and the changing role of the LEA, has meant that increasingly schools and governing bodies are being charged for these information and support services. Nevertheless, when asked if a direct charge was made for any of the aforementioned services only one-third of headteachers stated this to be the case. Some made reference to an all-inclusive fee, others to a basic entitlement with additional sessions being charged at various rates. In the six case study LEAs for example, some were still providing training and service at no cost, others charged for places on training courses whilst others had become business units, encouraging schools to use their devolved GEST funds to 'buy back' into various packages. Presumably the latter arrangement will become more common in the light of the GEST arrangements for 1995-96.

Respondents were also asked if they felt that the information provided for school governors by the LEA was sufficient to meet their needs. Table 4.7 shows that approximately three-quarters of respondents gauged this to be *'about right'*. (The earlier NFER survey found exactly the same percentage of heads and a higher percentage of governors (78 per cent) reporting the information provided by the LEA to be *'about right'*, (Keys & Fernandes, 1990). Respondents were also requested to indicate any topics or areas on which they would welcome additional information from the LEA in the near future. Insufficient responses were received from chairs or governors for any meaningful comparisons to be made but most heads offered suggestions for topics that they felt additional information from the LEA would be needed in the near future and these are shown in Table 4.8.

Table 4.7: Information provided for school governors by the LEA

	%		
Information provided by the LEA is:	**Heads**	**Chairs**	**Governors**
Not enough	13	12	16
About right	79	75	70
Too much	8	13	14
(n=	339	208	223)

Table 4.8: Topics on which additional information from the LEA will be needed

	%*
Suggested topics/areas:	**Heads**
OFSTED inspections	26
Finance, budget, LMS	25
Personnel issues	23
Assessment and national curriculum	19
Legal requirements/legislation	19
	(n=227)

*(*Percentages do not add up to 100 as more than one topic could be suggested.)*

The views of both chairs and governors (but not heads) on what should be the role of the LEA in relation to the work of the governing body are summarised in Table 4.9. In broad terms, governors were looking towards the LEA to provide governing bodies with advice, information, support, help and guidance. Interestingly, only two per cent of chairs and governors referred to the role of the LEA in monitoring or 'keeping an eye on' the governing body. Similarly, only a small number (four per cent) made a direct reference to the clerking function of LEAs. Clerking was specifically raised as a key issue in two of the case studies and, although no questions were directly asked on this issue in the survey, it was apparent that some LEAs continued to provide a direct clerking service, whilst others restricted themselves to the training and regular briefing of clerks. In fact, when respondents were asked in what ways (if any) could LEAs help governing bodies to fulfil their roles more effectively, the presence of a clerk or an LEA representative to sit on the governing body was mentioned by about one in eight of those responding. Table 4.10 shows the distribution of the various suggestions made and although there are similarities between the categories of respondent, a greater proportion of chairs and governors suggested LEAs could help governing bodies become more effective by operating in a more speedy, efficient and open manner, and by providing short, digestible, jargon-free information on educational matters. Interestingly, the single most frequent response from heads was to make a positive comment about what the LEA was providing or to state that it could do little more that it was currently doing. Several heads also made reference to the declining resource base of the LEA and the associated difficulties this has brought, such as the withdrawal of the LEA's presence (as clerks) at governing body meetings. The following comment from a primary head was representative of the many positive comments made:

> *The LEA should continue to offer the whole governing body training sessions plus the existing menu service. It should continue to clerk meetings, and continue to present 'digested' documents for noting, decision and/or adoption.*

Finally, respondents were asked if their governing body did **not** use the services provided by the LEA, to whom did it turn for information, support and training. As most made use of the LEA, there were few responses to this question. However, of those responding, the following were mentioned most frequently: the Diocesan Board; the head and senior management team (or some 'in-house' arrangement); private consultants; GM Schools Centre; professional bodies and national organisations (e.g. NAGM, SHA, NAHT, AGIT) and institutes of higher education.

Table 4.9: Views on the role of the LEA in relation to the work of governing bodies

	% *	
Role of LEA:	**Chairs**	**Governors**
To provide general advice and information	58	48
To offer support and help	57	56
To give impartial/neutral guidance	22	18
To provide specific expertise (e.g. legal, health and safety, personnel, premises)	19	17
To provide training for governors	11	12
	(n=200)	(n=200)

*(*Percentages do not total 100 as more than one view could be offered.)*

Table 4.10: Ways in which the LEA could help the governing body fulfil its role more effectively

	%*		
Suggestions made for the LEA:	**Heads**	**Chairs**	**Governors**
Acting more efficiently/openly	19	29	34
Provision of more training (both general and tailored to needs)	19	15	18
Presence of LEA representative or clerk on governing body	11	13	14
Provision of short, jargon-free information on educational matters	9	22	19
Greater devolution of funds to schools	9	9	8
Positive comment about LEA or 'None'	30	17	11
(n=	186	151	138)

*(*Percentages do not total 100 as more than one suggestion could be offered.)*

Training and support: the case studies

The training and support provided by the LEAs was explored in the case studies. Interviewees generally viewed favourably the support and training offered: in many cases comments were made about the high quality of current provision. But the take up of training amongst the case study governing bodies was patchy. Some governors having attended training courses 'in the early days' no longer felt they needed or had the time for further course attendance, whereas others simply refused to be trained, regarding, for example, participation in governing body meetings or 'on-the-job' training as sufficient. One governor had received no formal training and spoke of 'learning by doing': *'I want to be my own person: I don't want to be trained'*. Those heads and governing bodies who offered induction programmes or handbooks for new governors were able, to some extent, to ensure there was at least some preparation and training for what was generally considered to be a demanding role.

LEA governor trainers remarked that established or experienced governors often felt they did not need training, whereas the newer appointees had a different attitude and perceived the need for training and support, particularly on new issues and areas. The take-up of training generally however was reported to be buoyant:

> *There are individual governors who resist attempts to train them, but over 90% of governing bodies had sent at least one person on a course; I think we have increased the percentage this year. If every governor applied we couldn't cope, but some governors apply for more than ten courses at once (the record is 15). This is an exception. We need to do a survey to ascertain why some governors don't apply. We've agreed with the link governors to devise a grid which will show the total number of courses that we've run with a space down the side for governing bodies to put their names and each governor will be able to enter who attended what. I'd like to find out why people don't attend.*
> (LEA: GTC.)

In one of the case studies, the LEA provided an eight week foundation course (soon to be extended to ten weeks). The governor training coordinator remarked:

> *We are now spending less time on NC, but have to spend more time on other issues (e.g. OFSTED, special needs). This constitutes 20 hours of basic training. We have moved away from the title 'induction training' because we think people who have been governors for, say,*

eight years could benefit: they need the up-date because so many things are new. We run on average 4 sessions per term, during the day, in the evening or on Saturdays. The timings are rotated in each term and each locality. Since the funding for these courses comes out of category five GEST funding, all governors have free access. No devolved budget money has to be used. The foundation course has evolved largely because of the commitment and expertise of my colleagues: a detailed analysis is prepared and the content is evaluated and changed where necessary every term. At the end of the course governors have a manual of about 200 pages, which they have built up over the eight weeks and which aren't just copies of course handouts. Homework is given each week in the form of a case study, and the following week's session will start with this case study.

In one LEA, which offered a total package which school governing bodies could purchase, data were kept on the take-up of governor training and each governing body sent a print-out of course attendance. This also enabled governing bodies to ascertain whether or not they were making full use of the service to which they were subscribing.

Not all comments received about training were favourable and some case study governors felt disappointed with the training they had received. Criticisms tended to focus on the inability of some trainers to adapt to a mixed ability group or to put themselves *'in the shoes of governors'*. As a primary school chair remarked:

Courses should be very concentrated and the presenters very experienced who know the sorts of questions people are going to ask. For example, 'this is the precise nature of the responsibility, this is what you need to know, this is the extent to which you should interfere, this is what you do if you are concerned'. It is all in the handbooks but you need practical examples. I thought the courses were awful: I stopped going. (Chair: Primary.)

Other governors felt they had not been sufficiently encouraged to attend courses:

I asked about training and was told I could go if I wanted to but I received no encouragement from the headteacher or chair. By the time you get the (course) booklet you're usually too late for half of them anyway or they clash. I've just applied for one on 'Appraisal' and one on 'Appointing Staff', as now I'm on Personnel (subcommittee). I asked the clerk of governors what I did about applying for these courses but she wasn't sure. It seemed as if it was a most unusual question. I think there should be more encouragement, more emphasis on training. (Foundation governor: Secondary.)

Being a governor was a position of responsibility and surprise was expressed by some that training was optional:

I would have thought that governors would have been required to have training as opposed to having the option. Being a governor of a school is not like being on the committee of the tennis club - because of the responsibilities not only legal, but to the children. Whoever voted for me considered me to be suitable, so I have a responsibility. There is a very serious side to being a governor. (Parent governor: Secondary.)

However, regardless of the quality of the training provision itself, the value of meeting other governors was often acknowledged. As an LEA training coordinator remarked:

One of the things that comes through on evaluation sheets is the value at courses of meeting governors from other schools who are dealing with the same problems; so I think there will be a demand for formal training sessions as well as a greater demand for sessions working with the whole governing body. We have far fewer moans at training sessions than we used to, and are far more likely to get people who are pleased to meet and discuss mutual problems. I would therefore place a high priority on courses which enable governors from a variety of schools to come together.

Training for whole school governing bodies was also available and LEA training coordinators remarked that a growing proportion of their time was being spent on such activities. Some case study heads commented that they did not feel their governing body had yet reached the stage when it could be trained as a group. In their view, there were one or two governors who would resist such training, thus decreasing the likelihood of success. Others, however, were contemplating ways in which they could develop their governing bodies and become more effective. In one case, a residential weekend for the whole governing body had been postponed because of an impending OFSTED inspection. LEA training coordinators were asked to comment on their activities with whole governing bodies. One commented:

Most of those who wanted or needed training (as individual governors) have now been trained. We have taught them to swim, now we must improve their stroke.

In the view of another coordinator:

Schools are increasingly asking for training in school and it may well be that more training in the future is school-based - either team-building for the whole governing body or a whole staff activity. What we do at the moment in school-based sessions are things like developing school policies, team building, formulating a scheme of delegation (committee structures) and effective meetings. (LEA: GTC.)

In one LEA, all schools who subscribed to the service were offered a two-hour school-based training session and about two thirds had taken up the option. As the LEA coordinator remarked:

We try to encourage schools to book their session early. We send information out through the LEA asking governors about training sessions, so that it will have to go on the governing body agenda at least once a year. The sessions would include: any big issues the governing body felt it needed to deal with (e.g. special needs). There was, however, so much choice as to what we included that governing bodies didn't know what to choose. Whilst it is good for them to be able to choose, it sometimes means that they ask for training as a knee jerk response to a perceived inadequacy, and there is no planning ahead or development of training. We have now re-vamped the sessions into modules under five different headings. You can therefore choose a particular heading or pick and mix. The headings include 'development training' (e.g. what's involved in planning, the SDP, etc), 'building relationships' and 'the curriculum'. We will publish these so that governing bodies can choose over the year. The (school-based) session would usually be in the evening. There is flexibility of organisation (e.g. if a school joined with two others they would get three school-based sessions for the price of one; or they could elect to tag it on to the end of a meeting where the issue is being considered). To date, governing bodies have generally opted for sessions separate to the school and separate from other meetings. It does take a long time for schools to plan what they need to do.

Collective rather than individual training was most likely to be tailored to the needs of the governing body. Coordinators reported that in-house training for governing bodies involved looking at development and organisational issues - the way in which they organise their committees, record their meetings, and management issues. One coordinator explained that in his LEA, working with the whole governing body would only occur if there was a specific request from an officer or adviser. This request would be made because of the difficulties which a particular governing body was perceived to be having. Such requests however were not very frequent.

In another LEA, criteria had been developed for the provision of school-based training:

> *We do put on training for whole governing bodies. In addition to the usual courses, we do training in working as a team, having effective meetings and so on. The training advisory group worked out criteria for providing school-based training, because we have to pay the professional development unit for the staff to run this. The criteria they came up with were: if there were a lot of new governors on the governing body, or if there was a new head. If there were particularly difficult issues to deal with we would also provide support. This might come about in two ways: the governing body would ask for it, or it would come about as a result of my work with heads. The type/direction of the training would be decided by the professional trainer, having regard to the needs of the particular governing body. S/he would do a range of things (e.g. team building, analysis of strengths and weaknesses, time management, stress management etc.).*
>
> (LEA: GTC.)

A coordinator from another LEA remarked how working with governing bodies was often on request:

> *When I go out to schools, this is because I've been asked to, but there are different reasons for my being asked: the head may want me to raise the consciousness of the governing body to their responsibilities, or conversely to stop the governing body taking over the management of the school; sometimes the chair of governors wants to develop more team spirit, or the chair of governors doesn't think the head knows what the governors are trying to do. The hidden agenda must be understood.* (LEA: GTC.)

There was reported to be the beginning of a demand from governing bodies for some sort of evaluation of their effectiveness and the OFSTED inspection process had made governing bodies more aware of the need for this. However, concern was also expressed that LEAs and governor training coordinators were unable to be more proactive in relation to monitoring the effectiveness of governing bodies. A chair, who as a governor of another school had recently experienced an OFSTED inspection noted:

> *Personally, I think the LEA should monitor a bit better how the governing bodies are getting on. Nobody actually looks to see how we are getting on, whether we're coping or not, whether we are fulfilling our role or not. They see whether the school is doing its job but nobody sees whether we are. They have an auditor who checks the accounts. The government has the power to take away the governing body's powers but nobody checks up before that point. They inspect the schools but not governing bodies.* (Chair: Primary.)

A coordinator elaborated on the limited influence that the LEA could exert on the operation of governing bodies:

> *There is a significant number of heads who want to operate almost apart from the governing body, and occasionally heads are willing to take on all the work of the governing body themselves to maintain control. The LEA can still have some influence, but if the head is running the school well, it probably would not try to nudge the head to give the governing body more space. It would have to be done very sympathetically. There is no specific trouble-shooter if a school needs help.* (LEA: GTC.)

The LEA's role was seen by most case study governors not only as providing training – individual and collective – but also offering advice, helping to solve problems and providing a safety net.

Summary

Just under half of the headteachers participating in this study and more than three quarters of chairs and other governing body members had received formal training for their role as governors. Most had found it useful in helping them to understand and fulfil their responsibilities. Responses showed wide variation in relation to the amount of money that had been devolved to schools for training purposes. Whilst the monies had generally been spent on training courses, LEA training related services and the purchase of training materials, some respondents reported that these funds were not used exclusively for training but also for other aspects of governing body operations. (It will be interesting and important to monitor how funds are deployed under the latest GEST arrangements.) Very few governors had claimed reimbursement for expenses incurred in attending training sessions or in carrying out their duties. Most were unaware whether such reimbursement could be made or whether the LEA provided childminding facilities during training sessions.

The training undergone by respondents had covered a wide range of topics, though particular emphasis had been placed on local management of schools, the role and functions of governors, and personnel matters including staff recruitment and selection. The importance of these topics was confirmed by respondents' views of the future training requirements of governors, though it was also felt that the need for governing bodies to keep abreast of recent developments and issues in education should be addressed in future training programmes. Heads in particular were also keen for governing bodies to receive more information and training with regard to the demands made by OFSTED inspections.

A comparison with the findings from the NFER study carried out in 1990 showed that governors were now making greater use of the information and support services offered by LEAs. Newsletters or bulletins for governors, handbooks, guidance notes and instruments and articles of government were found to be especially valuable, though there was little recourse being made to training videos, telephone hotlines and reference collections in libraries.

Data from the case studies showed that training was usually valued and that there was a general trend towards collective as well as individual governor training. This trend was said to be partly a result of the need for governing bodies to consider their own effectiveness.

Chapter 5
Who Becomes a Governor and Why?

Whether or not governors are elected, they must first agree to have their names put forward for consideration as governors. Above all they are volunteers: nobody is obliged or coerced to sit on a governing body. It was noted earlier that the bulk of headteachers, given the choice, had decided to become members of their school's governing body. But what about other governors? What sort of people choose to become governors and what is known about their background? Also, which aspects of being a governor do they find most enjoyable, most time-consuming and most difficult? The earlier NFER survey provided detailed information on many aspects of school governors – their age, sex, occupational background, for example – and the current survey wished to examine, amongst other things, the extent to which these had changed. Was the typical governor today very different from that of the late 1980s?

Background details

The earlier NFER survey found that approximately half of governors but only 30 per cent of chairs of governing bodies were female (Keys and Fernandes, 1990). A virtually identical *gender* distribution was found for the current sample. Further analysis showed statistically significant differences between gender and school phase. Approximately two-thirds of primary school chairs and 80 per cent of secondary school chairs were male. Sixty per cent of secondary school governors were male, whilst in primary school governing bodies there was a more even balance between the sexes (54 per cent were female). A similar picture was found for the *age* distribution of chairs of governing bodies although not quite such correspondence was evident for governors (Table 5.1). (Where relevant, the percentages from the Keys and Fernandes' survey have been shown on the tables in brackets to enable comparisons to be more easily made.) Approaching half of the chairs completing the current questionnaire were aged 45 to 60 with a significant proportion – one-quarter – over 60 years of age. Governors tended to be younger – 42 per cent were under 45.

The position regarding the *ethnic origin* or background of chairs and governors was similar to the earlier survey, with the great majority (92 per cent) being of British origin (Table 5.2). The shortage of governors from ethnic minority backgrounds is noticeable and is not at all representative of their numbers in the population as a whole.

Table 5.1: Age of governors and chairs

	% of samples*			
Age:	Chairs		Governors	
Under 30	0.5	(0)	0.5	(2)
30-44	26	(27)	41.5	(51)
45-60	48	(44)	41	(36)
Over 60	25	(28)	15	(12)
Missing data	1	(1)	2	(0)
	100	(100)	100	(100)
	n=233	(n=614)	n=241	(n=2634)

(The percentages in brackets are taken from the earlier NFER survey in 1990. Due to rounding errors, percentages may not total 100.)*

Table 5.2: Ethnic origin of governors and chairs

	% of samples*			
Ethnic background:	Chairs		Governors	
English/Scottish/ Welsh/Northern Irish	92	(96)	92	(98)
Other European	2	(1)	0.5	(1)
Afro-Caribbean/ African	0	(0.2)	0	(0.3)
Indian, Pakistani or Bangladeshi	0.5	(0.2)	1	(0.5)
Chinese	0	(0)	0	(0)
Other	1	(1)	1	(0.5)
Prefer not to say	2	(0)	2	(0)
Missing data	2.5	(1.5)	3.5	(0)
	100	(100)	100	(100)
	n=233	n=614	n=241	(n=2634)

(The percentages in brackets are taken from the earlier NFER survey in 1990.)*

Tables 5.3 to 5.5 show how long governors and chairs of governing bodies had been involved in school governance. For chairs, as in the earlier survey, the median length of service *as governors* was eight years and, *as chairs,* four years (Table 5.3).

Governors, on the other hand, had generally served for a shorter period – a median of four years (see Table 5.5), a year longer than found in the earlier survey. The length of service on the governing body of their *current* school is shown in Table 5.4 (for chairs) and Table 5.5 (for governors). In the current survey, nearly a third of chairs of governors had held the position in their current school for three to five years and over one-fifth for one year or less. Chairs were found to have been governors at their current school for an average of 8.6 years (a median of six years), whilst they had been the chair of the governing body for a shorter period (a mean of 4.6 years and a median of 3.5 years – see Table 5.4). It is interesting to note that the latter figures were considerably lower than those found in the earlier survey. This was not the case, however, for governors. The median length of service on the governing body of their current school was four years for governors (compared with two years in 1990) with one quarter having been a governor (at their current school) for one year or less (Table 5.5).

Table 5.3: Chairs: Length of service as governor and as chair *(in total)*

	% of sample of chairs*		
No. of years:	Governor		Chair of governors
One year or less	1	(2)	17
2	4	(8)	11
3-5	24	(23)	23
6-10	24	(27)	18
11+	36	(33)	12
Missing data	11	(7)	19
	100	(100)	100
n=	233	(614)	233
Mean number of years:	10.8	(9.9)	5.9
Median number of years:	8.0	(8.0)	4.0

(The percentages in brackets are taken from the earlier NFER survey in 1990.)*

Table 5.4: Chairs: Length of service as governor and as chair *(at the school)*

	% of sample of chairs*			
No. of years:	Governor		Chair of governors	
One year or less	3	(1)	22	(11)
2	5	(8)	15	(18)
3-5	34	(33)	32	(43)
6-10	31	(31)	21	(18)
11+	26	(26)	6	(8)
Missing data	1	(2)	5	(2)
	100	(100)	100	(100)
n=	233	(614)	233	(614)
Mean number of years:	8.6	(8.3)	4.6	(8.6)
Median number of years:	6	(7.0)	3.5	(7.0)

(The percentages in brackets are taken from the earlier NFER survey in 1990. Due to rounding errors, percentages may not total 100.)*

Table 5.5: Governors: Length of time as governor *in total* and at *the school*

	% of govenors*			
No. of years:	Governor		Governor at the school	
One year or less	19	(29)	25	(37)
2	8	(18)	12	(21)
3-5	37	(27)	40	(24)
6-10	26	(16)	18	(12)
11+	10	(10)	5	(6)
	100	(100)	100	(100)
n=	241	(2528)	241	(2613)
Mean number of years:	6.0	(4.8)	4.3	(3.8)
Median number of years:	4.0	(3.0)	4.0	(2.0)

(The percentages in brackets are taken from the earlier NFER survey in 1990. The percentages have been calculated from those providing responses so as to make comparisons meaningful.)*

The *educational background* and qualifications obtained by the sample of chairs and governors is shown in Table 5.6. Nearly half of chairs of governing bodies and 44 per cent of governors held first or higher degrees with a third and a quarter of the sample respectively also possessing a professional qualification. (The previous NFER survey found similar evidence of a well-educated and highly qualified group of governors). Although the current survey did not seek details of the type of employing organisation, it is interesting to note the proportion of chairs and governors – about a quarter – who were in possession of a teaching qualification.

Respondents were also requested to provide details of their occupation or former occupation if retired or unemployed. The occupations were then classified using the *Standard Occupational Classification* and the results are shown in Table 5.7. Direct comparisons with the earlier NFER survey were not possible but a similar picture emerged of a significant proportion of governors in professional and intermediate occupations. Representation from manual workers was extremely low and non-existent from unskilled or semi-skilled occupations.

Table 5.6: Educational/professional qualifications of chairs and governors

	% of samples*	
Qualifications held:	**Chair**	**Governors**
GCSE/GCE O-levels/CSE/Secretarial	69	68
BTEC/Ordinary National Diploma or Certificate	3	8
BTEC/Higher National Diploma or Certificate	5	8
GCE A-levels	49	39
Full industrial apprenticeship	7	7
Teachers' Certificate	24	25
Degree or higher degree	49	44
Professional institute final qualification (e.g. accountancy, surveying, etc.)	33	24
Other	4	1
	(n=215)	(n= 226)

(Percentages do not total 100 as more than one response could be given.)*

Table 5.7: Occupation (or former occupation) of chairs and governors

Occupational classification:	% of samples	
	Chair	**Governors**
Professional occupations	24	21
Intermediate occupations e.g. managers	57	50
Skilled occupations (e.g. non-manual)	3	11
Skilled occupations (e.g. manual)	3	5
Partly-skilled occupations	*	0
Unskilled occupations	0	0
Self-employed	1	0
Student	0	*
Missing data	12	13
	100	100
	(n=233)	(n=241)

(1 respondent reported belonging to this category.)*

To summarise, compared with the *governors* responding to the current survey, the *chairs* of school governing bodies were more likely to be:

- *Male (71 per cent compared with 52 per cent).*
- *Older (a quarter were over 60, compared with 15 per cent of the governors).*
- *More experienced (a median length of service as a governor twice as long in general, whilst also having served longer as a governor in their* ***present*** *school - a median length of six years compared to four years for governors).*
- *More highly qualified (about half possessed a degree or higher degree compared with 44 per cent of the governors. However, compared with the population at large, the governors surveyed were also extremely well qualified).*
- *From professional and intermediate occupations (although the bulk of respondents had occupations in these categories, the proportion was lower for governors responding to the survey).*

Why become a governor?

Both governors and chairs of governing bodies were asked to give their reasons for deciding to become a school governor. They were not presented with a series of categories or options but simply asked to indicate their reasons. The responses from both categories of respondent are shown in Table 5.8 which suggests that there were several main reasons why individuals opted to become school governors. Both chairs and governors made most frequent reference to the fact that their children attended or had attended the school and that as a parent they were very interested in their child's schooling. Chairs and governors were also asked (if applicable) if their children attended the school of which they were a governor and Table 5.10 shows the respective percentages. In fact, if those not responding or answering *'not applicable'* are omitted from the calculations, approximately two-thirds of chairs and nearly three-quarters of governors reported that they had children who, at some stage, attended the school.

The other main reasons given for becoming involved in school governance centred on a sense of public duty or public service to the community, or being persuaded, encouraged or invited to put one's name forward to fill a governor vacancy. An interest in young people and education was also mentioned quite frequently. It is interesting to note that a similar proportion of chairs and governors – about one-in-ten – stated that they had decided to become a school governor because of their professional involvement in education (see Table 5.8).

Table 5.8: Reasons for becoming a governor

	%*	
Main reasons given:	**Chair**	**Governors**
• Children attend(ed) school/parental interest	30	30
• A sense of public duty/service	23	21
• Persuaded/invited to fill vacancy	20	22
• Interested in education/young people	20	17
• Desire to contribute to the school	11	16
• Professional involvement in education	10	11
• Councillor/LEA representative	10	3
• Appointed by church	10	4
• Enjoy being in school	9	8
• Concern over a particular matter	8	8
• Wished to be part of decision-making process	6	7

(Percentages do not total 100 as more than one reason could be given. The percentages have been calculated from the number responding to this question and not from the total samples.)*

The rewards and pitfalls of governance

The *most rewarding* aspect of being a governor invariably centred around developing relationships with others, particularly students and staff, and seeing the school improve or make progress. For heads, many of the reasons put forward would also probably account for why they were working in education. The pattern of responses for chairs and governors was quite similar with nearly one-third of both groups making reference to schools visits, meeting pupils and working with children. The main areas or aspects of governance that respondents found most rewarding are shown in Table 5.9.

Table 5.9: Most rewarding aspects of being a governor

	%*		
Main areas/topics mentioned:	**Heads**	**Chairs**	**Governors**
• School improvements/achievements	25	33	16
• Developing relationships/involvement with staff and pupils	16	34	22
• Working together	15	7	8
• Planning the school's future	15	7	5
• Responsible for resource allocation	9	3	6
• Visiting the school/meeting pupils	8	30	32
• Personnel matters	7	11	10
• Aspects relating to the running of school	6	8	13
• Short, productive meetings	6	13	4
• Meeting parents/community links	4	8	7
• Involvement in school events	1	12	11
• Making a contribution to the school and the community	0.5	2	8
(n=	220	215	219)

(* *Percentages do not total 100 as more than one area could be suggested. The percentages have been calculated from those providing responses and not from the total samples.)*

The *most time-consuming* aspects of being a governor tended to centre on two main areas: reading documents and other paperwork; and the meetings of the full governing body and its committees (Table 5.10). Perhaps unsurprisingly, for heads a third commonly mentioned topic or area concerned the preparation and production of reports and documents.

Details of the amount of time devoted to activities as a governing body member were given in Chapter 2, where it was reported that heads, on average, spent nearly three-and-a-half hours per week on such activities. Other research into headship has also suggested that the new governing bodies are, amongst other things, making increased demands on heads' time (e.g. Earley, Weindling and Baker, forthcoming).

Matters relating to finance and the school's budget (LMS) although commented on by approximately one-in-eight were not as frequently referred to by chairs as they were in the earlier NFER survey (Keys and Fernandes, 1990). A similar proportion of heads made reference to the time they had to spend in keeping governors informed of educational matters and issues (see Table 5.10). As a primary head remarked:

> *I find giving them sufficient knowledge to be incredibly time-consuming and I often think my time could be better spent. They have too much to decide. They rely on me heavily and this is an extra burden at a time when headship is becoming more demanding.*

A case study head made a similar point. She said:

> *(As a governing body) we don't feel we have the necessary qualifications, time or information to attend to all that is demanded of us. As head I feel governors lean on me far too much and look to me for advice and information as well as being the main governing body admin assistant.*

In relation to this matter of '*educating*' governors, several of the case study headteachers produced such things as a termly newsletter for governors and saw an important part of their job – as with members of the school's staff – as having a training and development function.

Table 5.10: Most time-consuming aspects of being a governor

Main areas/topics mentioned:	%*		
	Heads	Chairs	Governors
• Preparing/producing documents and reports	37	9	8
• Meetings of full governing body and its committees	36	31	47
• Reading documents/paperwork	24	48	32
• Informing governors of educational matters	12	2	0.5
• Budget/financial matters	11	12	7
• Personnel issues	4	10	6
• Keeping abreast of educational developments	4	5	9
(n=	246	204	204)

(Percentages do not total 100 as more than one area could be suggested. The percentages have been calculated from those providing responses and not from the total samples.)*

The main areas or topics mentioned as the *most difficult* aspects of being a governor are recorded in Table 5.11. The area commented upon most frequently by all three categories of respondent concerned personnel issues, particularly in relation to such areas as redundancy, capability, incompetence and the determination of salaries. Motivating governors to embrace their responsibilities was mentioned by about on-in-six heads, with a similar proportion of heads and governors making reference to the difficulties created for governing bodies by having to cope with constant changes. Interestingly, understanding of the budget or finance was mentioned by only one-in-ten governors who provided comments, slightly fewer than the number referring to pupil exclusions and discipline. Although reconciling the respective roles of heads and governors was not a difficulty reported by governors, about one-in-eight made some comment about 'working relationships' on the governing body, usually with a specific reference to the head or staff. Managing information or 'paperwork' did not appear to be as significant a factor as it was in the earlier NFER survey, or indeed, as reported by other surveys (e.g. P.E. International, 1993). Managing paper had proved to be time-consuming but it was not necessarily difficult.

Table 5.11: Most difficult aspects of being a governor

Main areas/topics mentioned:	%*		
	Heads	**Chairs**	**Governors**
• Personnel issues	22	22	16
• Motivating governors to embrace responsibilities	16	9	2
• Coping with constant changes	15	9	16
• Finding time	9	8	8
• Understanding finance/budget	8	10	11
• Managing information	6	0.5	2
• Reconciling roles of head and governors	6	0.5	0.5
• Pupil exclusion and discipline	5	13	10
• Managing effective meetings	3	9	4
• Parental cooperation/participation	2	9	3
• Working relationships	2	11	12
(n=	207	197	191)

(* *Percentages do not total 100 as more than one area could be suggested. The percentages have been calculated from those providing responses and not from the total samples.*)

Summary

Half of the governors but only 30 per cent of the chairs participating in this study were female. Chairs tended to be older and by far the majority of both chairs and governors were of British origin. Most governors had served for four years, whilst chairs had generally served as governors for eight years before taking on the chair. Governing bodies were composed of well-educated and highly qualified professionals.

The main reasons for becoming a governor were reported as having a child currently or formerly at the school, having a sense of public service, and being invited to serve. The most rewarding aspect of the role was in seeing the school improve and in developing good relations with staff and students. The most time-consuming tasks were dealing with the associated paperwork and attending meetings of the full governing body and its committees. The most difficult aspect of being a governor centred on personnel issues.

Chapter 6

What is an Effective Governing Body?

The last few years have seen no shortage of commentary about the nature of an effective governing body and advice on the various strategies which governing bodies can use to evaluate their own performance and improve practice (see for example, AGIT, 1994; Curtis, 1994; NAGM, 1994; Oxford Centre for Educational Management, n.d.; Sallis, 1993, 1994; Woodhouse, 1993). NAGM – a national voluntary organisation run by governors – for example, states that a governing body may be considered effective if it does two things:

- *it contributes significantly to what the school does to give pupils a good education*
- *it does its work efficiently and governors use productively and to good purpose the limited time they can devote to their duties.*

(NAGM 1994.)

Similarly, Woodhouse (writing on behalf of the national governor training organisation, AGIT) remarks that:

> *The effective governing body takes decisions within an agreed policy framework, planning for the future, budgeting to meet priorities. In doing this and monitoring the effects, it assures the quality of education of children in the school.*

Furthermore, she continues:

> *Governors in an effective governing body .... develop relationships both inside and outside the school; they learn to work together as a team; they set the framework for future decision-making through development planning, budget-setting and policy-making; they develop lines of communication with parents; and finally, they regularly evaluate their own performance and seek ways to become more effective.* (Woodhouse, 1993.)

All participants in the NFER research project were asked to give their views on the main features of an effective governing body. As might be expected, a large number of comments were received from respondents to this open-ended question. The most frequently mentioned features or attributes were coded and these have been listed in Table 6.1. As can be seen from the table, although there was a considerable degree of agreement between heads, governors and chairs of governing bodies on many features, there were nevertheless some interesting differences.

Table 6.1: Main features of an effective governing body

	%*		
Main features mentioned:	Heads	Chairs	Governors
• Gives time to school/committed	47	39	28
• Supports school, staff and pupils	40	29	27
• Knowledgeable of educational issues	32	28	18
• Balance of skills and expertise/ representative of local community	31	31	27
• Shared tasks & responsibilities within governing body/teamwork	30	39	30
• Works well with head and staff	29	34	35
• Visits school/see school 'at work'	26	25	21
• Involved in key functions (e.g. policy, monitoring, resource allocation)	23	24	32
• Acts as 'critical friend'	23	14	11
• Factors associated with meetings/ committees (e.g. short, well-attended, purposeful, good clerk)	20	22	24
• Promotes school in community/ develops links	18	22	24
• Aware of roles and responsibilities (governance v. management)	18	13	12
• Factors associated with Chair	18	8	18
• Knowledgeable of school and staff	15	15	9
• Clear view/understanding of school's aims, ethos, etc.	9	10	12
(n=	406	208	225)

(Percentages do not total 100 as more than one suggestion could be made.)*

For headteachers, the most commonly mentioned feature – referred to by nearly half of all those responding – related to the notion of *commitment* and the *giving of time and priority* to the school. Although chairs of governing bodies also frequently mentioned this factor (39 per cent), it was less often noted by governors (28 per cent) and further statistical analysis showed this be to a significant difference. Statistically significant differences between the three categories of respondents were also found in relation to the following attributes or features of an effective governing body:

- *supports school, staff and pupils*
- *acts as 'critical friend'*
- *knowledgeable of educational issues*
- *factors associated with the chair*

With the exception of the feature *'factors associated with the chair'* it was headteachers who were significantly more likely to make reference to the above attributes or characteristics of effective governing bodies. Headteachers, for example, clearly regarded the notion of a *critical friend,* offering objective guidance and commentary, to be an important feature of an effective governing body to a much greater extent than did their fellow governors. All three groups of respondents attached importance to having a balance of skills, expertise and local community interests represented on the governing body.

Concerning the *'awareness of roles and responsibilities'* or, as it is also sometimes termed, the differences between '*governance and management*', two points can be made. Firstly, it was not in the top ten most commonly mentioned factors by any group; and, secondly, it was more likely to be mentioned by heads than it was by chairs or governors. Bearing in mind the lack of clarity between the specific roles and responsibilities of governors and school managers (e.g. Morris, 1994; DFE, 1993) it is interesting to note the relative ranking given to this particular attribute of an effective governing body. Similarly, it is noteworthy that notions of clarity of purpose and *understanding of school aims, objectives and/or ethos* were mentioned by only approximately one in ten respondents.

Headteachers were also asked if there were any factors which prevented the governing body from being as effective as it might be. Just over two-thirds (67 per cent) of heads stated that there were negative factors at work. (There were no statistically significant differences between the responses of heads of primary or secondary schools.) Headteachers were also asked to provide details of any factors at work preventing the governing body from being as effective as it might (Table 6.2). A number of factors were mentioned and of those heads providing information, by far the most common reference (60 per cent) was to the *lack of time* available for the responsibilities and functions of governing bodies to be fulfilled. As a primary head remarked:

> *Governing bodies have far too much material to absorb. Governors have difficulties in 'coming to an understanding' of many issues. I have to spend too much time explaining and this all limits the quality of any meaningful debate. Quite honestly, they accept my recommendation always - in full but then I know what they are likely to approve!*

Another remarked:

> *Most governors are very ordinary people who know very little about complicated laws, finance, personnel issues, etc. They also have jobs and families which take up the majority of their time. Being a governor is seen as a minor role.*

Insufficient knowledge and understanding of educational issues by members of the governing body was the heads' second most common response (14 per cent) followed closely by a reference to individual governors not being prepared to undertake tasks or demonstrate any form of *commitment* (13 per cent). *Constant changes and initiatives or innovation overload,* which amongst other things was making long term planning difficult, was mentioned by nearly one-in-ten headteachers. *Political partisanship, lack of awareness of how the school works* and uncertainty of the governing body's *proper role and function* (its raison d'être) were also mentioned, albeit not commonly, as were a number of other factors.

Governors and chairs of governors were asked to describe any factors which prevented a) **them** from effectively fulfilling their role and b) the **governing body** from being as effective as it might. As far as their roles were concerned, a similar proportion made reference to the *lack of time* (65 per cent) and *insufficient knowledge and understanding of educational issues* (16 per cent of governors and 11 per cent of chairs) as significant factors preventing them from fulfilling **their roles** effectively. The responses of chairs and governors to the second part of the question relating to **governing body** effectiveness are shown in Table 6.2. In broad terms, a similar pattern of responses to the heads can be seen although more references were made to time constraints on **individual** governors rather than **collective** governing body effectiveness. Other items mentioned by more than ten per cent of respondents were: insufficient knowledge and understanding of educational issues, lack of commitment and an imbalance of expertise and experience. It is also noteworthy that just under one-in-ten chairs of governors providing comments were unsure of the proper role and function of the governing body, whilst one-in-twenty remarked that there were *too many demands and responsibilities* put on governing bodies for them to be effective. Not a single chair of governors made reference to the *headteacher* as a factor preventing the governing body from being as effective as it might, although reference was made to school leadership by a small proportion of governors (seven per cent). Chairs were in fact asked to whom they would turn if they had a problem about the role of the head or the role of the governing body. The results, shown in Table 6.3, point to the importance of the LEA's advisers and inspectors. Certainly, as shown in Chapters 4 and 7, the issue of who monitors the work of the governing body and the headteacher is crucial.

Table 6.2: Factors preventing governing body effectiveness

	%*		
Main factors mentioned:	**Heads**	**Chairs**	**Governors**
• Lack of time	60	44	30
• Insufficient knowledge and understanding of educational issues	14	15	15
• Unwillingness/lack of commitment	13	9	12
• Imbalance of skills/expertise/experience	11	11	8
• Constant change/innovation overload	9	8	8
• Political partisanship/factions	7	3	2
• Lack of awareness of how school works	6	4	4
• Unsure of proper role & function	5	9	5
• Information overload	3	7	1
• No clear idea of committees' roles	4	-	11
• Financial problems/funds retained at centre	3	7	12
• Overcrowded agenda	2	5	1
• Relationship with LEA	1	3	4
• Factors associated with the head	-	-	7
• Too many demands/responsibilities	1	5	2
(n=	321	163	119)

(Percentages do not total 100 as more than one factor could be mentioned. The percentages have been calculated from the number offering suggestions and not from the total samples.)*

Table 6.3: Bodies or organisations chairs would turn to if experiencing problems with heads or governing body

	A problem with the role of the:	
	Headteacher	Governing body
Individuals/organisations	% of Chairs**	
Headteacher/other heads	8	28
Governing body/other governors	25	12
Diocesan board*	7	6
LEA advisers/inspectors	52	37
LEA governor unit/trainers	3	9
Governor associations (e.g. NAGM, AGIT)	1	2
Grant Maintained Schools Centre*	1	2
Department for Education	0.5	2
Senior management team (school)	0.5	-
	(n=222)	(n=216)

(* *The percentages have been calculated from the total number of responses from chairs and not solely from chairs of Church or GM schools.*)

(** *Percentages do not total 100 as more than one response could be made.*)

For at least one secondary head the whole question of recognising an effective governing body was problematic, particularly in view of the potential conflict concerning the demarcation between school management and school governance. He remarked:

> *I am not sure that I would recognise an effective governing body in an objective sense. My governing body has many excellent people on it but there is inevitably a conflict between the responsibilities and real accountability of the head for the quality of education and the responsibilities (in the legal sense) of governors. The greatest difficulty is agreeing the divide between governing the school and managing it. The head, in my view, defines policies and runs the school. If the governors feel he/she is not successful they should be able to remove him/her. The real accountability from the client perspective is the headteacher. I have been fortunate in relationships with governors but legislation in Sex Education and R.E. has responded to views of tiny minorities – such an extremist view in a chair of governors could lead to horrific difficulties. Do we really want amateur governors to have such enormous responsibilities?*
>
> (Headteacher: Secondary.)

Although there was a view that the effectiveness of governing bodies was 'a sweepstake' or down to good luck, the attitude of the head towards the governing body was seen as crucial. The degree to which the governing body was able to act in an effective manner was, to a considerable extent, in the hands of headteachers. As one of the case study heads remarked in response to a question on the main features of an effective governing body:

> *I see the head's role as:*
> - *informing*
> - *liaising*
> - *involving*
> - *mediating*
> - *consulting*
> - *advising*
> - *training*
>
> *This should result in a responsive, harmonious governing body.*

The evidence from the survey suggests that the majority of heads wanted their governing body to operate effectively and as envisaged by current legislation, although as earlier discussed, with certain important reservations. As a secondary head remarked:

> *They bring a wider perspective to our decision making. They have been very supportive to the senior management and have influenced decision making. The chair and vice chair have a weekly meeting with me, which enables me to share my problems.*

Governing bodies were said to be a valuable source of support helping to reduce the isolation of headship inherent in the position. The case study heads, for example, often made reference to this, especially in the open, honest and trusting relationships they have developed (or were developing) with chairs of governing bodies. There was also a recognition that governors offered expertise that may not be otherwise available within the school and that an effective headteacher needed to make optimum use of this. Effective governing bodies were informed, committed, supportive, constructively critical and able to debate issues without rancour or reference to political partisanship. Some governors, it was suggested, had not given sufficient thought to their responsibilities in terms of having adequate time for attendance, preparation and training for the role.

The following written comments – from a primary head and two secondary heads – are offered as examples of attempts to delineate the main features of an effective governing body:

An effective governing body will have:

- *A positive/supportive chair who is wise and has humility.*
- *A chair who has had experience of 'running' an organisation herself.*
- *Good back-up from the vice chair.*
- *Good levels of respect for the professionalism of teachers and headteachers.*
- *Stability on the governing body.*
- *Absence of political influences.*

An effective governing body will have:

- *A realisation by the membership that this is a role of responsibility.*
- *Governors who give time and commitment to their role outside the meeting.*
- *A first hand knowledge of the school and positive relationships.*
- *Prepared well and are informed for governors' meetings.*
- *Good use of delegation (sub committees).*

An effective governing body will have:

- *A clear understanding of roles and responsibilities.*
- *Good committee/working group system to share workload.*
- *Good communication/interaction with school and parents.*
- *Mutual support and professional expertise from within the governing body.*
- *A close working relationships with the head, deputy heads and staff.*

In the case studies interviewees were also asked to elaborate on their views of an effective governing body. An LEA governor training coordinator and a primary head (from different LEAs) offered the following descriptions:

An effective governing body should have individual governors with a good knowledge of the school. They need an awareness of their roles and responsibilities, and how they can best put that into practice in the school. They should have an awareness of the strengths of the school, good communications within the school and through the correct channels. They need an understanding of where the buck stops (i.e. they need to grasp what are **not** *their roles and responsibilities). They need good relationships and interpersonal skills and a broad understanding of education. They need to ask themselves what they can do within this for the wider community. They should be able to listen to people, have interview techniques and so on.* (LEA: GTC.)

You can't have an efficient and effective governing body unless the governors know the school. They need to know the staff, the ethos, to be in classes, to see the school operating, to talk to the children. Basically, to know what we are supposed to be doing. They must also work together: there is no success if you have a governing body with one set of views and the school with another. They have to marry their philosophies and expectations and be realistic about what can be achieved with the members of staff you've got. That is true here but I'm not sure how much is from knowledge. They support because they think it is a duty rather than out of educational knowledge. Also you need balance. You are running a business as well as an educational establishment. You have to manage your books, to be mindful of value for money and to have people who could take some of those concerns away from you would be wonderful. You also need a commitment to the school.

(Headteacher: Primary.)

Perhaps the final word should go to chairs of governors who again stressed the difficulties and constraints which were preventing their governing bodies from being effective:

There has been too much change too quickly to assimilate and action. The learning curve of the chair is steep and to make any positive impact/contribution requires too much time for a 'working' chair.

The idea/principle behind the Education Act has its merits, if the government didn't keep moving the goal posts and changing the rules. It is most annoying and frustrating. We will be good 'partners' if they provide the **time** *and the* **resources** *we need.*

It was apparent that there was considerable variation in the degree of effectiveness of different governing bodies and, as remarked by a primary head, *'this rules out any uniformity of support for schools'*. Was it, as suggested by some heads, simply a matter of good fortune if the governing body was fully competent to discharge all of its responsibilities? The key question is therefore how can this support be made more universal.

Summary

For heads, chairs and governors the main features of an effective governing body were said to centre on its members' willingness to share tasks and responsibilities as part of a working team. It was, of course, also considered important that the governing body be able to work well with the head and staff of the school. Commitment in relation to the time and support members gave to the school was seen as critical, particularly by heads and chairs. Heads also felt it important for members to be knowledgeable about educational issues, whilst all three groups of respondents recognised the value of having a balance of skills, expertise and local community interests represented on the governing body.

More than two-thirds of the heads believed that there were factors preventing the governing body from being as effective as it might be. For all groups of respondents, the predominant factor was lack of time, followed by insufficient knowledge and awareness of educational matters. Finally, chairs were asked to indicate where they would seek help if they were experiencing problems with the head or governing body. Their responses indicated that LEA advisers and inspectors have an important role to play here.

Chapter 7
The Case Studies

Although the previous chapters have drawn, to varying degrees, on the responses of the interviewees from the case studies, it is the intention of this chapter to make further use of this data to illustrate a number of *key issues* which appeared to be related to notions of effectiveness. It will be recalled that the case study school governing bodies were selected by the researchers using a number of criteria but generally because their survey returns indicated varying levels of effectiveness. (Two of the six case studies had not been involved in the questionnaire survey.) In this chapter the following issues or areas are examined:

- the roles and responsibilities of governing bodies
- relations between headteachers, chairs and governors
- links with the school and notions of partnership
- governors and school improvement.

These areas and issues are considered not by presenting individual case studies or 'cameos' of governing bodies at work but rather by drawing upon all six to illustrate points where relevant. (Further details of each case study school, headteacher, chair of governors and governing body is given in Appendix 2. Details are also provided of the governors interviewed and the meetings attended.)

Roles and responsibilities

In order to tease out views and gain insights into the actual *practices* of governing bodies, interviewees were asked to comment on the model guidelines which have recently been produced by AGIT (Holt, 1993). These guidelines suggest that the respective roles and responsibilities of governors and heads should not be defined too rigidly and that there is a need to achieve room for manoeuvre. The various partners, it is suggested, should be able to work them out for themselves. The AGIT guidelines state that governors were there to:

- *advise;*
- *provide a different perspective and alternative information;*
- *make policy and set priorities;*
- *mediate different views, initially amongst themselves;*
- *support and promote, but with careful thought about the kind of support required;*
- *monitor, bearing in mind the Secretary of State's intention to place greater accountability on the governing body and the head together.* (Holt, 1993.)

The following extracts from the interviews give an indication of the views held in relation to the above six areas of responsibility.

a) Advise

As far as advice was concerned, a number of interviewees made reference to the fact that advice was offered to the head by the governing body, *where and when it was felt appropriate*. However, it was often stated that it was the governing body who looked to the head for advice, especially in relation to matters that were deemed to be 'professional'. Without exception, the headteacher was seen as the professional adviser to the governing body. As one remarked: *'governors understand that the head has professional expertise and they haven't'*. It was considered to be unwise to seek specific or specialist advice from governors on, for example, the content and organisation of the curriculum but governors could usefully advise on such things as the reactions of the community, parents or the business world and thus provide a wide range of views. As another head commented:

> *I'd look for advice on premises, repairs, lettings; I'd draw on their skills (e.g. accounting). Also I 'd look to the health and safety rep for advice. Some things I would baulk at. Some governors have different agendas, for example a political agenda that we have to be careful about. Some governors would be full of ideas for day-to-day management which is down to me and the staff. I also take advice on contractors.* (Headteacher: Primary.)

A teacher governor stated that generally the governing body did not advise, adding that:

They do (advise) on specific issues (e.g. one governor has expertise on buildings and can offer invaluable advice, another with knowledge of catering, offered advice on contracts). They don't offer advice on curriculum matters – they do question, but they accept the head's view. They might ask, for example about exam pass rates, but they accept the head's response. The governing body is not really critical of the head – they accept his explanations or statements without looking for proof.

(Teacher governor: Secondary)

A governor from another school supported this view:

We tend towards the headteacher's advice on the majority of things. Perhaps we give advice on buildings or grounds maintenance. Education-wise it is very difficult. I wouldn't want someone who didn't know my job to come and give me advice.

(LEA-appointed governor: Primary.)

b) Provide a different perspective

This was generally considered to be an important and necessary function or responsibility of governing bodies. Governing bodies were said to provide alternative information and to act as critical sounding boards:

My governors are pretty well read, with connections with professional people. For example when discussing GM, we had a teacher placement officer who had been in GM schools who was pro-GM. The vice-chair who had been an officer in an LEA took the opposite view. Governors will say: what about this or that? Everyone can freely express views because the meetings are closed. We prefer it that way so that the LEA does not know what we are doing. As headteacher I present choices and the governing body questions them. It is their policy and they have the right to modify and change. I don't want a rubber-stamping body. Generally, they do go the way I expected but they do add, take out, change. (Headteacher: Primary.)

The head was also asked to comment on the general response of his primary headteacher colleagues. He remarked that:

The bulk fall into one of two categories: either the governors 'eat out of my hand' or 'they are difficult because they ask awkward questions'.

He added:

I think it is their duty to ask questions. They must know. They give a critical edge.

The mix of perspectives that a governing body can offer was seen as valuable:

> *Very often schools are like little islands in the middle of their communities. They often don't know what the temperature is outside; how parents see the school and the difficulties they have in understanding what the children are being taught and why in that way. We get to talk to lots of them outside in other situations.*
>
> (Chair: Primary.)

However, not all the case study heads had found governing bodies provided that critical perspective:

> *I can't think of any example where the governing body has acted as a critical friend. As for a sounding board - yes, I'll bring up something and ask which of X or Y we should do.*

What is more as this head added:

> *This can be dangerous because I have thought things through and they are making a decision on the spot. They really need time to chew it over but because governor body meetings are few, decisions need to be made. Also snap decisions at 10 pm. when everyone is tired at the end of a long day can be dangerous.* (Headteacher: Primary.)

c) Make policy and set priorities

There was broad agreement that governing bodies did make policies in certain areas (e.g. health and safety, pay) but in general, especially in curriculum areas, governors tended to respond and adapt draft policies that had been drawn up by the school and presented to them. According to the case study heads, the school's senior management and staff devised policies and set priorities which were then presented to governors who should monitor and ensure implementation. The following interview extracts give examples of how heads and governors perceived their role in relation to policy-making. The first, from a primary head, indicates how a curriculum policy and a pay policy were formulated:

> *Let's take curriculum policy as an example. The curriculum group meets. There is a chat from the curriculum coordinator, usually the governors will then say 'fine, we'll need to look at this again: will you report back to us, when can we have a draft?'. We then go away as a staff and hammer out how we think it should be. The draft comes back to the curriculum working group. The governors have copies of the draft well in advance (usually three weeks). They go through it thoroughly and have made notes. They ask for explanations or say they don't like a particular point. The meeting can last two hours. It's*

almost like a third reading in the House (of Commons). The final draft is presented to the full governing body. It is still called a draft but recommended by the working group, and is finally accepted and minuted as such.

As for the pay policy, this was drawn up by the personnel committee (chair, vice chair, clerk, treasurer, head, deputy head). As headteacher I would be expected to advise. Then the treasurer who is actually in private education will advise on how he sees it, then the clerk who is in a magistrate's court will say how they do it. It will be decided where we want to get to and how we are going to get there. The LEA has not advised on pay policy but the professional associations have and the governors have leaned very heavily on them in the past.

(Headteacher: Primary.)

Another head remarked of his governing body:

They don't make policy. We make the policy within the school and it will then be referred to governors for comment. They don't start out with a blank piece of paper e.g. sex education policy. My specialist in health education will prepare a draft sex education policy, submit it to me – I make some changes – and then put it before the appropriate committee. The teacher concerned attends the committee. They may amend it and then it goes to the full governing body. I never ask the governing body to write a policy. I guess they set priorities at the moment of the budget. Again, it will be very strongly advised by us.

(Headteacher: Secondary.)

A governor from the same school remarked:

The school takes the lead very much in everything - it has to. How can the governing body make the policy? It is initiated by the school, taken to the subcommittees who generally agree (with minor amendments) and then it goes to the full governing body which again usually accepts with minor amendments. (Foundation governor: Secondary.)

A governor from a different school commented on policy-making:

We do this in that we are presented with policy documents for approval by the school. We don't automatically rubber stamp: we go through the documents quite carefully. We do have a role in setting priorities in the SDP: we would expect to spend a meeting discussing this with the head. This is important because the SDP will inform our decisions on spending, etc. Our two major priorities are the SDP and premises. We are not given so much of a lead from the teaching staff on premises.

(Coopted governor: Secondary.)

An LEA governor training coordinator felt that governing bodies needed to be more proactive and that they should be working more closely with schools on policy formulation and priority setting. This, he suggested, was being made difficult by a misuse of governors' time:

Far too many governing bodies receive reports of what has happened (e.g. the headteacher's report is a retrospective account of what has happened). The legal requirement is for one report per year which is retrospective and summarises the work of the school. The head shouldn't be going through this - governors should have read it: this frees the time to look forward. They would then have the time to make policy and set priorities. Most governing bodies are given the school development plan, and have not participated in this. Too many staff in schools want to make the policy. There should be joint working parties with governors and teachers working together. At the school where I am a governor I chair a curriculum working party consisting of myself, two other governors, the deputy head, the KS1 coordinator and the KS2 coordinator. We looked at the resourcing of the curriculum for the next year (staffing, materials, equipment such as computers etc.) We then worked in a larger group looking at priorities, and the curriculum committee then put forward those priorities to the finance committee.

d) Mediate different views

Governing bodies were seen as mediating different views, initially amongst themselves but not among other members of school - as one head remarked that was his job:

If there are widely differing views among members of the governing body then they must sort that out themselves but if there are widely differing views amongst the school staff that's the job of the school management to sort out. (Headteacher: Secondary.)

A parent governor of a secondary school commented:

In a time of such change there are so many views but in a governing body they must really be unanimous to be effective. You can have a lot of dissent but you must come to a group decision that's going to support the school policy or else you'll be bogged down in politics with a small 'p'. The quality of the information brought to us by the headteacher and bursar are of such a nature that you can come to an informed decision. There is no real danger of anyone going along to a meeting and saying 'I don't really understand it but I'll go along with it'.

Political differences of opinion were however occasionally still found:

> *The governing body is divided politically down the middle. You know beforehand how they will vote if it is a political issue. Otherwise it will be a full, open debate.* (Teacher governor: Secondary.)

e) Support and promote

The majority of governors felt most comfortable performing the aspect of their role that concerned promotion and support (see Chapter 3). *'Governors see themselves as supporting the head and the school'* or *'this is the head's school, we're here to support the head'* were common views of the interviewees.

> *Having appointed the headteacher, it is the governing body's bounden duty to support him, through hell and high water. If he is doing wrong, then, fine, they tell him but outside they support him en bloc - equally the teachers. We should promote the school, to the extent everyone wants to send their children to this school. Equally you've got to promote it in the minds of the pupils.*
> (LEA-appointed governor: Secondary.)

> *They do (provide support) and they try very hard to . The support is largely limited to moral support but practical help in the school does go on. They are caring people, they help with reading, etc. The support comes from decisions made in committee: it's not a tangible thing. The school sees the governing body as supportive. It's not 'us and them'.* (Teacher governor: Primary.)

f) Monitor

Governing bodies were said to have a monitoring role but comments from interviewees suggested that this was sometimes problematic, particularly in relation to professional practices.

> *Monitoring is a professional process; lay people will monitor informally and quite properly, but it is wrong for lay people to be involved in a professional monitoring exercise. OFSTED is one monitoring device but it is also the job of management. The governing body does monitor in that it receives regular reports, etc. The chair of the finance committee monitors the finances of the school.*
> (Headteacher: Secondary.)

> *Monitoring? I think we do this. It's in the nature of the regularity of the meetings we hold, that we look to see what we discussed last time, and what's happened since. As a matter of routine we look closely at*

exam results and the school's overall performance. This year we asked the staff to prepare a much more detailed document comparing performance over the last few years.

(Coopted governor: Secondary.)

We keep a very close eye on the budget. The chair of finance is an employee of the county council. We go through the budget with a fine toothcomb. The chair of curriculum subcommittee examines the results and talks about them at full governor meetings. The head rang me when the results came out and asked me to look at them with him before they went to the governing body. (Chair: Secondary.)

However, as an LEA governor training coordinator remarked, monitoring can be misinterpreted to mean inspect:

Governors are not there to inspect but to ensure that certain guidelines and regulations are in place (e.g. appraisal - they are not there to be appraisers but to ensure that it takes place.) The majority of headteachers are governors and therefore it's difficult to separate the two. The governors are not there to make critical assessments but to understand and support the school. They should make sure the school is operating efficiently and effectively. If, for example, a subject area was underperforming, it would be the governing body's responsibility to ensure that the proper procedures were being carried out to deal with it, with due regard to what ensuing developments could be; they would also need to bring in appropriate expertise to assist. It is ultimately the collective responsibility of the governing body and they would have to decide whether or not to act, even if the head did not wish to. (LEA: GTC.)

The issue was also raised of who monitors the operation of governing bodies. A chair of governors, who was also a governor of another school which had recently been the subject of an OFSTED inspection, spoke of the limited value of the process in eliciting objective views about the effectiveness of the governing body. During the inspection the OFSTED inspector had asked her if she was able to raise up difficult or controversial issues in meetings of the full governing body. She had tried to be as diplomatic as possible and replied to the inspector that she could with some but not with others. The case study chair felt that if she had been honest she would have had to say to the inspector that this was not the case. She had found herself in a difficult position as she did not want to be critical of the school because of the implications of this for the

OFSTED report. The resulting adverse publicity could have negative effects on pupil intake and hence resources. She felt there was no in-between situation and was concerned that nobody was monitoring the governing body. It was, she suggested, difficult to go to the LEA and invite them into difficult schools. As she said *'the LEA have to be invited and I can't see any head doing any such thing!'*

Relations between heads, chairs and governors

It was generally recognised that relations between heads and governors, particularly chairs, was crucial to the success of any partnership. The exact nature of the relationship between the head and the chair was explored in each of the case studies. The following interview extracts give an indication of how positive relationships had developed:

> *We meet very briefly to make sure key issues are covered in either the headteacher's or chair's reports. I would always tell him of any issues I was going to raise. I wouldn't spring them on him nor would he spring anything on me. We make sure the agenda is properly prepared. We don't plot the outcome in any sense. We don't manipulate the meeting. It is not wrapped up but common sense indicates you must make sure there is coverage. There are two outstanding items on our agenda. The head's report and the chair's report. Sometimes it will be a report on something we've been doing together. We then have to decide which of us will report it. We clear the undergrowth. He checks the draft agenda and so do I. I see the chair two or three times a week anyway for this or that. He is retired so he is quite available. Our contact is entirely informal. I might not see him for a day or two. Perhaps he comes in for an interview. I might ring him. I take the view that it is my job to keep him informed. Nothing comes as a surprise to him. If I foresee any difficulties on the horizon I will give him a ring and say, "We've got this problem arising, this is what I'm proposing to do, do you think this sounds right?" He'll say "yes" or "we ought to check that out". There is a comfortable relationship but we don't get together and plot.*
>
> (Headteacher: Secondary.)

> *An effective governing body could be one where the chair comes in perhaps once a week. I'd be happy with that: it's a model that I could happily work with. I agree there is a need to develop a healthy working relationship with the chair, but not being seen as this pair making all the decisions, or 'sewing things up' before the meeting of the full*

governing body. Because our chair isn't in the school very much, when he does come in it's greatly valued by staff. I don't think that the other governors would say that the head and the chair have sewn things up. (Headteacher: Secondary.)

Some governing bodies can become meddlesome and interfering, which can hinder the school. The relationship between the head and chair of governing body is therefore crucial. Any head needs support and a good chair will support the head to the hilt if the school is being properly run. (Deputy head/clerk: Secondary.)

There was, however, a recognition that the relationship between the head and the chair should not become 'cosy' or that they should become the key decision-makers to the detriment of other members of the governing body. As a governor and chair commented:

If you have a very good headteacher and a strong chair there could be a tendency for a number of matters to be determined outside the governing body or pre-determined so that the governing body doesn't have the opportunity to play its part.
(Foundation governor: Primary.)

Inevitably some decisions are made outside the meeting, things that need urgent attention. At the moment we are trying to get to grips with getting the subcommittees properly organised so that we can designate what things it's OK to make decisions about - to get it all written down and sorted out properly, to delegate what and to whom. For urgent decisions it used to be the chair and headteacher but some others might have felt excluded. When the Buildings Committee wanted to do something I suggested they spoke to Finance and the headteacher and then I agreed, so quite a group of governors were involved. It is not good for the headteacher and the chair on their own to make too many decisions. (Chair: Primary.)

Governing bodies and heads were often having to define their respective roles and responsibilities to ensure each knew what was expected of them. As a chair remarked of her governing body:

We're almost starting from scratch. When we started (and I suspect this is true of most schools) neither the staff nor the headteacher, governors or pupils had any idea what it was going to involve. We had some real problems with areas that should have involved governors and where the headteacher was doing things as he always used to. He found it difficult when we said "you shouldn't have done that", e.g. changing the school day - he hadn't talked to governors about that. He sent a letter to parents who were asking us about it. It wasn't his fault, the governing body had not laid down very clear guidelines where his responsibilities began and ended. (Chair: Primary.)

An LEA governor training coordinator –an ex-head himself – remarked that, in his experience, there were some heads, particularly the long-serving, who were not comfortable with the new role and responsibilities of governing bodies. He stated that:

It is a key test of a good head if you can go into a school and find the head using the governing body as a resource. It has to be a sharing relationship and each side has to given something. The head has to realise that ideas will be tested/questioned by the governors, and the governors have to realise that the head is responsible for the day to day management of the school. If there is friction between the head and the chair, you should talk to them together and emphasise their ***joint responsibility****.* (LEA: GTC.)

Another commented that in his LEA:

We have the whole spectrum, in terms of 'partnership' between the school and the governing body - from schools with very autocratic heads to governing bodies who have the bit between their teeth and want to run the school, and do interfere with the running of the school. In the middle are some examples of good partnership: heads should be able to regard chairs and governors as critical friends. There must be a lot of trust to develop this relationship (LEA: GTC.)

Also of critical importance was the relationship of the head and the teacher governors. As a case study head commented:

The two teacher governors here are not afraid to come forward and say to me that I ought to be aware of this or that; but equally they give me public support in the governing body meeting. When I first came here, the teachers did not trust the governors. Indeed I don't think they really knew who they were. The teacher governors have been involved in pairing up departments and governors, and getting them to visit the departments. I try and remember what it was like when I first started teaching. The governing body was not important to you and all you could recall was there was probably one on your interviewing panel. I never knew who the governors were, although I think these times have changed. I think the average teacher's view is to say that it is the head and the teacher governors who have to deal with other governors, and that we trust them - the governors - to make sure that the finances are in order or, if applicable, the head is in order. I think teachers' responses depend largely on how long they've been here. If they've been teaching here for 25 years, they will have seen four chairs of governors. But other teachers will judge a governing body on how it responds to a particular issue. For example, a few years ago we had a major discussion of the poor exam results. As a result of this the governors assumed a higher profile in the staff's minds, because they were looking at reasons for such poor performance. The bond between the governors is usually that much stronger because of the up-front exchanges that take place. The teacher governors here will meet with me after they've seen a draft of the head's report. We will discuss it. I've never yet had a bombshell drop on my lap at a governing body meeting. If there is an issue on the governing body agenda that we need to discuss I will invite them to talk about it. If there was, for example, a disciplinary action then I would inform the teacher governors of this. If anything breaks out in the staffroom there are the teacher governors that teachers can go to. They tend to act as ambassadors or friends. They tend to do this rather than the union representatives. It's a style of management that I prefer.

(Headteacher: Secondary.)

Another facet of an effective governing body concerned the parent group. This group of governors, it was suggested, should be supportive yet critical and the case study governing bodies had worked hard to try to achieve this. In most cases parent governors visited the school in session more often than did other categories of governor.

One case study head was asked what advice he would give to a new headteacher in relation to the governors. He replied:

Governors are a crucial group to whom you are answerable, and it's more important to work to them than to the LEA. So I think I would work very hard at developing those relationships. It's not that you neglect the LEA, but governing bodies are, in this LEA at least, very important. A crucial relationship is that between the head and the chair. You've got to make sure that you get to know each governor individually - especially parent governors. I think the notion of pairing up governors with departments has worked reasonably well.

Specifically with this governing body I think one also has to be aware of parochialism. Don't get too cosy too quickly. I've been here seven years now, and I think there's a point when you become anaesthetised. I think if you're not careful it can become a bit cosy. I ask myself would we really tell each other if we thought things were going badly. I'd like to think we would, but I don't know. (Headteacher: Secondary.)

Links with the school and notions of partnership

It was a commonly voiced concern by both governors and heads that not enough time was spent on site or 'seeing the school at work'. In one case, for example, the governors were invited to spend half a day in school and were then debriefed. What did they see? What did they like? Was it what they expected? As the head of the school remarked:

The half a day in school is worth its weight in gold. Governors must know what schools are about. They need an insight into their duties and responsibilities but the curriculum must come first.

A secondary case study head commented that governors did not visit the school as much as either the staff would like or the governors themselves would like. He remarked:

An example would be the parent governor whom you saw this morning. He lives locally and he used to work not far away, but now he works in X. He used to pop in regularly but he no longer does, or at least not as frequently. I welcome governors into the school and the opportunity that it gives them to see the school as it really is. Governors also bring a perspective or vista from the community: they can, for example, tell us how we are perceived locally. It's important for governors in paid employment to be given time off to come into school. This doesn't present a problem with some of our governors. Another governor is in school quite a lot, but I'm not aware of any of our governors getting paid leave. You ask if constantly coming into the school by governors would be bordering on the interfering. I guess this all depends on who the individual governor is! It comes back again to what is an effective governing body, and it's all a matter of trust between the senior management team and governing body as a whole. If trust is there, then the word 'meddling' is not appropriate.

(Headteacher: Secondary.)

It was generally agreed that if governors came into school regularly and built relationships with staff they were seen as less of a threat. There were, however, differing views expressed about the attitudes of teachers towards governors' visits to the school and its classrooms. In one junior school it was 'open house' and classroom observation was not seen as a threat by teachers. In fact it was welcomed:

> *The staff recognise the hard work of the governing body and appreciate it. Governors are always welcomed in the school and are helpful. All the staff know the governors and welcome them into the classroom - all are used to it. The staff are not at all inhibited. On the governing body the teacher governor's views are always welcomed. All members of the governing body are valued for what they bring to the meeting.* (Teacher governor: Primary.)

> *The governors act very much as a questioning, challenging group. We have to justify ourselves to them.. Every governor is attached to a department and works with the head of department so that each governor knows in detail the work of one department. If an appointment is made in that department we try to get the attached governor involved.* (Headteacher: Secondary.)

A governor from the same school remarked that:

> *Some of the most valuable work I do is just going into my department. I support CDT and food and textiles technology. If I don't ring up and make an appointment the head of department will ring me to ask if I'm coming in this term. I'm not quite sure what I do. I enjoy going. I'm very happy to see how much things have changed since I was at school. They send me invitations to things in their department and seem genuinely pleased. I think they feel supported - I suppose it's showing an interest. I'm now linked with the 6th form. I saw the acting head of 6th. He said I must come into a School Council and a 6th form assembly. I got a letter last week detailing all of them, showing they are interested in my coming.* (Foundation governor: Secondary.)

Another school had introduced the attachment of governors to departments. A teacher governor offered the following comment on its introduction:

> *There was initially quite a lot of opposition from staff and suspicion in spite of careful introduction of the scheme and detailed planning of the designated afternoon. Generally, the scheme helps to build up relationships but a lot of governors have no idea what goes on in school, so it's a long process. One parent governor does come into school every week and helps in the classroom but this is the exception.*

The teacher governor who did the arrangements now tries to get heads of department to write to governors giving a range of dates, and to encourage governors to reply, so that heads of department can arrange a programme for them. (Teacher governor: Secondary.)

However, as a head of department in another school noted:

It could be difficult if I had a governor who did not understand language teaching and wanted me to teach verbs. Governors do not come and sit in classes. They respect the principle that they come by invitation. (Teacher governor: Secondary.)

Finally, one of the case studies had devoted a staff meeting to consider the links between teachers and the governing body and how they might be improved. Six or seven governors (at least one of each category) had attended the meeting which had been arranged by the teacher governors. The staff had divided into groups – each with a governor – to consider a number of questions about governance. The staff were said to have welcomed these deliberations and a number of suggestions had been put forward as ways to improve the links between governors and staff, thereby further developing the partnership. Staff reported valuing the different things that governors brought with them, whilst governors felt they needed to be able to make a valued contribution. (The questions addressed and the suggestions put forward have been reproduced as Appendix 4.)

Governors' role in school improvement

At the end of each interview, heads, governors, chairs and LEA governor training coordinators were asked if, in their view, the quality of education for pupils within the school had *improved* as a direct result of the increased responsibilities of the governing body. A range of views were expressed with governors invariably being quite humble, pointing to the crucial role of high quality staff in school improvement:

No, I don't think it's made any difference. I think the quality of education here is excellent – was excellent – and it's down to the head and the staff. (Foundation governor: Secondary.)

That seems a little vain as we are merely facilitating professional people to do their work. We provide the physical environment so that perhaps the professionals can do a better job, enhancing surroundings and equipment. Perhaps at curriculum meetings we put something into the pot, adding a dimension. (Vice-chair: Primary.)

Frankly I doubt it. The headteacher here is good and that is probably the most important feature of a school. After all it is the teachers who run the school. If the headteacher were not good, it might be different, they'd be here as a safety net. (Parent governor: Secondary.)

For others, however, the governing body was seen as having played a more significant role, particularly in the spheres of improving the learning environment and the appointment of teachers.

Quality is the responsibility of the headteacher and the deputy head. The governing body as a whole has the responsibility for appointing people to the school. It is a great responsibility to choose the right people. It is a crucial role. Also the school is helped by the governing body taking interest. We cannot function well without it.

(Teacher governor: Primary.)

Some governors were of little doubt about the role of the governing body:

If the governing body wasn't there it would make an enormous difference to the headteacher. He has the rest of the governors to turn to for advice, support, anything. In the past we had no funds, now we can channel funds in the best interests of the children, e.g. carpets throughout. Having one's own budget makes the governors more interested - they feel they can do something. It's a big boost to the staff that we can decide our own priorities. Improving the environment makes the children happy. (Governor: Primary.)

It definitely is helping to improve things for pupils. In the past too often things were done for the benefit of the staff rather than the pupils. But now, because there is this body who have been given the authority to look into what is going on and take more responsibility, that schools are taking things more seriously. In the previous governing body, we used to have one meeting per term which lasted approximately half an hour. No one put any questions. Everybody was expected to say 'well done' and show appreciation even if we were concerned about something. There was no mechanism for challenging.

(Chair: Primary.)

Improvements in education came from the professionalism of the headteacher and the teaching staff and the governing body was seen as being able to affect the climate in which the school operated. One head made reference to the existence of a direct correlation between the governing body and improvement in the quality of learning and compared the position to when governors had a passive role and were kept in the background. Another spoke in some detail of how this was occurring:

> *If we look at various crude measures, like exam results, we'll see that they have gone up year by year, and I like to think that's part of the jigsaw in terms of devolution and being able to target resources where you think they are needed. We've also been able to be more flexible regarding staffing. The environment too has also been improved. I think having governors in the school has given us an informed lay opinion or view. The role of the governing body has taken some of the power from the headteacher. Another example which I think has led to an improvement would be the needs-led bidding by department heads. This was a scheme that was pushed heavily by our chairman of finance. I don't think we'd have done this if he'd not pushed it so hard. This has been a success, and has been welcomed by the heads of department. As you can imagine, the chair said 'I told you so'! The school had operated for years with a set formula of resource allocation to departments. So I think it's these sort of areas where the governors can have a greater say and an impact. They do act as checks and balances. I'm not sure if there's been an improvement across the board, but there has in particular instances. The governor attachment to curriculum areas has, I think, helped. What we've been able to do with weak department areas is to attach a good governor, who has been able to look at the work of the department and write a report alongside an LEA adviser. Those two reports together did have a desired effect. There have been other cases where there were concerns - e.g. exam results, uptake in years 10 and 11. So to get a governor involved in these areas can be very beneficial. They are able to do some things that the head really can't do.*
>
> (Headteacher: Secondary.)

Another secondary head commented that there had been no tangible effect on the quality of teaching and learning but governors had worked to improve the resource base of the school. They also had supported policies for enhancing the learning environment.

Finally, in response to this question about governors' role in school improvement, the views of two LEA governor training coordinators are worth noting, focusing as they do on the key question of governing body effectiveness:

The answer to this question would express how effective the governing body has been. Some governing bodies are geared up to the slick meeting, but it doesn't help the teaching and learning in the school. The question 'what have you done to enhance teaching and learning?' might be a good one to evaluate the performance of governing bodies.
(LEA: GTC.)

At the end of the day the governing body should be more effective so that the children in the schools derive benefit. If the quality of teaching and learning in schools has not improved, then we must question that. I think the quality of governors in schools now is better - they are sharper, leaner and have a genuine interest in the school. I think there are signs that children are beginning to benefit. The partnership between the governing body, the school and the staff/head is now working much better. There is now generally a much closer partnership between the chair and the head. (LEA: GTC.)

Chapter 8
Towards Effective School Governance

The key question is: do governing bodies make a difference to the overall quality of schools? Do they 'add value' or would schools be better off without them? In the previous chapter, effectiveness was defined in terms of governing bodies being able to make a contribution, in either a direct or an indirect way, to improving the quality of the teaching and learning process. Effective governing bodies helped create the climate for effective teaching and learning to take place. This was achieved in a number of ways. If the governing body was not making an impact on the quality of the school then it was, by definition, ineffective and as such created extra work for school managers without commensurate benefits for their schools.

Some of the ways in which governing bodies contribute to *school improvement* have been documented. There is now a growing body of research evidence which points to a number of key factors which are central to *governing body effectiveness* and thus to school improvement. Both the current and the earlier NFER research projects (Baginsky *et al*, 1991) highlight what might be termed, basic or 'bottom line' factors or competences which have to be met for governing bodies to achieve minimal effectiveness. These would include such factors as the conduct of meetings, chairing, clerking, clarity of purpose of subcommittees, and the regular attendance and appropriate commitment of members. Without these – and the research has shown they should not yet be taken for granted – the chances of school governing bodies 'making a difference' to pupils' learning are significantly reduced.

In order to achieve effectiveness there is also a need for governing bodies to have a clear understanding of the nature of their roles and responsibilities and how these coalesce and complement those of the head and senior managers. Again, it appears that such clarity was not always to be found. How rigidly the respective roles should be defined or clarified is a matter of current debate, with some arguing for flexibility and negotiation, whilst others would prefer to see a much clearer outline of the respective responsibilities and a sharp demarcation between 'governance' and 'management'. However, whether or not governors 'move into management' (Thody, 1992) there is a need for the parameters of the respective roles of chairs, governors and heads to be agreed so as to establish how best all parties can *work together*. An effective governing body, as the research has highlighted, was seen as one which worked well as a **team** both within itself and with the school. The benefits said to exist where there was a working 'partnership' were many and varied. The term partnership is, however, a much overused word and subject to a great deal of rhetoric; so there is a need for governing bodies to decide what is the precise nature of that partnership and how it might be achieved.

Governors have to be seen as an important part of the school. Others have argued for the need to avoid governor decision-making becoming a separate and bureaucratic layer removed from the reality of school life and for existing school management structures to include governors (e.g. Burt, 1992). This is important to note, particularly as research into LMS and school governance suggests that one of the most significant effects of devolved budgets has been to increase the power of *headteachers* (see, for example, Levacic, 1992; Shearn, *et al*, 1993; Deem and Brehony, 1993; Maychell, 1994). As the role and influence of the local education authority has decreased, governing bodies have not always been *able* or *allowed* to act in the manner envisaged by recent legislation, with the result that some heads are in a more powerful position than hitherto. It is clear that some headteachers are continuing to keep governors 'at arms length' and wanting them to act solely in a rubber stamping capacity. How extensive such practices are and the strategies heads use to achieve such a state of affairs is an area in need of further analysis. Research at Sheffield University Management School, based on in-depth analysis of 21 school governing bodies, has made a useful start and delineates the different ways in which responsibility is divided between heads and governors (Shearn, *et al*, 1993). Similarly, Deem and Brehony (1993), in a study of 10 governing bodies over four years, provide insights into the micropolitical processes taking place amongst heads and governors. However, the current NFER research suggests heads see much value – both for themselves and their schools – in working closely with an *effective* governing body. The isolation of headship for example – which, if anything, has been accentuated by the application of market forces to education – can be partially overcome by the existence of an effective governing body. Similarly, an informed group of governors can provide school managers with an external perspective and a constructively critical edge, as well as performing other key functions.

An effective governing body has to be integral to the school, an important part of it, not an adjunct. Sallis has recently set out the arguments for collaborative decision-making, pointing to some of the dangers when either heads *or* governors 'go it alone' (Sallis, 1994). The greatest leadership challenge currently facing heads, she says, is for them to ensure that governing bodies are involved in schools in a meaningful and effective manner. This does not mean, however, being involved in the day-to-day management of the school. Governors do not *require* or *expect* such involvement as the case studies have shown. However, the current study also demonstrated that it was not unusual for governing bodies still to have amongst their members a number of 'passengers' or less-committed members. Heads may well find, therefore, that attempts to create a meaningful partnership involving collaborative decision-making are thwarted or not always readily taken up. The reluctance of governing bodies to become more involved may be of their own making and not the heads'. It was apparent that some governors, for various reasons, did not wish to embrace the full extent of their 'new' responsibilities, although, as suggested by the GTCs in the current research, there was a breed of governors emerging who showed the necessary degree of commitment and interest. Prospective governors need to be made aware of their responsibilities and the time that will be required to fulfil them. 'Busy' people perhaps need to ask themselves if they will be able to find the time that will be required for them to act in an effective capacity.

Workload factors were clearly important and the data suggest that although that of both heads and chairs has recently increased, chairs, to a greater degree than heads, were taking on more, whilst governors appeared to be spending less time than previously on governing body matters. An effective governing body is more likely where there is a more equitable distribution of work. It may be, as some have argued, that the number and range of governing body duties and responsibilities is simply too extensive – 861 according to one interviewee! – for a group of part-time volunteers. This makes effectiveness an impossible ideal. Should governing body responsibilities be limited to more global, strategic matters leaving the school management team to have the prime responsibility for their achievement? Whether or not this is the case, the situation is not helped when a few governors have to undertake the bulk of the work. Greater involvement of all governing body members would, of course, also reduce the possibility of 'cosiness' existing between the head and chair or the development of factions or subgroups of governors. In addition, the question has to be asked if governing bodies are currently spending too much time on some things and not enough on other, more important, matters. Is it a matter of working 'smarter rather than longer' and at some things rather than others?

Relations between heads and governors, especially chairs, were said to be crucial to the effective functioning of governing bodies. Trust and mutual understanding and respect were hallmarks of the case studies. However, such practices are not necessarily very 'newsworthy'. It is often the case that when relationships between the various parties break down they attract the attention of the educational and national media. Such reporting can give a highly misleading picture of the general state of governing body operations and ignores the many examples of existing good practice. Without doubt, there have been instances where the behaviour of heads *and/or* governors has left much to be desired. Partly in response to such deviant or maverick behaviour, suggestions have been made of the need for a governors' code of conduct. Indeed, some LEAs have already produced such codes. Interestingly, the Further Education Funding Council has recently issued a guide to the duties and responsibilities of governors in FE colleges, modelled on the one produced for higher education institutions in 1991 (FEFC, 1994). The FEFC guide, which was produced by a working party in response to requests from chairs of governing bodies, covers much of the same ground as the DFE equivalent for schools (DFE, 1993). The guide points to the role of the college governing body in strategic planning, financial control, the effective use of physical and human resources and the delivery of the curriculum. However, it also includes a 12-part code of conduct which suggests governors behave and act in a certain way (e.g. to work cooperatively with other governors; to base views on an honest and objective assessment of the available facts; to respect confidentiality; to give priority, as far as practicable, to attendance at meetings; to support the majority decision of the governing body). The code does not, of course, guarantee the end of inappropriate behaviour by governors but it should help to minimise it. An equivalent national code for school governors might therefore be of value.

The FEFC guide also states that each governor should 'take or seek opportunities to enhance his or her effectiveness as a governor through participation in training and development programmes and by increasing his or her own knowledge of the college' (FEFC, 1994). As has been shown, both are key factors for school governing body effectiveness. The NFER research highlighted the importance of governor training and support both for individual governors and for whole governing bodies. It was suggested that governors were becoming more aware – perhaps as a result of a growing maturity and/or a forthcoming OFSTED inspection – of the need to evaluate their own effectiveness. This was being facilitated by LEA training coordinators, some of whom were making use of self-evaluation instruments or providing a tailored programme to meet needs. The refocus from individual governor training to working with whole governing bodies was seen as crucial to their overall effectiveness and empowerment (see also Burt, 1992; Curtis, 1994).

The research, however, also highlighted two further factors which may have a significant bearing on governing body effectiveness: the existence of a training and development culture, and monitoring. Firstly, although the survey data demonstrated that most governors had received some formal training, the case studies suggested that in many cases this occurred several years ago and that there was a reluctance on the part of some governors – especially the more experienced – to attend training events. Reluctance to attend may have been due to a previous negative experience, an inability to find the time or the cost to the school. Governing bodies appeared to have different *cultures* of training and development. As is the case with any social group, governing bodies develop their own cultural identity and this includes norms and expectations, about, amongst other things, training and development. In some case studies, the bulk of training and induction activity was 'in-house' and on-the-job. Without wishing to downgrade the significance and need for such internal activity, it is clearly important that governors continue to have access to high quality external training in addition to that offered in-house. This should ensure, amongst other things, that they benefit from contact with governors of other schools. Insularity needs to be avoided and governors made aware of different 'cultures' and ways of working effectively.

Improving governor and governing body effectiveness is about engaging in a learning and development process. The training and development culture will be at various stages of development. It will be interesting to see to what extent governing body development becomes a more central issue for those schools about to be inspected by OFSTED, and for those schools who wish to become '*Investors in People*' – a national standard for training and development. It will also be very important to monitor the effects of the new GEST funding arrangements – which devolves a greater proportion of training funds to schools – on both the access and extent of governor training, and the support and information which LEAs are able to continue to provide. There have been serious concerns expressed, for example by the governor training organisations, that the greater devolution of funds to schools will significantly reduce the amount of training undertaken by governors and have deleterious effects on the support LEAs are able to offer. It is too simple to say that if such support is valued – and the research shows it is – it will be purchased by schools and their governing bodies. School governing bodies, given the choice, may prefer to channel such funds into staff training or other areas deemed more important than their own individual or collective development.

A second factor affecting governing body effectiveness highlighted by the research centres on *monitoring*. Concern was expressed that there were few mechanisms currently in place for monitoring the operation of governing bodies. Governing bodies could engage in an evaluation of their practices in the ways mentioned above but essentially this practice was *self-driven*. Also LEAs were said to have always had a limited monitoring role. Unless the situation had so developed that the school governing body was in danger of having its delegated budget withdrawn, there was little that could be done. The opportunities to be proactive with governing bodies who were operating in a less than effective manner were very few, especially if the head or chair did not invite LEA participation.

Also, although OFSTED includes an evaluation of governing body effectiveness as part of its four-yearly inspection cycle, evidence from the case studies showed that this was not without its problems. Firstly, there may be a certain reluctance on the part of governors to be open and totally honest with inspectors because of the implications an adverse OFSTED inspection report may have on pupil numbers and hence resources. Secondly, taking into account the range of activities OFSTED are expected to examine, it may not be possible to undertake much more than a superficial or cursory analysis of the operation of the governing body. Indeed, initial research into the inspection process conducted by the author suggests this to be the case. (A more positive picture of the OFSTED experience by governors is however found in RISE, 1994.) In addition, it has also been suggested that conceptions of governance held by many inspectors are outdated and do not reflect the expectations currently made of governing bodies. However, the role of governing bodies in the preparation and monitoring of post-inspection action plans may well encourage governors to give greater consideration to their overall way of working. (A useful set of questions governors might ask in relation to action or development planning is provided by OFSTED in a booklet on school improvement, OFSTED, 1994.) The monitoring of the effectiveness of governing bodies is clearly a major issue; adequate mechanisms to ensure this takes place continue to be absent.

The research suggests that although much progress is being made there is room for improvement in the way many governing bodies currently operate, particularly in the priorities they give to the various roles they are asked to perform. For example, it suggests there is a need for them to move beyond the provision of support – which most appear to do well and see as their main function – to be able to offer an informed and constructively critical approach to the school and its operations, including its management. The case study heads welcomed such a supportive yet critical approach. Support had to be earned and not just given (see also Corrick, 1994). Was there a need for a harder edge in which to judge the school's performance in an educational world increasingly driven by market forces? As the research has shown, governors were able to perform a useful role without necessarily usurping or replacing the important role of the LEA or other professional bodies.

Continuous improvement – the *sine qua non* of total quality management – was more likely to be an integral part of a school's way of working if the governing body was involved in a manner which went beyond the mere provision of support and encouragement. As is the case with a school's staff, the governing body is an important resource and, as with any resource, there is a need to monitor its effectiveness on a regular basis. Schools who are unable or unwilling to make optimum use of this resource are *disadvantaged*. Ultimately the quality of the teaching and learning process will be adversely affected by such actions. There is a distinct possibility that the gap between those schools with effective governing bodies and those without will widen, with deleterious effects on the latter schools. Already, there is evidence from the research that inner-city schools and schools with a high proportion of pupils entitled to free school meals were experiencing difficulties in recruiting governors, and their governing bodies were seen as less likely to have the correct balance of skills, expertise and interests. The policy implications of such findings are for others to decide, but clearly there is a need to ensure that schools are not disadvantaged by factors which may, to a large extent, be outside of their control.

Essentially, improving governing body effectiveness - and thereby school effectiveness - is about management development. Management development is the means of increasing the capacity of school management 'to create the conditions which enable teachers and pupils to achieve effective learning' (SMTF, 1990). The focus of a good school is effective learning. Effective schools are invariably characterised as having, amongst other things, good leadership, collaborative decision-making structures, and participative and open models of management. Interestingly, within the effective schools literature there is a noticeable absence of reference to school boards or governing bodies, although partnerships with outside agencies and the local community are frequently cited (SMTF, 1990). Few would agree with the view that the marginalization of governors makes sense. There is much to be gained from a greater degree of governing body involvement in the management of schools. This has to be seen, however, at a broad strategic planning and policy-making level: budgetary control, resource allocation, monitoring and the setting of priorities in relation to the school development plan are key functions of the governing body. Governors should not be involved nor do they wish to be involved in the *day-to-day running* of the school. Some governors have become involved in such a manner but it should be stressed that this was never perceived to be their proper role. For more governing bodies to become effective, there will be a need for change on the part of governors as well as heads and/or school management. There needs to be an acknowledgement and an acceptance of the legitimate role of each.

As Curtis states: 'there is no single correct model of "the governing body" and how it should operate just as there is no "best way" to manage and organise' (Curtis, 1994). She further notes that governing bodies will have to examine the models of best practice that become available to them and adapt them to their own situations. There is clearly a need for more models to become available. However, it is hoped that the research reported here provides heads, governors and others involved in the 'business' of governing with some ideas and approaches to governance which might inform their own thinking and practice. If it does this it will have made at least a partial contribution towards the achievement of more effective school governance/ management.

References

ACTION FOR GOVERNORS' INFORMATION AND TRAINING. (1994). How effective is our governing body? A pack for self-appraisal of the governing body. AGIT/NAGM: Coventry.

BAGINSKY, M., BAKER, L. and CLEAVE, S. (1991). *Towards Effective Partnerships in School Governance*. Slough: NFER.

BAGLEY, C. (1993). *Governor Training and Equal Opportunities*. Slough: NFER.

BURT, C. (1992). 'Governing training: doing things right, or doing the right things?' *Journal of Teacher Development*, Vol. 1. No. 2.

CORRICK, M. (1994). 'Stand and deliver...', *Times Educational Supplement*, 22 July.

CURTIS, A. (1994). 'Effectiveness and efficiency: views from South Oxfordshire', in Thody. A. (ed). *School Governors: Leaders or Followers*? Harlow: Longman.

DEEM, R. (1993). 'Education reform and school governing bodies, 1986-92: old dogs, new tricks or new dogs, new tricks?' in Preedy, M. (ed.) *Managing the Effective School*. London: Paul Chapman Publishing.

DEEM, R. and BREHONY, K. (1993). 'Consumers and education professionals in the organisation and administration of schools: partnership or conflict?' *Educational Studies*, Vol. 19. No.3.

DEPARTMENT FOR EDUCATION. (1993). *Drawing the Lines: A Report of the DFE/HMI Governors' Conference*, Cambridge, November, 1992. London: DFE.

DEPARTMENT FOR EDUCATION. (1993). *School Governors: A Guide to the Law*. London: DFE.

EARLEY, P., WEINDLING, D. and BAKER, L. (forthcoming). 'Building partnerships: headteachers' relationships with governing bodies and LEAs', *Managing Schools Today*.

FURTHER EDUCATION FUNDING COUNCIL. (1994). *Guide for College Governors*. Coventry: FEFC.

HOLT, A. (1993). 'A governor's perspective,' in *Drawing the Lines*, DFE Conference Report.

KEYS, W. and FERNANDES, C. (1990). *A Survey of School Governing Bodies: Report for the DES (2 volumes).* Slough: NFER.

LEVACIC, R. (1992). 'Local management of schools: aims, scope and impact', *Educational Management and Administration,* Vol. 20. No. 1.

MAYCHELL, K. (1994). *Counting the Cost: The Impact of LMS on Schools' Patterns of Spending.* Slough: NFER.

MORRIS, R. (1994). 'School management and governance: can a dividing line be drawn?', *The Heads Legal Guide* Issue No. 55. Croner, April, pp 2-4.

NATIONAL ASSOCIATION OF GOVERNORS AND MANAGERS. (1994). *The Effective Governing Body.* NAGM Paper No. 42, Birmingham. (2nd edition).

OFFICE FOR STANDARDS IN EDUCATION. (1994). *Improving Schools.* London, HMSO.

OXFORD CENTRE FOR EDUCATIONAL MANAGEMENT. (n.d.). 'The effective governing body', Oxford Centre for Educational Management. Oxford Brookes University.

P.E. INTERNATIONAL. (1993). *A Survey of School Governors.* Department for Education, April.

POUNCE, M. (1993). 'Governor training', *Managing Schools Today,* Vol. 3. No. 3. Nov/Dec. pp 25-28.

RESEARCH AND INFORMATION ON STATE EDUCATION TRUST. (1994). *The OFSTED experience: A governor's eye view*, Conference Report, London, 14 April.

SALLIS, J. (1993). 'Good teamwork for governing bodies: A do-it-better guide.' AGIT: Coventry.

SALLIS, J. (1994). *Heads and Governors: Building the Partnership.* AGIT: Coventry.

SCHOOL MANAGEMENT TASK FORCE. (1990). *Developing School Management: The Way Forward.* London: HMSO.

SHEARN, D. et al. (1993). *Headteachers, Governors and LMS*, Paper presented at BERA conference, Liverpool University, September.

THODY, A. (1992). *Moving to Management: School Governors in the 1990s*. London: David Fulton.

TOMLINSON, J. (1993). *The Control of Education.* London: Cassell.

WOODHOUSE, C. (1993). 'The effective governing body', *Managing Schools Today,* Vol. 3, No 1, September.

Abbreviations and Acronyms

AGIT	Action for Governors' Information and Training
DFE	Department for Education
ESL	English as a Second Language
GEST	Grants for Education Support and Training
GM(S)	Grant Maintained (School)
GTC	LEA governor training coordinator
INSET	In-Service Education and Training
LEA	Local Education Authority
NAGM	National Association of Governors and Managers
NAHT	National Association of Head Teachers
NC	National Curriculum
NFER	National Foundation for Educational Research
OFSTED	Office for Standards in Education
SDP	School development plan
SHA	Secondary Heads Association

Appendix 1
Details of Questionnaire Samples

The Schools

Background details of the schools were obtained from headteachers (n=428)

Table 1: Status of school

School status or type:	% of schools
LEA: maintained	63
LEA: voluntary-aided	14
LEA: voluntary-controlled	11
Grant maintained	8
Other/missing data	4
	100
	(n=428)

Table 2: Number on roll

	% of schools	
	Primary	Secondary
up to 150 pupils	31	0.5
151-300	48	5.5
301-500	19.5	12
501-750	1.5	31
751-1000	-	25
1001-1250	-	16
1251-1500	-	8
1500+	-	3
	100	101
	(n=216)	(n=212)

Table 3: Percentage of pupils in receipt of ESL support and entitled to free school meals

Approx % of pupils	% of schools	
	Needing ESL support	**Entitled to free school meals**
0	25	1
1-10	36	34
11-20	6	24
21-50	7	20
51+	2	7
Missing data	24	14
	100	100
	(n=428)	

Table 4: Type of catchment area

	% of schools
Country town &/or rural	43
Suburban	30
Inner urban/inner city	23
(Missing data)	4
	100
	(n=428)

The Headteachers

Table 5: Number of years in headship in total and at present school

	% of sample	
	No. of yrs a head	
No. of years	in total	at present school
0-5	40	49
6-10	25	26
11-15	17	14
16+ yrs	16	8
Missing data	2	3
	100	100
Mean	8.6 years	6.9 years
Median	8.0 years	5.0 years
	(n=428)	

The Governors

Background details of both governors and chairs of governing bodies are given in Chapter 5. Data were not collected on category of governor for chairs.

Table 6: Type or category of governor

Category of governor	% of sample
LEA-appointed governor	17
Teacher governor	8
Parent governor	27
Co-opted governor	23
Minor Authority governor	2
Foundation governor	16
First governor (GM)	3
Missing data	4
	100
	(n=241)

Appendix 2
Background Details of Case Studies

Case study 1

School:

- LEA voluntary-controlled junior school (220 pupils).
- Rural community.
- Shire county.
- Nearly one-quarter of pupils require ESL support and just under 10% are entitled to free school meals.
- Delegated budget only since April '92.

Headteacher:

- Male.
- 5 years as head at school (9 years in total as head).
- Chosen to be a governor and attends all subcommittees.

Chair:

- Female (age 45).
- Governor of 2 schools (LEA appointed but formerly a parent governor).
- Governor for a total of 10 years; 4 years at present school and chair of governors only since September '93.
- Children attended school.
- Part-time music teacher.

Governing body:

- 12 governors (no current vacancies). Some difficulty in recruiting parent governors as 3 schools in a small village.
- 3 Foundation but no co-opted governors. (Vicar is *ex-officio* but is no longer chair.)
- Met 7 times last year.
- Main (sub)committees are: Staffing, Buildings, Curriculum, Finance and Pastoral/Community. (Each has delegated powers.)
- 3 out of 4 governors are women.
- Amount of devolved funding for training and development = £250 (spent mainly on LEA provided training and support, and materials).
- Used to be a joint governing body with Infants school.

- High levels of governor attendance.
- No business representative (although 2 parent governors are bank clerks!).
- No link governor (clerk acts in this capacity).
- Clerk appointed by governing body. Several years without a clerk. (No LEA clerking for many years.)

Governors interviewed:

- Headteacher.
- Chair of governors (twice).
- Teacher governor (deputy head).
- LEA-appointed governors (2).
- Parent governors (2).

Meetings attended:

- Full governing body.

Case study 2

School:

- LEA voluntary-controlled, 11-18 comprehensive (1780 pupils).
- Country town.
- Shire county.

Headteacher

- Male.
- 11 years as head at school (18 years in total as head).
- Chosen to be a governor.
- Provides induction training for new governors.

Chair:

- Male (over 60 years of age).
- Foundation governor (formerly an LEA-appointed governor of 3 schools).
- Governor for a total of 9 years at the school and chair for 3 years.
- Children attended school.
- Retired, formally a primary school headteacher.

Governing body:

- 19 governors (2 current vacancies, including co-opted governor). Only 6 candidates for 5 parent governor vacancies.
- 4 Foundation governors.

- Met 6 times last year.
- Main committees are: Premises, Personnel, Financial Management, Curriculum and Foundation Management. (All have delegated powers.)
- Only 3 female governors.
- Amount of devolved funding for training and development = £200 (spent on attendance at LEA short courses).
- High levels of attendance.
- No link governor.
- Clerk (school administrative officer). No LEA clerking since 1974.

Governors interviewed:

- Headteacher.
- Chair of governors.
- Teacher governor (Head of Department).
- LEA governor (chair of subcommittee).
- Foundation governor.
- Parent governor.

Meetings attended:

- Full governing body.

Case study 3

School:

- LEA voluntary-aided junior school (310 pupils).
- Country town/village.
- Shire county.
- Just over 10% of pupils are entitled to free school meals.

Headteacher:

- Male.
- 5 years as head at present school (first headship).
- Chosen to be a governor.
- Produces a termly governors' newsletter.
- Member of all subcommittees.

Chair:

- Male (60 years plus) and local vicar. Governor of only one school and appointed to his first chair 6 years ago.

Governing body:

- 12 governors (2 current vacancies).
- 7 Foundation and 5 representative governors (former must outnumber latter by 2) includes business representation. No co-options.
- Main committees are: Curriculum, Finance, Personnel, and Health and Safety/Buildings. (Only Finance has delegated powers.)
- Met 7 times last year. If meetings not finished in 2 hours there is a guillotine.
- Clerked by a Foundation governor (who is a barrister).
- Link governor.
- Approximately equal number of men and women.
- High levels of attendance.
- Degree of continuity (e.g. parent governor serving second term of office and Foundation governors serve for up to 7 years).

Governors interviewed:

- Headteacher.
- Chair of governors.
- Foundation governor (vice-chair).
- Teacher governor (deputy head).
- LEA-appointed governor.
- Foundation governor (clerk).
- Parent governor.

Meetings attended:

- Full governing body.

Case study 4

School:

- LEA-maintained nursery and infant (190 full-time and 80 part-time pupils).
- Inner city, urban community.
- London borough.
- 75% of pupils are entitled to free school meals and 40% need ESL support.

- Delegated budget only since April 1992.
- Parents' association recently established.

Chair:

- Female (age 40).
- Co-opted governor.
- Formerly vice-chair and been chair for just over one year. (Recently resigned as chair to be replaced by another co-opted governor.)

Governing body:

- 17 governors (joint governing body with junior school).
- 2 vacancies (parent governors). Some difficulty in recruitment.
- Met 9 times last year.
- Main subcommittees are: Finance, Personnel, Premises and Lettings. (Limited delegated powers).
- Many of the governors are parents (only 3 have no connections with the school).
- Fairly young governors with no retired members.
- Amount of devolved funding for training and development = £300 (spent mainly on LEA provided training and support).
- Link governor.
- Mainly female.
- Attendance levels variable (especially with parent governors).
- No clerk (have not had one since LEA stopped clerking meetings 3 years ago).
- Insufficient funds to employ a clerk (intend to offer overtime to school administrative assistant).

Governors interviewed:

- Headteacher.
- Chair of governors.
- Co-opted governors (2).
- LEA-appointed governor.
- Teacher governor.

Meetings attended:

- Full governing body.

Case study 5

School:

- LEA-maintained, 11-19 comprehensive school (900 pupils).
- Country town.
- Shire county.
- 9% of pupils are entitled to free school meals and 3% with ESL.

Headteacher:

- Male.
- 7 years as head at school.
- Chosen to be a governor.
- Usually attends subcommittee meetings.

Chair:

- Male (age 50).
- Co-opted (formerly LEA-appointed governor).
- Governor for 10 years and chair for 8 years.
- Employed full-time (local government officer).
- Attends Finance and General Purposes Subcommittee (vice-chair attends all 3 subcommittees and has frequent contact with Chair).

Governing body:

- 19 governors including 6 co-opted governors.
- No current vacancies and no difficulty in recruitment (e.g. 10 parents stood for 5 places).
- Good attendance (only 2 'passengers').
- Met 3 times last year.
- Main committees are: Sites and Buildings, Staffing and Personnel, Finance and General Purposes. (Delegated powers and governing body usually accepts recommendations of committees.)
- Governors assigned to curriculum areas/departments and contribute to presentation of department reports.
- Two thirds of governors (approx) are male.
- Amount of devolved funding for training and development is 'very small' (spent mainly on LEA provided training and support).
- Clerked by head's secretary (LEA stopped clerking meetings 8 or 9 years ago).
- Link governor.

Governors interviewed:

- Headteacher.
- Chair of governors.
- Teacher governors (2).
- Parent governors (2).
- Co-opted governor.
- Clerk to governing body.
- LEA-appointed governor.

Meetings attended:

- Full governing body.
- Subcommittee.

Case study 6

School:

- Grant-maintained since April 1992. 11-18 comprehensive school (1050 pupils).
- Suburban.
- 20% of pupils are entitled to free school meals.
- Outer London borough.

Headteacher:

- Male.
- 9 years as head at school.
- As GM head has to be a governor (*ex-officio*), but was a governor when school was LEA-maintained.
- A member of 2 (sub) committees but attends all committee meetings.

Chair:

- Male (aged mid 40's).
- First (formerly parent) governor.
- Governor for 9 years and chair for 8 years.
- Employed full-time (research scientist).
- Chair was not a member of committees but often attended meetings.

Governing body:

- 17 governors, including 9 First governors (appointed for 7 years) and 5 parent governors (appointed for 4 years).
- 2 current vacancies, (1 First governor and 1 teacher governor). Only 1 nomination had been received for most recent parent governor vacancy and some difficulty in filling vacancy for teacher governor.
- All First governors had previously been governors at the school.
- Met 4 times last year. Each subcommittee meets twice per term.
- Main committees are: Curriculum, Finance, Personnel and Premises (with delegated powers not requiring approval from full governing body (unless otherwise specified)). Two members of the Senior Management Team are attached to each of the 4 main committees and service them. (Other subcommittees include: Appeals committees (2) for pupil admissions and pupil discipline, and for staff discipline; pupil discipline and staff discipline committees (2) and an admissions committee.)
- *A Guide for Staff and Governors on the Governance and Management of the School* had been authorised by the governing body which specified roles and responsibilities and terms of reference of committees.
- Good attendance.
- Clerked by deputy head (part of job description). A governor is deputy clerk.
- Three out of 4 governors are male.
- Approx. £1000 for governor training, most of which was spent on LEA training and support. (Governing body inducts new members.)
- Used to have a link (or training) governor but this is now clerk's function.

Governors interviewed:

- Headteacher.
- Chair of governors.
- Parent governor.
- First governor.
- Teacher governor (Head of Special Needs).
- Clerk to governing body (deputy head).

Meetings attended:

- Full governing body (2).
- Subcommittee.

Appendix 3

Terms of Reference for Governing Body Committees

An Example

This case study governing body – of a large secondary school – had four main committees: Finance, Premises, Personnel and Curriculum for which the terms of reference have, with kind permission of the school, been reproduced below:

A. Financial Management Committee

1. **The Financial Management Committee** will act for the Governing Body in all matters relating to the Governors' financial responsibilities under the law, and in accordance with LEA practice and requirements.

2. **Responsibilities**

   The Financial Management Committee is responsible to Governors:

   a. To oversee financial planning within the school in the context of the School Development Plan and the policies and objectives of the school.

   b. To set and monitor the LMS budget and to circulate the approved budget to all Governors with the appropriate minutes.

   c. To assist in liaison with the LEA on financial matters.

   d. To be a channel of communication with staff on financial matters.

   e. To ensure all actions and decisions are reported to the next available meeting of the Governing Body.

   f. To be satisfied that the school bank accounts are audited correctly, and are free from any VAT implications.

3. **Membership**

   a. Five Governors (to include Vice-Chairman and at least one LEA, parent and teacher Governor) to be appointed at the first meeting of the Governing Body in each academic year.

   b. The Headteacher.

   c. Four teaching staff, elected by all members of the teaching staff on a single transferable vote system, serving for two years with elections for two places every year.

   d. One member of the support staff, elected bi-annually by all non-teaching staff on a single transferable vote system.

e. Ex-officio members: The Deputy Headteachers
The Bursar
The Senior Accounts Assistant
The Clerk to the Governors

In addition, the Committee may, from time to time, wish to co-opt members with particular expertise, e.g. the Director of Studies.

4. Meetings

a. Meetings will be held at least once a term.

b. Additional meetings may be called as required in exercise of the Committee's responsibilities for budget setting and monitoring.

c. Three Governors will form a quorum.

d. Governors, other than those appointed to the Committee, may attend and speak if they wish, but may not vote.

e. Only appointed Governors are entitled to vote at meetings of the Committee.

5. Standing Orders

a. The Chairman shall be appointed annually by the Committee at the first Committee meeting of the new academic year (and after the meeting of the Governing Body has appointed five Governors to the Committee).

b. Only Governors appointed to the Committee (excluding the Headteacher) are eligible to serve as Chairman.

c. The Agenda for each meeting will be distributed to all Governors at least seven days before the meeting.

d. All meetings will be minuted and the minutes circulated to all Governors and Committee members as soon as possible after the meeting.

e. Where there is an equality of votes on any issue, the Chairman may have a second and casting vote.

6. Working Practices

a. Copies of the most recent LEA printout (or similar school printout) shall be made available at each meeting.

b. Details will be provided at each meeting confirming that the bank account and the school's own financial accounting system balance for all preceding months.

c. The school budget shall be approved by the Committee in time to meet the LEA submission date deadline of 15th April each year.

d. At the first meeting of each academic year, the Committee will review the terms of the "School's Own Financial Regulations", whereby Governors delegate an authorised spending and virement limit to the Headteacher. Any virement/spending decision required outside this limit shall be referred to the Committee Chairman, or in his/her absence, the Chairman of Governors.

B. Premises Committee

1. Composition

a. The Premises Committee will consist of *five* Governors.

b. There will be *one* Teacher Governor and at least *one* Governor from each of the three constituent groups.

c. The Head will be a member of the committee *ex officio.*

d. Other Governors may attend and speak at the meetings but may not vote.

e. The quorum for the committee is *three* Governors.

f. The committee will elect its own Chairman and Vice-Chairman.

g. The minutes and agenda of meetings will be circulated to all Governors.

h. The Chairman (or Vice-Chairman in his/her absence) will give a verbal report at each Governors' meeting.

2. Responsibilities

The Premises Committee is responsible to the Governors for:

a. seeking to ensure the provision of adequate buildings and grounds for the delivery of the curriculum;

b. ensuring that the maintenance of the premises is such as to provide a positive environment for the pupils and staff, with particular regard to Health and Safety requirements;

c. assess, evaluate and monitor contracts for the cleaning of the buildings and the maintenance of the grounds;

d. ensuring that all reasonable measures are taken to protect the premises from burglary, vandalism and fire;

e. ensuring that the premises are used effectively and efficiently for activities beyond the normal school day, bearing in mind the need for financial profitability alongside community accessibility.

3. Sources of Information

In pursuit of the above objectives, the Premises Committee will be serviced *inter alia,* as appropriate, by:

a. the Director of Studies and the Senior Timetabler who will provide information relating to the curriculum needs and the buildings and grounds;

b. i the Bursar and the LEA Property Manager who will provide regular reports on the physical conditions of the buildings;

ii the Deputy i/c Health and Safety who will report on any problems identified and measures taken or recommended;

c. the Bursar who will advise, with external specialist helps as required, on the contractual arrangements for cleaning and grounds maintenance;

d. the Bursar who will report on security;

e. the Bursar, who, with information provided by the Lettings Officer, will report on the commercial and community use of the buildings.

4. Actions

The Premises Committee will determine, in the light of recommendations made by the Head and Bursar and within the financial constraints of the overall budget:

a. the submission to be made to the LEA in connection with further capital building projects;

b. the programme for re-decoration and maintenance;

c. the recommendations to the Governing Body for the award of contracts for cleaning and grounds maintenance

d. the charges for the use of the premises, including the extent of the flexibility delegated to the Head, Bursar and Lettings Officer in these matters.

C. Personnel Committee

1. Composition

a. The Personnel Committee will consist of *six* governors, including the Headteacher.

b. There will be *one* Teacher Governor and at least *one* governor from each of the three constituent groups.

c. Others Governors may attend as non-voting observers, except when the Committee is fulfilling its disciplinary function.

d. The quorum for the committee is *three*.

e. The committee will elect its own Chairman and Vice-Chairman.

f. The minutes and agenda of meetings will be circulated to all Governors.

g. The Chairman (or Vice-Chairman in his/her absence) will give a verbal report at each Governors' meeting.

2. Responsibilities

The Personnel Committee is responsible to the Governors for:

a. appointing the agreed number of teaching and non-teaching staff, within overall financial constraints, delegating to the Head as appropriate;

b. establishing, reviewing and implementing the Pay Policy. (This is a separate document);

c. ensuring that the working conditions for all staff are the best that can be achieved within the prevailing physical and financial limitations;

d. ensuring that procedures are in place for the appraisal of teaching staff to be carried out according to statutory requirements and in line with best practice;

e. ensuring that all staff have fair access to In-service and professional development opportunities;

f. Carrying out any necessary disciplinary procedures in relation to staff. (This is a separate document.)

3. Sources of Information

In order to carry out the above responsibilities, the Personnel committee will be serviced, where necessary, by:

a. the Head and/or Deputy i/c staffing who will provide regular reports on the staffing complement;

b. the Head and Deputies, who will provide such information as is required for the implementation of the Pay Policy, including the Annual Review;

c. the Head, Deputies and, as appropriate, the Chair of the Common Room Committee who will report on measures taken on behalf of the staff;

d. the Deputy Head i/c Appraisal;

e. the Deputy Head i/c INSET;

f. the Head.

g. the Bursar.

4. Actions

The Personnel committee will determine, in the light of recommendations made by the Head and Deputies, when appropriate:

a. the policy for appointing staff, including delegated powers to the Head;

b. the pay structure for all staff;

c. any measures to be taken for staff welfare;

d. the appraisal procedures;
e. the INSET policy;
f. the staff disciplinary policy.

5. Appeals committee

In the personnel matters outlined above, staff have the right of appeal against certain decisions. The Governors will therefore establish an Appeals Committee which will consist of *five* Governors (excluding the Head) other than those serving on the Personnel Committee.

D. Curriculum Committee

1. Composition

a. The Curriculum Committee will consist of *five* Governors.
b. There will be *one* Teacher Governor and at least *one* Governor from each of the three constituent groups.
c. The Head will be a member of the committee *ex officio*.
d. Other Governors may attend but will not vote.
e. The quorum for the committee is *three*.
f. The committee will elect its own Chairman and Vice-Chairman.
g. The minutes and agenda of meetings will be circulated to all Governors.
h. The Chairman (or Vice-Chairman in his/her absence) will give a verbal report at each Governors' meeting.

2. Responsibilities

The Curriculum committee is responsible to the Governors for:

a. ensuring that the curriculum offered meets all statutory requirements;
b. ensuring that, within the prevailing financial constraints, the curriculum meets the needs of all the pupils and students in the school, of whatever ability, gender, race or social background;
c. ensuring that testing and assessment are carried out in accordance with statutory requirements and that all reasonable steps are taken to achieve the highest possible quality of education;
d. ensuring that the school discharges its wider pastoral and disciplinary responsibilities to the best of its ability;
e. ensuring that the extra-curricular opportunities are as appropriate, varied and numerous as can be achieved within our human, financial and physical limitations.

3. Sources of Information

In pursuit of the above objectives, the Curriculum Committee will be serviced *inter alia,* as appropriate, by:

a. i. the Deputy i/c Curriculum and the Director of Studies, who will report on the curriculum proposals made by the Academic Planning Committee

ii other members of staff as needed in relation to those aspects of the national curriculum for which the Governors have direct responsibility and on which they must seek the approval of the full Governing Body:

- sex education (teacher i/c health education)
- religious education (Head of R.E.)
- personal and social education (Head of P.S.E.)
- collective worship (Heads and Deputies)

b. other members of staff, either in person or in writing, who have responsibilities such as Learning Support, Very Able Pupils, Equal Opportunities etc.

c. Head and Deputies in their role as quality assurance monitors of teaching departments, together with relevant reports from the Statistics Officer;

d. Head and Deputies, with members of the pastoral staff as appropriate, including those with special responsibilities such as Equal Opportunities (Gender and Race), Bullying etc.

e. Head and Deputies, with other members of staff, either in person or in writing, who have responsibilities for Music, Drama, Sport, Duke of Edinburgh Award Scheme, educational visits, etc.

4. Actions

The Curriculum Committee will determine, in the light of recommendations made by the Head and Deputies, what to recommend to the Governors in relation to:

a. the curriculum plan and the detailed statutory arrangements;

b. the grouping policy;

c. the quality control policy;

d. the pastoral programme and policy;

se. the extra-curricular policy.

Appendix 4
Developing the Links between Staff and Governors

The following paper, which has been reproduced with the kind permission of the school, was presented to a meeting of the full governing body. It outlines a series of questions which staff and governors were asked to consider during a staff meeting on staff-governor links. It also puts forward a number of suggestions for improving links which emerged from the deliberations.

A) The following are the **questions** addressed by the groups in discussion:

Who sets the agenda for meetings?

Are there any other ways of linking governors?

What do governors do with the information gained from visits?

What do governors do?

How could staff be dismissed?

Can governors be dismissed?

What influence do governors have on the curriculum?

Why does a teacher want to be a governor?

How involved should governors be in the day-to-day running of the school?

How can we get the governors to understand us?

Is there a clash of interests when governors are supposed to be attached to a department and yet are supposed to remain detached?

Is there a continuity problem when a new governing body is elected?

Would direct contact between the governors and pupils be of benefit?

How easy is it for governors to get to know the school?

How much discussion is there about individual departments?

Is the link governor automatically on the interview panel for that department?

What is the training programme for governors?

How often should governors visit the school?

What makes a good governing body?

What makes a bad governing body?

How balanced is the input from different types of governors?

Do situations arise where governors vote on things they know nothing about?

B) The following suggestions were put forward as ways to improve staff-governor links:

1 Other forms of linking could be tried, e.g. with year groups.
2 Visits could take place during non-contact time to allow greater discussion.
3 Meetings with new staff should have a focal point.
4 Governors could 'shadow' a pupil or member of staff, (e.g. year tutor) for a day. Different roles could be looked at on different visits.
5 Lunches are a good idea but with smaller numbers.
6 The new school council could be a vehicle for pupils meeting governors.
7 More governors could visit the family room.
8 Invite interested staff to observe governing body meetings.
9 Invite governors to observe meetings, e.g. HoDs, Year Tutors', Staff Council/Association.

DEPREMİN HAKÎKATİ

ZİLZÂL SÛRESİ

إِذَا زُلْزِلَتِ الْأَرْضُ زِلْزَالَهَا

Derleyen
CEMÂLNUR SARGUT

NEFES

NEFES

ZİLZÂL SÛRESİ
Depremin Hakîkati
CEMÂLNUR SARGUT

ISBN: 978-625-8185-30-0
1. Baskı: Şubat 2024

REDAKSİYON: Çiğdem Yazır
KAPAK TASARIM: Özle Çetinkaya
SAYFA DÜZENİ: Melik Uyar

İÇ BASKI/CİLT: Çınar Matbaacılık ve Yay. San. Tic. Ltd. Şti.
Yüzyıl Mah. Matbaacılar Cad. Ata Han No:34 K:5 Bağcılar/İstanbul
Sertifika No: 45103

NEFES YAYINLARI
Bağdat Cad. No:167/2 Çatırlı Apt. B Blok D:4
Göztepe/Kadıköy/İstanbul
Tel: (216) 359 10 20 Faks: (216) 359 40 92
www.nefesyayinevi.com
irtibat@nefesyayinevi.com
/nefesyayinevicom
/nefesyayinevi
/nefesyayinevi
KÜLTÜR BAKANLIĞI YAYINCILIK SERTİFİKA NO: 52382

İYİLİK YAYINCILIĞI

Nefes Yayınevi, Tuti Kitap ve Genç Tuti olarak dünya çapında yepyeni bir proje başlatmanın mutluluğunu yaşıyoruz.

Adı: İyilik Yayıncılığı

Peki "iyilik yayıncılığı" nedir? İyilik nasıl yayılır?

Bu logonun bulunduğu kitaplarımızdan satın aldığınız takdirde, doğrudan bir iyilik hareketinin parçası oluyorsunuz! Çünkü bu logoya sahip kitapların her biri, bir iyiliği destekliyor.

"İyilik Yayıncılığı" hareketi bünyesinde belirlenen yerlere, kitaplarımızdan elde edilen gelirler doğrultusunda destekte bulunuyoruz.

Böylece "iyilik yayın" kitaplarımızdan satın aldığınız an, siz de bir iyilik sürecinin parçası oluyorsunuz. Hem kitabınızı keyifle okuyor hem de ihtiyaç sahiplerine el uzatıyorsunuz...

İyilik Yayılsın...

CEMÂLNUR SARGUT

TÜRKKAD İstanbul Başkanlığı görevini yürütmekte olan Sargut, İstanbul doğumludur ve Kimya Mühendisliği bölümü mezunudur. 30 yılı aşkın süredir tasavvuf alanında çalışmalar yapmakta ve hizmet vermektedir. Yayınlanmış kitapları arasında Kur'ân-ı Kerîm üzerine büyük mutasavvıfların yorumlarına dayalı çalışmaları ve Fusûsu'l-Hikem şerhleri yer almaktadır. Halka açık olarak Mesnevî ve Fusûsu'l-Hikem dersleri vermektedir. Almanya, Amerika ve Hindistan'da çeşitli üniversite ve kuruluşlarda İslâm Tasavvufu alanında düzenli seminerler vermektedir. North Carolina Üniversitesi Dinî Etütler Bölümü'nde (2009), Pekin Üniversitesi Beşerî Bilimler Enstitüsü'nde (2011) ve Kyoto Üniversitesi'nde (2016) "Kenan Rifai Distinguished Professorship on Islamic Studies" kürsülerinin kurulmasına öncülük etmiştir. Bakü Avrasya Üniversitesi kendisine fahrî doktora unvanı vermiştir (2014). Halen Üsküdar Üniversitesi Rektör Danışmanlığı yapmakta olan Sargut, Üniversite'nin Tasavvuf Araştırmaları Enstitüsü'nde de dersler vermektedir.

İÇİNDEKİLER

ÖNSÖZ

Eğer kıyâmet vücudî kıyâmetse, hâdiselerde sadece Rabb'ini gördüğünden erir, nefisler sarsılır. Bu eğer maddî bir sarsıntı ise, aslında gören için bu sarsıntı, Cenâb-ı Hakk'ın nurunun her şeyi sarışıdır. Bu kimse yapanın yaptıranın O olduğunu idrak ettiğinden ve O'nun rahmetinin gazâbını daima örttüğünü bildiğinden hâdiseleri hakîkatinden seyreder. Bu kişi er kişidir. Hâli ise, hâdisede hizmet etmek, itiraz etmemektir.

Görülüyor ki iki çeşit kıyâmet vardır: Küçük ve büyük kıyâmet.

Küçük kıyâmet kulun idrak etmeye başlaması ve bu idraki geliştirerek iki âlemin arasında kalacak seviyeye erişmesidir. Büyük kıyâmet ise herkesin mutlaka kendi hakîkatini göreceği günü anlatır.

Buradan anlaşılıyor ki herkesin kendi âyân-ı sâbitesini idrak etmesine, yani kendi hakîkatini görmesine büyük kıyâmet deniyor, ki bunlar amel defterlerini sağdan alanlardır. Bazıları ise taşıdıkları ismin hakîkatinden bîhaber olduklarından şaşkınlık ve pişmanlık cehennemine girecekler, ki bunlar amel defterlerini soldan alanlardır.

Âcizane derim ki:

Amel defterini sağdan almak, dünyada gayretini mânevî yolda sarf etmek demektir. Soldan almak, nefsanî yolda sarf edilen bir ömür demektir.

Cemâlnur Sargut

ZİLZÂL SÛRESİ

إِذَا زُلْزِلَتِ الْأَرْضُ زِلْزَالَهَا

İzâ zülzileti'l-'ardu zilzâlehâ

Âyet 1: *"Yeryüzü şiddetli bir şekilde sarsıldığında."*

وَأَخْرَجَتِ الْأَرْضُ أَثْقَالَهَا

Ve-ahracati'l-'ardu eskālehâ

Âyet 2: *"Yer, içindeki ağırlıkları dışarı çıkardığında."*

وَقَالَ الْإِنسَانُ مَا لَهَا

Ve-kāle'l-insânu mâ lehâ

Âyet 3: *"Ve insan, 'Ne oluyor buna!' dediği vakit."*

يَوْمَئِذٍ تُحَدِّثُ أَخْبَارَهَا

Yevme'izin tuhaddisu ahbârahâ

Âyet 4: *"İşte o gün (yer) üzerinde olup bitenleri anlatır."*

بِأَنَّ رَبَّكَ أَوْحَىٰ لَهَا

Bi-enne rabbeke evhâ lehâ

Âyet 5: *"Rabb'inin ona bildirmesiyle (bunu yapar)."*

يَوْمَئِذٍ يَصْدُرُ النَّاسُ أَشْتَاتًا لِّيُرَوْا أَعْمَالَهُمْ

Yevme'izin yaşduru'n-nâsu eştâten li-yurav a'mâlehum

Âyet 6: ***"O gün insanlar amellerini görmeleri (karşılığını almaları) için grup grup kabirlerden çıkıp hesap yerine gelirler."***

فَمَن يَعْمَلْ مِثْقَالَ ذَرَّةٍ خَيْرًا يَرَهُ

Fe-men ya'mel mişkāle zerretin hayran yerâh(u)

Âyet 7: ***"Kim zerre miktarı hayır yapmışsa onu görür."***

وَمَن يَعْمَلْ مِثْقَالَ ذَرَّةٍ شَرًّا يَرَهُ

ve-men ya'mel mişkāle zerretin şerren yerâh(u)

Âyet 8: ***"Kim de zerre miktarı şer işlemişse onu görür."***

- Adını ilk âyetinin son kelimesinden alır ve ez-Zelzele, İzâ zülzilet Sûresi diye de anılır. Medenî veya Mekkî olduğu hususunda farklı görüşler ileri sürülmüştür. Taberî ve Kurtubî, Medenî diye kaydetmiş (*Câmi'u'l-beyân*, XXX, 337; *el-Câmi' li-ahkâmi'l-Kur'ân*, XX, 100), Süyûtî de bunu tercih etmiş (el-İtkān, I, 36), İbn Âşûr ise Mekkî olduğunu söylemiştir (*et-Tahrîr ve't-tenvîr*, XXX, 437). Sekiz âyet olup fâsılaları ا، م، ه harfleridir. Sûrenin konusu kıyâmetin kopması ve insanların dünyada işledikleri ameller için hesaba çekilmesi hakkındadır.

Zilzâl Sûresi yerin büyük bir sarsıntı ile sarsılacağı ve içindeki ağırlıkları (eskāl) dışarıya atacağı günü hatırlatılmakla başlar. Diğer âyetlerde sûra üfürülmekle vuku bulacağı ifade edilen bu olayın (ez-Zümer 39/68) ikinci üfleyişle meydana geleceğini söylemek mümkündür. 2. âyette yer alan "eskāl" kelimesi Taberî ve İbn Kesîr'e göre yerin karnındaki (kabirlerdeki) ölüleri anlatır. Buna yerküresinin kendi içinde sakladığı çeşitli maden ve hazineler de eklendiği takdirde bu yer sarsıntısını birinci ve ikinci üfleyiş olarak kabul etmek gerekir. Ardından, tasvir edilen durum karşısında inkârcılar veya bütün insanlar hayrete düşüp, "Arzın bu hali nedir?" diyeceklerdir. O gün Cenâb-ı Hakk'ın ilhamıyla, yerküresi üzerinde işlenen bütün amelleri haber verecektir. Dünyada peygamberlerin tebliğlerine doğrudan veya dolaylı biçimde muhatap olan insanlar tek başlarına ve dağınık şekilde hesap yerine geleceklerdir. Zerre kadar iyilik yapan da zerre kadar kötülük yapan da karşılığını bulacaktır.

Sûrenin tefsiri hakkında rivayet edilen hadislerden biri şöyledir: Abdullah b. Ömer'den nakledildiğine göre sûre nâzil olurken orada bulunan Ebû Bekir ağlamaya başlamış, Hz. Peygamber bunun sebebini sorunca sûrenin kendisini ağlattığını söylemiş, bunun üzerine Hz. Peygamber şöyle buyurmuştur: *"Siz hiç hatâ etmez, günah işlemez olsaydınız Allah Teâlâ sizden sonra hatâ edip günah işleyen bir ümmet yaratır ve -tövbe etmeleri üzerine- onları affederdi."* (Vâhidî, s. 368; Heysemî, VII, 141). Resûl-i Ekrem, yerin içinde sakladığı haberlerden bahseden 4. âyete atıfta bulunarak yerin sakladığı haberlerin ne olduğunu sormuş, yanındakiler bunu Allah ve Resûl'ünün bildiğini söyleyince şöyle demiştir: "Yerin içinde barındırdığı haberler, Allah'ın her erkek ve kadın kulunun yer üzerinde işlediği amellere şâhitlik edip şöyle demesidir: 'Benim sırtımda filân ve filân günde şu ve şu amelleri işledin; evet yerin haberleri bundan ibarettir.'" (*Müsned*, II, 347; Tirmizî, "Şıfatü'l-ḳıyâme", 7; "Tefsîrü'l-Ḳur'ân", 99).

Sûrenin fazileti hakkında rivayet edilen hadîse göre bir sahâbî Resûlullah'ın huzuruna gelip kendisine Kur'an okutmasını istemiş, Hz. Peygamber "elif lâm râ'", "hâ mîm" veya tesbih kavramıyla başlayan sûrelerden okumasını söylemiş, sahâbî bunların her biri için, "Yaşım ilerlemiş, kalbim sıkıntılı hale gelmiş, dilim de kalınlaşmış" şeklinde mazeret beyan ederek kendisine özlü bir sûre okutmasını talep etmiştir. Resûl-i Ekrem ona Zilzâl Sûresi'ni okutmuştur. Sahâbî okumasını bitirince, "Seni Hak peygamber olarak gönderen Allah'a yemin ederim ki hayatımın sonuna kadar buna başka bir şey ilâve etmeyeceğim." demiş ve oradan ayrılmıştır. Bunun üzerine Hz. Peygamber şöyle demiştir: "Bu adam kurtuluş yolunu bulmuş, kurtuluş yolunu bulmuştur." (*Müsned*, II, 169; *a.e.* [Arnaût], XI, 139-141; Ebû Dâvûd, "Şehru ramażân", 9; İbrâhim Ali, s. 302-303, 360-361).[1]

- Zeyd b. Eşlem'den (r.a) rivayet edildi ki: Bir adam Hz. Peygamber'e (s.a.s) gelip: "Allah'ın sana öğrettiği şeyden bana da öğret." dedi. Rasûlullah onu, kendisine Kur'an öğretmesi için birisine gönderdi. Adam, *"izâ zülziletü'l-ardu"* sûresini öğretti. *"Kim zerre ağırlığında bir hayır işlerse…"* mealindeki âyete gelince: "Bana yeter." dedi. Durum Rasûlullah'a haber verilince: *"Onu bırak, adam fakih oldu (anladı)."* buyurdu.[2]

- Allah Teâlâ Kehf Sûresi'nde şöyle buyurmuştur:

"Mûsâ, genç arkadaşına, *'Ben iki denizin birleştiği yere ulaşmaya yahut yıllarca yürümeye kararlıyım.'* (Kehf, 60) dedi."

İki deniz, peygamberlik ahlâkı olan şerîat ilmiyle Mevlâ'nın hakîkat ilmidir. Hıdır'ın, Mecmau'l Bahreyn (iki denizin birleştiği yer) de olması, onun her iki ilme sahip bulunmasına; Allah'ın Mûsâ Aleyhisselâm'ı Hıdır'a göndermesi, insan kemâlinin ancak ledünnî ilimle tamam olacağına; birinci ilim her ne kadar ulü'l-azm peygamberlerde, ikinci ilim rütbe itibarıyla onlardan aşağıda olanlarda ise de ikincisinin arandığına, ledünnî ilim sahibine Allah'a ibâdet edecek kadar şerîat öğrenmesinin kâfi olduğuna işarettir. Bunun içindir ki Hz. Peygamber Aleyhisselâm amel edeceğini söyleyen insana "Âdem tefakkuh etti, anladı." buyurmuştur. Zilzâl Sûresi'ni görünce adam öğrenimi terk etmişti. *Avârif*'te ve diğer eserlerde de böyle yazılıdır.[3]

- Abdullah b. Abbas'tan rivayet edilen bir hadiste de Resûlullah, Zilzâl Sûresi'nin Kur'ân'ın yarısına, İhlâs'ın üçte birine, Kâfirûn Sûresi'nin de dörtte birine denk geldiğini söylemiştir (Tirmizî, "Feżâ'ilü'l-Ḳur'ân", 10; İbrâhim Ali, s. 360-363; Kâfirûn Sûresi'yle ilgili beyanın sıhhati hakkında bk. *DİA*, XXIV, 149). Şehâbeddin Mahmûd el-Âlûsî, Zilzâl

1 Bekir Topaloğlu, *Zilzal Suresi*, *DİA*, c. 44, s. 420-421.

2 İsmail Hakkı Bursevî, *Rûhu'l-Beyân Tefsîri*, c. 10, s. 143-144.

3 Niyazî-i Mısrî, *İrfan Sofraları*, Elli Sekizinci Sofra, s. 146-147.

Sûresi'nin Kur'ân'ın yarısına denk gelişini onun içerdiği hükümlerin dünyaya ve âhirete dair olmasına, sûrenin âhiret ahkâmını kısaca içermesi özelliğine bağlamıştır (*Rûḥu'l-meʿânî*, XXX, 602).[4]

- Bursevî ise bir hadîs-i şerifte: "İzâ zülzilet Sûresi Kur'ân'ın dörtte birine denktir." buyurulduğunu aktarır. Onun dört kez okunması Kur'ân'ın tamamının okunması gibidir.[5]

Hz. Peygamber'in "Zilzâl Sûresi Kur'ân'ın yarısına denktir sözü, Zilzâl Sûresi'nin fıkhî yönden Kur'ân'ın yarısını temsil ettiğini belirtir. Bursevî'nin tefsirinde aktardığı "İzâ zülzilet Sûresi Kur'ân'ın dörtte birine denktir." hadîsi ise Zilzâl Sûresi'nin hakîkat yönünden Kur'ân'ın dörtte birini anlattığını söylemektedir.[6]

- **Zilzâl Sûresi'nin Önceki Sûre ile Bağlantısı ise şudur:** Önceki sûrede *"Onların Rableri katında mükâfatları Adn cennetleridir."* (Beyyine, 8) buyruldu. Bu sûrede, o mükâfatın verileceği zamandan bahsedildi. Sanki inkâr eden kimse "Bu cezâ ve mükâfat ne zaman verilecek?" diye sormuş, ona cevap olarak, *"Yerküre şiddetli bir sarsıntıyla sallandığı zaman."* denilmiştir. Peşinden gelen Âdiyât Sûresi'nde ise o günü inkâr ederek hiçbir hazırlık yapmayanların göreceği azap anlatılmıştır.[7]

Buradan anlaşılıyor ki herkesin kıyâmete hazırlık yapması lazım. Bu kıyâmet şeklî bir kıyâmetse devamlı bir sarsıntı ile ortaya çıkıyor. Vücudî sarsıntı ise idrakle ortaya çıkıyor ve idrak tekrarlanıyor. Her iki sarsıntı da şakî ile saidi ayırmış, saidin müjdesi şakînin felaketi olmuştur.[8]

---

4 Bekir Topaloğlu, Zilzal Suresi, *DİA*, c. 44, s. 420-421.

5 İsmail Hakkı Bursevî, *Rûhu'l-Beyân Tefsîri*, c. 10, s. 143.

6 *Derleyenin Notu.*

7 İbn Acîbe, *Bahrü'l-Medîd*, c. 11, s. 99.

8 *Derleyenin Notu.*

ÂYET 1

"Yeryüzü şiddetli bir şekilde sarsıldığında."

• Yerin o zilzali, zelzelesi. Yerin, hareketi-i arz (yer hareketi) dediğimiz zangır zangır sarsıntısıdır. "Zell", hareket mânâsı ifade ettiği için zelzele ve zilzâl onun muzaafı olarak tekrar etmeyi ifade eder. Bilhassa izafetle ifade edilmesi, yerin mümkün olabilen bütün şiddet ve dehşetiyle sarsıntısına işarettir ki, maksat Hac Sûresi'nde geçtiği üzere *"Şüphesiz kıyâmet vaktinin depremi müthiş bir şeydir."* (Hac, 1). Vâkı'a Sûresi'nde ve daha birçok sûrelerde: *"Yer şiddetle sarsıldığı, dağlar parçalandığı, dağılıp toz duman haline geldiği zaman."* (Vâkı'a, 4-6) gibi âyetlerle açıklanmış ve haber verilmiş olan kıyâmet depremidir.[9]

• *"Yer"* kendine mahsus, daha ötesi olmayan *"şiddetli bir sarsıntı ile"* tekrar tekrar *"sallandığı..."* Aynı harflerin tekrarlanışı, sallanmanın da tekrarlanacağını gösterir.[10]

• *"Yeryüzü şiddetli bir şekilde sarsıldığında."* Yani yeryüzü şiddetli bir şekilde, peş peşe kuvvetle sarsıldığı zaman. Bu sarsılma yüce Allah'ın

9 Elmalılı Hamdi Yazır, *Hak Dini Kur'an Dili*, c. 9, s. 401.

10 İsmail Hakkı Bursevî, *Rûhu'l-Beyân Tefsîri*, c. 10, s. 140.

dilemesine göre kendisine has çok ayrı bir sarsılmadır. Öyle bir sarsılır ki daha ötesi yoktur.

Yahut yer öyle bir sarsılır ki derecesi ölçülemez.

İbn Arafe der ki: Âyette sarsılan yerden kasıt, yerin birinci tabakasıdır, çünkü yerin ikinci tabakasında (kıyâmet kopunca dışarı çıkarılacak) ölüler yoktur. Gök bilimcilere göre gökler, tabaka halinde birbirini sarmaktadır. Yerler de böyledir. Bize göre, göklerin arasında belli bir boşluğun olması mümkündür. İsrâ ve mi'rac olayını anlatan hadîsin zâhirî ifadelerinden bu anlaşılıyor. (Çünkü Hz. Peygamber [sallallahu aleyhi vesellem], bir gökten diğerine mi'racla yükselerek gitmiştir. Demek aralarında bir mesafe vardır.)"[11]

Yerden dibe doğru, gökten de arşa doğru çeşitli tabakalar vardır. Bunlar aynı zamanda insandaki tecellîlerdir.[12]

- *"Arz şiddetli bir sarsıntı ile sallandığı vakit." "...sallandığı...vakit"* Yani beden arzı, insanî ruhun çıkarılması ölüm esnasında hayvanî ruhla kuvvetler sarsıntısıyla sallandığı zaman. Çünkü bedenin harap olacağını, bünyesinin yıkılacağını ilan eden bu durumda beden kaçınılmaz olarak sarsılır.[13]

- Malûmdur ki kıyâmet üç kısımdır.

Biri küçük kıyâmet. Hadîs-i şerifte de buyrulduğu üzere, insan öldüğü vakit kıyâmeti kopmuş demektir.

İkinci kıyâmet, sûr üflendiği vakitte bütün mevcûdatın dağılmasıdır.

Üçüncü kıyâmet ise, ikinci defa sûr üflendiği zaman herkesin kendi cesedinde ve hesabı görülmek üzere mahşerde dirilip toplanmasıdır ki, orada ne olacak ne bulacaksak, bunlar kendi amellerimizin neticesidir.[14]

---

11 İbn Acîbe el-Hasenî, *Bahrü'l-Medîd*, c. 11, s. 101-102.

12 *Derleyenin Notu.*

13 Muhyiddin İbn Arabî, *Tefsîr-i Kabîr Te'vilât*, c. 2, s. 1477.

14 Ken'an Rifâî, *Sohbetler*, s. 194.

- Kıyâmet gününde sûra üfürülecektir. Sûr, içinde mahlûkatın nefesleri sayısınca delikleri olan boynuz şeklinde bir mahlûktur. Sûrun içinde her varlığın bir deliği olduğundan, evvelce düşüp ölmemiş varlıklar onun sesinin tesiriyle gaşyolur (mest olmak).

Sûra üfleyen İsrâfil'dir (a.s). Ruh bir safta (taraf, yer), melekler diğer bir safta bulunur. Emr-i ilâhî ve melekler buluttan gölgeler içinde gelecektir. (...)

Sûra halkın bayılıp düşmesi için üfürüldükten sonra tekrar dirilip kalkmaları için de üfürülecek ve insanlar bundan sonra Hakk'ın kendilerinden neyi murad ettiğine bakıp bekleyeceklerdir.[15]

- Kıyâmet öldükten sonra ebedî hayata dönüştür. Bu da üçe ayrılır:

Birincisi, ölünün dünya hayatındaki hâline göre, tabiî ölümden sonra ulvî veya süflî berzahların birine gönderilmesidir. Nitekim Hz. Peygamber şöyle buyurmuştur: *"Nasıl yaşarsanız öyle ölürsünüz, nasıl ölürseniz öyle dirilirsiniz."* Ölümün bu türü Hz. Peygamber'in *"Kim ölmüşse kıyâmeti kopmuş olur."* [Deylemî, I, 285; Aclûnî, II, 386] hadîsiyle işâret buyurdukları küçük kıyâmettir.

İkincisi, irâdî bir ölümle kuds âleminde ebedî kalb hayatına döndürülmektir. Nitekim şöyle denilmiştir: *"İradenle öl ki, tabiî olarak yaşayasın."* Ölümün bu türü *"Ölü iken dirilttiğimiz ve insanlar arasında yürüyebileceği bir ışık verdiğimiz kimse..."* [En'âm, 122] âyetiyle işâret buyrulan orta kıyâmettir.

Üçüncüsü, Allah'ta fânî olduktan sonra Hak ile bâkî olurken, hakîkî hayata döndürülmektir. Bu büyük kıyâmettir. Nitekim âyette şöyle buyrulmuştur: *"Büyük kıyâmet geldiğinde..."* (Nâzi'ât, 34) (Kâşânî, 146).[16]

- İbnü'l-Arabî şöyle der:

"Allah âlemde iki kıyâmet yaratmıştır: küçük kıyâmet ve büyük kıyâmet (büyük toplanma). Küçük kıyâmet, misal âleminden bir bedende kulun dünya hayatından berzaha intikalidir. Büyük kıyâmet ise insan-

15 Ahmed er-Rifâî, *Mârifet Yolu*, s. 210.

16 *Metinlerle Tasavvuf Terimleri Sözlüğü*, s. 557.

ların toplanacakları diriliş ve büyük toplanma kıyâmetidir. Burası herhangi bir tartışma olmaksızın, amellerin kula sunulacağı gündür (*Fütûhât*, c. III, 389)."

Küçük kıyâmet kulun idrak etmeye başlaması ve bu idraki geliştirerek iki âlemin arasında kalacak seviyeye erişmesidir. Büyük kıyâmet ise herkesin mutlaka kendi hakîkatini göreceği günü anlatır.[17]

Küçük kıyâmet: Kulun ölümü ve âhiret hayatının örneği:

"'*Yakîn gelinceye kadar Rabbine ibâdet et.*' (Hicr, 99). Yakîn'in gelmesi, bu şeyleri müşâhede etmekle gerçekleşir. O da küçük kıyâmet demektir (*Tecelliyat*, 6)."

Küçük Ölüm, büyük ölümün zıddına (ölüm göçmesi) uykuda göçmektir.

İbnü'l-Arabî şöyle der: "Uyku, mevt-i asgar, yani küçük ölümdür. O da, uyuyanın göçtüğü mertebenin ölünün de göçtüğü mertebenin aynısı olması yönünden ölümün ta kendisidir. Uykudan sonra uyanmak, ölümden sonra dirilmek gibidir (*Fütûhât*, c. IV, 424)."

Hz. Mevlânâ da bu konuda Mesnevî'de "Uyumak ölmektir. Ruh incecik bir bağ vâsıtasıyla vücuttan ayrılır, hakîkatine gider. Nefs vücutta kalır fakat ertesi gün uyandığında ruh tekrar vücuda dönmüştür." der.[18]

"İnsan büyük ölüm veya küçük ölüm sayesinde berzaha göçtüğünde, küçük ölümde uyanıkken tahayyül ettiği bazı şeyleri berzahta duyulur şeyler olarak görür. Onlar, uyanıkken duyularına ilişen ve bu nedenle inkâr edemeyeceği şeyler gibidir (*Fütûhât*, c. IV, 99)."[19]

Yani insan hakîkî diriyken aklın almayacağı şeyleri de idrak eder.[20]

Ey kendileri hakkında irâde edilenden gâfil olanlar! Kıyâmet ânını düşünün! Özel ve büyük kıyâmeti düşünün! Özel kıyâmet sizden birisinin ölmesidir. Büyük kıyâmet ise Allahu Teâlâ'nın vadettiği kıyâmettir. Allahu Teâlâ'nın şu buyruğunu düşünüp hatırlayın: *"O gün müttakîleri vefd olarak Rahmân'ın huzûrunda haşrederiz. Mücrimleri ise vird olarak*

---

17 *Derleyenin Notu.*

18 *Derleyenin Notu.*

19 Suad el-Hakîm, *İbnü'l-Arabî Sözlüğü*, s. 435.

20 *Derleyenin Notu.*

cehenneme sevk ederiz." (Meryem, 85-86). "Vefd" cemaat demektir. "Vird" ise susuz demektir. Müttakîler haşredilirler; mücrimler ise sevk edilirler. Allahu Teâlâ bu günü dünya hayatında iken düşünmüş olan kuluna acır da, onu müttakîler arasına katar ve onlarla haşreder.[21]

- ***Avni Konuk Hazretleri buyuruyor ki:*** Kıyâmetin türleri vardır.

Bunlardan birincisi; her ân ve sâatte vukû bulandır. Çünkü âlemler her ânda gaybdan şehâdete ve şehâdet âleminden gayb âlemine dâhil olur. Ve bu âlemlerin bozulup yok olanlar ve var edilenler ve ma'nâlar ve cisimler gibi bütün türlerinin şehâdetten gayba ve gaybdan şehâdete dâhil oluşunu ve çıkışını, ihâta yolu üzere, ancak Cenâb-ı Hak bilir. Çünkü bu ilim ilâhi zevk (deneyim) ilminin zevkinden ibârettir. Bunda hiç kimsenin ortaklığı yoktur.

İkincisi; "mecbûri ölüm" ile gerçekleşendir. Nitekim (s.a.s) Efendimiz: *"Ölen kimsenin kıyâmeti kopar."* buyururlar.

Üçüncüsü; "isteğe bağlı ve irâdeye ait ölüm" ile olur. Sâlik bu ölüm ve kıyâmetten sonra âlemde âhiret oluşumu üzerine yaşar. İşte buna dayanaraktır ki, ölüye açılmış olan hâller seyri sülûku sırasında sâlike de açılmış olur. Ve bu hâle "küçük kıyâmet" ismini verirler. ***(Birinci Sûr'un üflenişi)***[22]

Dördüncüsü; ârifîn-i billâh hazarâtına fenâ-fillah ve baka-billâhtan sonra tam vahdet ve çokluğun yok olması hâlinin meydana gelmesidir. Ârifin nefsinde gerçekleşen bu tecellîye de "büyük kıyâmet" derler. ***(İkinci Sûr'un üflenişi - ölmeden önce ölmek.)***[23]

Beşincisi; bütün kâinât için takdir olunmuş ve beklenen kıyâmettir ki, Hak Teâlâ'nın celîl âyetlerindeki: *"İnne's-sâate âtiyetün lâ raybe fîhâ"* ya'nî *"O saat muhakkak gelecektir, onda hiç şüphe yoktur."* (Hac, 22/7) ve *"inne's-sâate âtiyetün ekâdu uhfîhâ"* ya'nî *"O saat muhakkak gelecektir, onu gizliyorum."* (Tâ-Hâ, 20/15) ve benzeri Kur'ân-ı Kerîm âyetleridir.[24]

---

21 Abdülkâdir Geylânî, *Cilâü'l-Hâtır*, 2. Meclis, s. 13-14.

22 *Derleyenin Notu.*

23 *Derleyenin Notu.*

24 Ahmed Avni Konuk, *Fusûsu'l-Hikem Tercüme ve Şerhi*, Ondokuzuncu Kısım: Kıyâmet, s. 95.

- Soru: Küçük ve büyük kıyâmet ne demektir?

Cevap: "Küçük kıyâmet", *"Kim öldü ise onun kıyâmeti kopmuştur."* hadîs-i şerîfi gereğince her bir ferdin ölümüyle gerçekleşen kıyâmettir. Ölüm de iki türlüdür; birisi "irâdî ölüm", diğeri "kaçınılmaz ölüm"dür. "İrâdî ölüm", Hakk yoluna sâlik yâni yolcu olanların şiddetli riyâzât ve çok mücâhedeler yapmasıyla nefsâni sıfatlarını imhâ etmeleriyle zuhûra gelir. *"Ölmeden önce ölünüz."* hadîs-i şerîfinde emr buyrulan ölüm budur. Bu hâle gelen sâlikin bakışında ne kendi vücûdu ve ne de âlem çokluklarının vücûdu kalmaz. Her nereye baksa "bir" olan vechi görür. Belki onun görmesi, Hakk'ın kendisini görmesi olur (***yukarıda anlatılan 3. ve 4. kıyâmetlerin mânâsıdır).***[25] "Kaçınılmaz ölüm", hâllerin hakîkatlerinden habersiz olan ve hayvâni hayatta bütün hayvânlar ile ortak olan perde ehlinin ölümüdür. Bu bahsin detayları uzundur. Bu kadarı yeterli olur.

"Büyük kıyâmet"te âlemin bütün her şeyiyle Âdem'in izâfi vücûdu gibi vâkti gelince fenâ bulmasıdır. Çünkü âlemin tamamı, Âdem gibi bütün ilâhi isimlerin görünme yeri olduğundan hakîkat ehli "büyük insan" olarak isimlendirmişlerdir. Eceli gelince küçük insan nasıl ölür ve izâfi vücûdu muzmahil yâni yok hükmünde olursa, büyük insan da öylece ölür ve izâfî vücûdu mahvolur. Ve bu anda da yukarıda îzâh edildiği üzere Allah, Vâhid ve Kahhâr isimlerinin kemâlâtı açığa çıkar. Çünkü halkediliş öncesi olan ulûhiyyet ve vâhidiyyet ve kahhâriyyet ile halkediliş sonrası olan ulûhiyyet ve vâhidiyyet ve kahhâriyyet arasında icmâl ve ayrıntı itibarıyla fark vardır.[26]

- Âlem ve Âdem, zât-ı ehadiyetin esmâ ve sıfatla tecellîsinden vücud buldu.

Ne vakit? "Mufassal" (kısımlara ayıran, adâlet eden) isminden zuhuratı tamam olduktan sonra.

"Ve O'na döneceksiniz…" (Yûnus, 56) âyet-i kerîmesi uyarınca icmale reddolundu ve nispetlerden, izafetlerden hâsıl olan arızî şeyler zail oldu, kayboldu.

25 *Derleyenin Notu.*

26 Ahmed Avni Konuk, *Fusûsu'l-Hikem Tercüme ve Şerhi*, İdrîsiyye Fassı, s. 315.

Şu var ki bu dönüş; bazılarına "Fenâ" yolu ile iradî bir ölümle daha bu dünya âleminde, bazılarına da ıztırarî ve tabiî bir ölümle hâsıl oldu.

Ve bu iki ölüme de küçük kıyâmet derler.

Âlem Âdem'in aynadaki aksidir. Bu aksin vücut bulması, küllün yani bütünün parçalara ayrışması ile olur. İsimlerin zâtının birliğini temsil eden Âdem'den ilk aynada âlem gözükür, sonra isim ve sıfatlar ayrışır. Fakat hepsinin gayesi O'na dönmektir. O'na dönmenin mânâsı da bu farklılıkların yok olup birliğin ortaya çıkmasıdır. Bu iki şekilde olur: Bazısı fenâya ererek çokluktan birliğe ulaşır. Yani kendi varlığından, nefsinden fenâ bulur (yok olur) ve ölmeden önce ölür. Bazıları da vücuttan kurtularak normal ölümle bu hâle erişir. Bunlara küçük kıyâmet denir.[27]

Ve âlemin bütün cüzlerinin yok olmasına da büyük kıyâmet derler. Zira bu kıyâmet, cümle fâni cüzleri müştemildir (içine alır) ki, onun üstünde kıyâmet yoktur. İşte bu cihetten, büyük kıyâmete fenâ-i ekber deniyor. (***Yokluğun en güzel hâli; büyük yokluk.***)[28]

Dolayısıyla, halk yönünden de en büyük kıyâmet budur. Nitekim onun büyük kıyâmet olduğu şu âyetin delâletinden de açıkça anlaşılıyor: *"Elbette yerin ve semâların yaratılışı, insanların yaratılışından daha büyük bir iştir..."* (Mü'min, 57).

Yani, yer ve semâlar; ki bunlar âfak (ufuklar) ve tafsil âlemidir, delâlet yönünden, enfüs (nefsler, ruhlar, yaşayanlar) ve icmalden (özet) daha büyüktür. Zira, enfüs metin; afak şerh gibidir ki metin, şerhe göre muhtasar (kısa, öz) ve mücmel (özetlenmiş) olduğu gibi, âdem dahi âleme göre böyledir. Ve

Hakîkatta âdemi gören, âlemi görür
Âlemi gören de âdemi görür.[29]

- Can, eğer bu kalıptan ayrılırsa kalıp, hasta ve harap olur. Bir gök gibi olan başın yıldızları, göz, kulak, ağız ve burundan ibaret olan

27 *Derleyenin Notu.*

28 *Derleyenin Notu.*

29 İsmail Hakkı Bursevî, *Kenz-i Mahfi*, s. 45-46.

hasseleridir. Bunların hepsi de işe yaramaz bir hale gelirler. Dökülürler ve yok olurlar. Bunun gibi kol, bilek, kalça, diz, el ve ayak, damar, sinir, mafsallar ve vücudun bağlarından ibaret olan geri kalan bütün uzuvlar da birbirinden ayrılır ve dökülürler. Zerre zerre olurlar. İşte bu âlemin, varlığın kıyâmeti de böyle kopar. Allah nurunu bu âlemden keserse âlem cansız kalır. Ağaçların meyveleri, her yıl olgunlaşınca yere düşüp yok oldukları halde, ağaçlar daha uzun müddet nasıl yaşarlarsa, âlemin meyvesi ve bir parçası olan insanlar da yetmiş, seksen sene yaşadıktan sonra ölürler; buna göre bütün olan âlemin ömrü daha uzundur. Âlemin eceli gelince, ki bu kıyâmet günüdür, âlemin başı olan gök parça parça olur ve dökülür, gökler yarılır ve parlak, ışıklı güneş kararır, yıldızlar dökülür, dağlar yerlerinden oynar, yırtıcı hayvanlar birbirine girer, denizler ateş kesilir. Ve yine âleme ölümsüz diyen ve onun son bulmasını inkâr eden kimselerin basîretsizliğine karşı Allah şöyle buyuruyor: *"Gökler yarılır, yıldızlar aşağı dökülür, denizler birleşir, mezarlar yerlerinden oynar ve alt üst olurlar."* (İnfitâr, 1-2). *"Dağlar pamuk gibi atılır."* (Kâri'a, 5).[30]

• *"Gökler yarılır."* (İnşikâk, 1) ve *"yer yerinden oynadığı zaman"* (Zilzâl, 1) bu sana işarettir. Yani sen kavuşma tadını tattın. İşte bir gün gelir ki bu parçaların ayrılığı tadını tadar, o âlemin genişliğini de müşâhede eder ve bu darlıktan kurtulursun, demektir. Mesela birini çarmıha gerseler, o orada rahat olduğunu zannederek kurtulma zevkini unutur. Halbuki çarmıhtan kurtulunca ne azap içinde olduğunu anlar. Bunun gibi çocukların da rahatı ve gelişmesi orada ellerini bağladıkları halde, beşikte olur. Fakat büyük bir adamı beşiğe koysalar, burası onun için zindan ve azap olur. Bazı kimseler güllerin açılıp goncalardan baş çıkarmasından hoşlanır; bazısı ise bütün gül yapraklarının birbirinden ayrılıp, kendi asıllarına bağlanmış olmalarından zevk duyar. İşte bazıları hiçbir dostluk, aşk ve sevgi, küfür ve îman kalmamasını, böylece asıllarına kavuşmalarını isterler. Çünkü bütün bunlar duvardır. Darlığa, sıkıntıya ve ikiliğe sebep olur. Halbuki o âlem genişliği, huzur ve mutlak birliği muciptir.[31]

30 Sultan Veled, *Maârif,* Fasıl 10, s. 49-50.

31 Mevlânâ, *Fîhi Mâfîh*, Fasıl 51, s. 297-298.

• Nefislerin toprağı yani fıtratı (mânevî terbiye altında) kendine has bir şekilde sarsıldığında, nefis ilâhî tecellîler ve hâllerle hareket ettirildiğinde ve insan bütünüyle nefsinden gaybet hâlini (ondan tamamen sıyrılıp Hakk'a yönelmeyi) elde ettiğinde, irfan güneşi parlar, bu güneş bütün varlıkları sarar; o güneş aydınlığında kalp her şeyde Allah'ı müşâhede eder."[32]

Mürşitle kıyâmetin kopması bu demektir ki, mürşit nefse yokluğunu idrak ettirir. Bu idrak vücudun Hakk'a yönelmesini sağlar. Kalp aydınlanır ve her an Allah'ın yeni bir ismini müşâhede eder.[33]

• Öyle kalpler vardır ki, kendisine tecellî eden Rabb'inin heybetinden erir, gönül dağı yerle bir olur, nefislerin arzı sarsılır. Bir tanesi bu mânâda nazım halinde şöyle demiştir:

"Eğer gözlerin ilâhî tecellî ile nefislerin arzının sarsıldığı ve gönüldeki dağların yerle bir olduğu günü görecek olsaydı, o sarsıntı esnasında Cenâb-ı Hakk'ın nurunun her şeyi sardığını görürdün. Bir de bu âlemde kimin gerçek er kişi (ricâlullah) olduğunu bilirdin."[34]

Eğer kıyâmet vücudî kıyâmetse, hâdiselerde sadece Rabbini gördüğünden erir, nefisler sarsılır. Yukarıda söylendiği gibi bu eğer maddî bir sarsıntı ise, aslında gören için bu sarsıntının Cenâb-ı Hakk'ın nurunun her şeyi sarışı olduğunu bilir. Bu kimse yapanın yaptıranın O olduğunu idrak ettiğinden ve daima rahmetinin gazâbını örttüğünü bildiğinden hâdiseleri hakîkatinden seyreder, itiraz etmez. Bu kişi er kişidir. Hâli ise, hâdisede hizmet etmek, itiraz etmemektir.[35]

• *Benlik ve nefsaniyet dağını, kazma ile, külünk ile yerinden söküp atacak bir hamiyyet, bir gayret nerede?*

Böyle yapılacak olursa, belki onun cüzlerine bir mânâ ayının nuru düşer. Belki ay ışığı ona yol gösterir.

32 İbn Acîbe el-Hasenî, *Bahrü'l-Medîd*, c. 11, s. 105.

33 *Derleyenin Notu.*

34 İbn Acîbe el- Hasenî, *Bahrü'l-Medîd*, c. 1, s. 354.

35 *Derleyenin Notu.*

Kıyâmet gününde dağlar yerinden sökülecek, senin de bir davranışın ne vakit bu lütfu gösterecek ve mânevî kıyâmet koparacak da benlik dağın paramparça olacak, hallaç pamuğu gibi atılacak?

Bu davranışın, bu silkinmen o kıyâmetten nasıl olur da aşağı olur? O kıyâmet yaradır. Bu kıyâmet merheme benzer.

Kim bu merhemi gördü ise, yaradan emindir. Bu güzelliği gören her kötü kişi ihsan sahibi olur.

Ne mutlu o çirkine ki, bu güzele eş olur. Vay o gül yüzlüye ki, kış gibi soğuk bir kişiye dosttur.[36]

- ***Ahmed er-Rifâî buyuruyor ki:*** "Bu mânevî hilâfeti son olarak bütün yönleriyle üslenen, bu zayıf, âciz, güçsüz, hiçbir şeye mâlik olmayan bendenizdir. Ki bunu bana, kadîm ve mukîm olan Hz. Allah, sadece kereminin bir neticesi olarak bahsetmiştir. Ayrıca rahmet peygamberi Hz. Muhammed de (s.a.s), kurbiyet derecesine ulaşanlar arasında ve onun mânevî huzurunda bulunan askerlerinin yanında, beni bununla müjdelemiştir. Allah'ın razı olduğuna biz de razı olduk. Bu, Allah'ın celâl sıfatının mahcûb kalplerde bir sarsıntısıdır. Ki bu sarsıntı, bazı insanların korkmaları ve Allah'ın kudretinden ibret almaları için olup, Cenâb-ı Hakk'ın depremlerle sarp ve yalçın dağları sarsmasından daha şiddetlidir. Ancak bu mânevî hilâfeti üslenen bazı kimseler de vardır ki, onlar sükûn üzere olup bu sarsıntıdan çok az etkilenirler. Şartların değişmesiyle kalplerinin paramparça olduğunu görürsün."[37]

36 Şefik Can, *Mesnevî Tercümesi*, c. 2, s. 363-364 beyit 1335-1341.

37 Ahmed er-Rifâî, *Sohbet Meclisleri*, s. 108-109.

ÂYET 2

"Yer, içindeki ağırlıkları dışarı çıkardığında."

- *"Yer, içindeki ağırlıkları dışarı çıkardığında."*: Yerin ağırlıklarını çıkarmasında iki rivayet vardır. Birisi: Ölüleri kabirlerinden fırlatıp çıkarmasıdır, ki *"Kabirlerin içindekiler dışarı çıkarıldığı zaman."* (İnfitâr, 4) âyetinin mefhumudur. Bu ise dirilmek demek olacağından ikinci sûrun üflenmesine işaret olur. Diğeri de içindeki definelerin, hazinelerin, madenlerin meydana çıkarılmasıdır ki, bunun da ilk sûra üflemede, yani ilk zelzelede olması açıktır. Bazı haberlerde kıyâmet alâmetlerinden olan Deccal'ın günlerinde yerin hazineleri meydana çıkacak diye vârit olmuştur. Bunu da bazıları ona yormuş ise de o, zelzeleden önce olan çıkarmalar olduğu, halbuki burada maksat zelzele ile meydana gelecek çıkarmalar olması açık bulunduğu cihetle demişlerdir ki, Deccal'ın zamanında çıkarılanlardan başka olarak kalmış olan bütün hazinelerin ve definelerin deprem ile fırlatılıp çıkarılmasıdır.

Burada iki tür zelzele anlatılıyor. Bugün yaşadığımız zelzele felâketinin de toprağın içindeki hazineleri ortaya çıkarmak için olduğu muhakkak, çünkü bu, Zilzâl Sûresi'nde anlatılan zelzelenin aynısı. Yani tekrar eden ve çok şiddetli, Vâkı'a Sûresi'nde de anlatıldığı gibi her şeyi mahveden, dağları, ovaları, her şeyi yok eden bir zelzele.

Demek ki zelzele, o bölge için bir çeşit kıyâmeti anlatıyor.

Bir de, vücutta birinci sûrun üflendiği anda, yani idrakin başladığı andaki zelzele var. Bu zelzele insanı çok sarsan ve ondan sonra artık her idrakte devamlılık arz eden bir zelzele. Fakat idrakle îman başlayınca, ikinci sûr üflenmiş oluyor. Ve bu da hakîkatin yani içinde ona ait hakîkî ismin ortaya çıkışıdır. İçindeki hazinelerin -cemâl veya celâl- zuhur edişidir. Bu hâl her tür kıyâmette böyle; büyük kıyâmette de böyle, küçük kıyâmette de böyle.[38]

Ancak ilk sûra üflemede mi, ikinci üflemede mi? Bunda da her iki ihtimali söyleyenler olmuştur. Bazıları demişlerdir ki: Bu depremden maksat, birinci depremdir. Yer o zaman hazinelerini çıkaracak, yeryüzü altın dolacak da ona iltifat eden olmayacak. Altın o zaman sanki insana şöyle bağıracak: Sen benim için dinini ve dünyanı yıkmıyor muydun? Sonra onun çıkarılmasının sonucu bir de *"Kıyâmet gününde biriktirilen malların üzerleri cehennem ateşinde kızdırılacak ve onlarla sahiplerinin alınları, yanları ve sırtları dağlanacak. Kendilerine: 'İşte kendiniz için biriktirdiğiniz budur.'"* (Tevbe, 35) hükmünün açıklanması olur ki, bu da ikinci sûr üflemesinden sonra olur.[39]

Dünya depreminde de aynı şey oluyor. Para, mal, biriktirilen her şeyin insanlara yük olduğu aşikâr oluyor. Yani biriktirdikleri şeyler, taptıkları şeyler onlara mezar oluyor. Taptıkları şeylerin yok oluşu insanların vücutlarını dağlıyor.

Mânevî kıyâmette de insan hiçbir şeyin öneminin olmadığını anladığı anda zaten o vücutlar yalnız Hakk'a dönüyorlar; mesele orada.[40]

- *"Yer ağırlıklarını çıkardığı..." "Ağırlıklar"*dan maksat, yerin içindeki hazineler ve ölülerdir. Mânâ şudur: Yer, kıyâmet alâmetlerinden olan ilk sûra üflemenin verdiği sarsıntı ânında olduğu gibi, içerisinde bulunan hazinelerini ve gömülü olan şeyleri, ikinci nefhanın sarsıntısı ânında da ölülerini çıkardığı zaman...

---

38 *Derleyenin Notu.*

39 Elmalılı Hamdi Yazır, *Hak Dini Kur'an Dili*, c. 9, s. 401.

40 *Derleyenin Notu.*

Âyette, kuvvetli ve tekrarlanan bir sarsıntıdan bahsediliyor. Bu sarsıntının sebebi de, içindeki ağırlıkların çıkarılışı, yani celâlin içinden cemâlin çıkarılışı gibidir.

Birinci sûrun üflenmesinde, insanın içinden hakîkatleri çıkar ve kim olduğu ortaya çıkar. Toprak da vahyolunmuş olduğu için, "Deprem, Peygamber gibidir." diyor Hz. Mevlânâ. Deprem, celâlle cemâli ayırır ve cemâl ehlinin cemâlini, celâl ehlinin celâlini hazine gibi dışarı çıkarır (şakîde ölülük, saitte ise hazine ortaya çıkar). Bu, birinci sûrun üflenişidir, herkesin hakîkatini ortaya çıkarır.

Toprakta ise bir yok oluş vardır, ama o yok oluş var oluşu getirir. Yani o toprak içinden güzel olanlar, çok güzel çıkar. Zâhirî depremde öbür âleme intikal edenler ise, şehit olarak giderler. Allah, onların bütün günahlarını affederek kabul eder; bu da büyük bir lütuftur.

Fakat buradan canlı çıkanlar iki bölükte çıkarlar; ya cemâl ehli, ya celâl ehli. Şakî şakîliğini, said saidliğini görür.

Eğer buna "vücûdî kıyâmet" açısından bakarsak da, birinci sûrun üflenişi muazzam bir sarsıntıdır, çünkü insanlar ilk defa idrake kavuşurlar. Bu idrakle içlerindeki bütün hazineler, yani ezelî hakîkatleri ve kim oldukları ortaya çıkar.

Toprak sallandığında nasıl içindeki değerli madenler dışarı çıkıyorsa vücut toprağı sallandığında da herkes kendi hakîkatini görür.[41]

Bir hadiste şöyle denilmektedir: *"Yer ciğerinin filizlerini altından sütunlar halinde kusar (atar.) Katil gelip: 'Ben bunun için öldürmüştüm.' der. Akrabalık bağını kesen: 'Ben bunun için akrabalığı ihmal ettim.' der. Hırsız gelip: 'Benim elim bunun için kesildi.' der. Sonra hiçbirisi bir şey almadan onu terk ederler."*

*"Ciğerinin filizleri"*nden maksat, içerisinde gömülü olan hazinelerdir. Resûlullah, yerin onları çıkaracağını bildirmiştir.[42]

Hakîkatler vücuttan da çıkıyor (ciğerden de çıkıyor), yerden de çıkıyor.[43]

41 *Derleyenin Notu.*

42 İsmail Hakkı Bursevî, *Rûhu'l-Beyân Tefsîri*, c. 10, s. 140.

43 *Derleyenin Notu.*

• Yeryüzünün bu sarsıntısı sûra ikinci defa üfürülmesi esnasında olacaktır. Bunu şu âyetten anlıyoruz: *"Yer içindeki ağırlıkları dışarı çıkardığında."* Yani yer, içindeki ölüleri ve hazineleri dışarı çıkaracaktır. Bu âyette yerin açıkça söylenmesi olayı kesin olarak ifade etmek içindir. Ayrıca bunda, yerin başka bir yere çevrileceğini de işaret vardır.[44]

Maddî sarsıntıda topraktakilerin dışarı çıkması gibi, vücuttaki sarsıntıda da ölü olanla hazine sahibi olan ayrılır. Ölünün hakîkati, müminin de hazinesi ortaya çıkar.[45]

• Bilmelisin ki, Allah sûretlere üfleyip kabirlerinde bulunanları dirilttiğinde, insanlar ve vahşiler toplanır. Bu bağlamda şöyle der: *"Yeryüzü ağırlıklarını çıkartır."* (Zilzâl, 2). Artık yeryüzünde kendisinden başka kimse kalmaz ve onları -bitirme şeklinde değil- kendinden çıkartma tarzında izhar eder. Zâhirî dünyanın yaratılışıyla âhiretin zâhirî yaratılışı arasındaki fark budur. Birincide bizi Allah yeryüzünden bitirmiş ve nasıl ki bitkilerin cisimleri dereceli bir şekilde bitip uzar ve enleşir, biz de dereceli bir şekilde bittik. Âhiret yaratılışı ise Allah'ın bizi dilediği bir sûrette "çıkartma" yoluyla gerçekleşir ve bu nedenle meşiyet ve irade, Allah'ın kendisini "bitici" diye nitelediği yerde yenilediği sûretlerin neşrine bağlanmıştır. Bu durumda sûret önceki bir misal olmaksızın biter, çünkü yeni sûret ilkine benzer değildir. Âhiret yaratılışı da böyledir. Allah onu daha önce olan ve benzeyeceği bir misal olmayan bir sûrette yaratır. Bu durum *"Sizi var ettiğimiz gibi iade edilirsiniz."* (A'râf, 29). Başka bir âyette *"İlk yaratmayı gördünüz, öğüt almaz mısınız?"* (Vâkı'a, 62) ve *"Sizi bilmediğiniz şekilde yaratırız."* (Vâkı'a, 62) ve *"Yeryüzü ağırlıklarını çıkartır."* (Zilzâl, 2) buyrulur. Yeryüzü içinde saklamış olduğu herhangi bir şeyin kalmadığını bildirir.[46]

• *"Ve toprak ağırlıklarını..."* beden arzı, *"...dışarı çıkardığı...vakit."* Metaını dışarı attığı zaman. Çünkü beden, kuvvetlerden, ruhlardan, amellerin heyetlerinden ve kalpte kökleşmiş inançlardan oluşan bu

44 İbn Acîbe el-Hasenî, *Bahrü'l-Medîd*, c. 11, s. 102.

45 *Derleyenin Notu.*

46 İbn Arabî, *Fütûhât-ı Mekkiyye*, c. 13, s. 358.

metalarla değerlenir. Âyette geçen *"eskal"* kelimesi "sakl"in çoğuludur ve ev eşyası anlamına gelir.[47]

- Şeyh Ebü'l-Abbas-ı Mürsî (r.a) bu konuda nazım halinde şunu söyle der:

"Nefislerin şiddetle sarsıldığı ve tabiatların yerle bir edildiği günü görseydin, o gün Hakk'ın güneşinin her yanı sardığını ve aydınlattığını görürdün. İşte o gün gerçek er kişiler, Allah dostları ortaya çıkar."

Nefisler ilâhî aşkla sarsılıp nurla temizlenince, içindeki ilimleri ortaya çıkarır.[48]

- Resûlullah: *"Nûrun kalbe girdiğine alâmet, bu gurur dünyasından baş çevirip sürur dünyası olan âhirete teveccüh ve ölüm gelmezden evvel ona hazırlanmaktır."* buyuruyor.[49]

- "Aşk geldi mi kıyâmet koptu demektir, aşk geldi mi tövbe kapıları kapanır."[50]

- İsrâfil, elindeki sûr ile kıyâmeti bekleyedursun, ben ki o aşkın nefesi ile dirildim, hemen arkasından ikinci bir nefes ölüm sûrunu çaldı ve beni öldürdü. Ne garip ki bu öldürücü aşk, diyetimi verecek bir kimse aradı, bulamayınca gene kendine verdi.[51]

- Beşeriyet mertebesinde olanlar, tamamıyla ve küllî olarak Allah'ın nurunda fânî olanların mertebesinden nasıl dem vurabilirler? Ve onlar ile kendilerini nasıl kıyaslayabilirler? Onların varlık gösteren yok olmuş vücutları Tûr'u, Hakk'ın cezbesi tecellîsinin sarsıntılarıyla kendinden

47 Muhyiddin İbn Arabî, *Tefsîr-i Kebîr Te'vîlât*, c. 2, s. 1477.

48 İbn Acîbe el-Hasenî, *Bahrü'l-Medîd*, c. 11, s. 105.

49 Ken'an Rifâî, *Sohbetler*, s. 569-570.

50 Sâmiha Ayverdi vd, *Yirminci Asrın Işığında Müslümanlık*, s. 231.

51 Sâmiha Ayverdi, *Yaşayan Ölü*, s. 140.

geçip tamamıyla muzmahil olmuş, silinip gitmiştir. İşte o zaman bunların iki âlemi kendinde toplamış olan Tûr-ı Sînâ'ya benzeyen varlıkları dağından zuhur eden kavil ve fiil, in'ikâs (aksetme) yoluyla, Rahmân'ın iktizalarıdır (gereklilikleridir).[52]

- *Mustafa (s.a.s), beden binektir dedi; ruh, yahut akıl, nasıl olur da binek olur?*

Onun sözünce bedeni binek bil de varlık âleminde aramaya kalkışma.

Şu halde iyice anlaşıldı ki gökle yer, aşağılık nefse ahır kesilmiştir.

Sen de binek değilsen, denizde incinin çıktığı gibi şu ahırdan dışarıya çık.

Katre sedefte inci oldu mu, artık o sedefte kalır mı hiç?

Kuş cücesinin kanadı çıktı mı, yumurtayı kırar, baş gösterir.

İster serçe olsun ister ankâ, yumurtayı kırar, göğe kanat aça.

Çocuk da ana karnında dokuz ayı doldurdu mu, dışarıya çıkar, darlıktan gamdan kurtulur.

Dışarıya çıkmazsa onu ana karnında ölmüş bil, yahut da hiç ana karnına düşmemiş say.

O, ciğerden kopan yele benzer; yeli çocuk sanmışlardır.

Çocuk olsaydı hoş bir tarzda baş gösterir, ana karnından şu âleme çıkardı...

Şu geniş, büyük âleme, yerle, gökle bezenmiş dünyaya gelirdi.

Âlemin dağı, ovası sayısızdır; suları, denizleri kıyısızdır hani. Sen de o nurlardan gebeysen şu karanlıklar dünyasından baş çıkar.

Ey aranıp duran, Meryem'e benzeyen bedenden Îsâ gibi babasız doğuver.

Kendine gel de o madendensen, varlığında, benliğinde kalma; cansan, bu bedene gönül verme.

Ana karnında oynayışın sevgi yüzündense, yel gibi saçma, abes oynayış değildir bu.

Bir kere daha dünya bedeninden çık da akıl ve ruh âlemine yürü.

52 Ken'an Rifâî, *Sohbetler*, s. 162.

Hani hâlis gümüşün toprakla karışmış bir halde bulunması gibi.

Gümüş toprakta gizlidir ya; toprak, bedene benzer, gümüşse candır.

Gümüş, topraktan çıktı, arındı mı, toprak, hor-hakir olur, bir işe yaramaz bir halde kalakalır.

Toprağın değeri gümüş içindir; yoksa gümüşsüz toprak, değersizdir.

Toprak da gümüşün çıktığı madenden çıkmıştır ama gümüş gibi tartılmaz ki.

O toprak, bir kez daha varlığından doğmadıkça, toprak olarak öylece kalakalır.

Hiçbir işe yaramaz; nerden gümüş para gibi değerli olacak da sürülecek?

Yahut da a aklı-fikri eren, denizden sağlam olarak çıkarılan sedef gibi hani.

O sedeften inci doğmadıkça onu, gümüş verip, altın verip alırlar mı?

O sedefin değeri, her ihtiyarın, her gencin katında, nerden inci gibi belirecek?

O halde yürü, gümüşün, altının, topraktan çıktığı gibi sen de varlığından geç de bir kez daha doğ.

Doğ da kurtul, tehlikeden emîn ol, Allah amanında yurt edin,

Melek gibi gökte, ölümsüzlüğe er de Allah, can şarabını sunsun sana.

Toprakla karışmış maden, ateşe vuruldu mu erir, güzelleşir, işi iş olur.

Horluktan kurtulur, yücelir; topraksa kalakalır ama gümüş yürür, yüceliğe erer.

Sen de istekliysen aşk ateşinde eri; gerçeklik potasında sızdırılmış bir hâle gel.

Gel de şu varlık perdesinden kurtul; Allah şarabıyla sarhoş ol.

Çünkü iki kere doğmak şarttır: Biri anadan, öbürü bedenden doğmak.

Biri, şu aldanış dünyasından doğmak, öbürü beden karanlıklarından doğmak.

İlk doğuş mukadder oldu, şu dünyaya geldin ya; ikinci doğuma da çalış ki nur olasın…[53]

53 Sultan Veled, *İbtidâ-nâme*, s. 5-7 beyit 33-70.

Sultan Veled, ikinci doğum olabilmesi yani insanın idrak kabiliyetine kavuşabilmesi için tamamen yıkılıp yeniden yapılması gerektiğini anlatıyor, ki bu da bir mânevî zelzele gerektiriyor. Bu mânevî zelzele kimi zaman cezbe-i Rahmân, kimi zaman sille-i Hüdâ şeklinde olur.[54]

Kenan Rifâî Hazretleri Sohbetler'inde, dervişlerin huzurlu hayatlarından ve iç âlemlerinin zevkinden bahsettikten sonra şöyle buyuruyorlar:

- "Mahşer günü kâfirler diyecekler ki: Yâ Rabbî, sen bizi iki kere öldürdün. Biri, bizim kalbimizi ölü olarak dünyaya getirdin ve sonra da ecel gelip bizi tabiî ölümle öldürdü. Âşıklar da diyecekler ki: Yâ Rabbî sen bizi iki kere dirilttin. Biri, anamızın karnından ayrıldığımız vakit, diğeri de bizi kendiliğimizden nefsimizden öldürüp seninle dirilttiğin vakit...

Hazreti Îsâ'nın sözüdür: *'Kim ki iki defa ölmezse melekût ve semâvâtı geçemez.'* Onun için dervişlerin ilâhî kokular ile mest olarak ve nefislerinin çirkinliklerinden, ağırlıklarından kurtulmuş bulunarak geçirdikleri hayat, elbette ki huzurlu, rahat ve mes'uttur."[55]

- Ba's, diriliş iki türlüdür. Biri zâhirî, diğeri mânevî. Ba'sin lügat mânâsı, yerinden koparmak demektir.

Sûrî olan ba'ste, insan ıztırârî yani tabiî ölümle öldükten sonra mezara girer ve kabirde nice müddet medfun kaldıktan sonra cesetler dirilip haşrolur. Böylece de kıyâmetin sırrı ve hakîkati o gün zuhura gelir ve hakîkatler herkese o gün ayan ve aşikâr olur.

Bir de mânevî ba's, mânevî diriliş vardır ki, bunda insan, ihtiyarî ölümle ölüp fânî olduktan ve mecazî vücut kaydından kurtularak zat nurları içinde birçok müddet medfun olduktan sonra Cenâb-ı Hak onu: *"Benim sıfatlarımla ortaya çık, seni gören beni görür."* (Hadîs-i kudsî) sözünün gereği üzere, fenâ mertebesinden bakâbillah yani yokluktan sonra Hak'la var olmak derecesine, Allah'ın sıfatlarıyla sıfatlanmış olduğu halde ba's ve

54 *Derleyenin Notu.*

55 Ken'an Rifâî, *Sohbetler*, s. 231.

ihrac eder. Ve o kimse bu mertebede Hakk'ın bekâsıyla bâkî ve rabbânî hayat ile dirilmiş olarak her ne işlerse hemen Hak'la işler. Bu mertebede o, eşyayı Hak'tan başka görmediği gibi, Hakk'ı da eşyadan gayrı görmez. Belki halkı Hak'la kâim ve Hakk'ı cümle eşya ve mahlûkatın aynasında zâhir ve tecellî eylemiş görür. Bir kesret görür ki hakîkatte vahdetin ta kendisidir. Bir vahdet görür ki eşyanın kesretinde kendini göstermekte bulunmuştur. İşte bu mertebede ona zâhir, bâtının kendisi ve bâtın da zuhuru itibarıyla zâhirin aynı göründüğü gibi, âhir aynı evvel ve evvel ise aynı âhir görünür. O kimse bu mertebede: Evvel âhirdir, âhir evveldir. Zâhir bâtındır ve bâtın da zâhirdir! der. Şeyh-i Ekber'in: "O izhar ettiği eşyanın ta kendisidir." kavli ve Hazreti Ali'nin: "Ölüm gözümden örtüyü kaldıracak olsa, bu dünyada gördüğümden fazla bir şey görmüş olmayacağım!" demesi de yine aynı mânâyı doğrular. Zeyd Hazretleri'nin gözleri de riyâzat ve ilâhî nurlarla aydınlandıktan sonra bu âlemde mahşeri görmemiş miydi?

Demek oluyor ki, ölmezden evvel ölüp dirilenlere ve Hakk'ın nuruyla bu eşyaya nazar edenlere, eşyanın hakîkatinin bu dünyada açılıp tamamıyla görünmesi kabil oluyormuş.

Sadece sûrette kalanlara hakîkati anlamak haram oldu. İşte bu hakîkatleri onlar ancak kıyâmet gününde görüp idrak edebileceklerdir.

Zâhir bâtın içinde; bâtın da zâhir içindedir, dedik. Öyle değil mi ya... Bakınız bu ba's, bu diriliş meselesinin biz yalnız birinci kısmını yani ana rahminden doğuşu biliyorduk. Fakat bundan bir de mânevî diriliş hakîkatini ortaya koyunca, bâtının, aynı zâhir olduğu meydana çıktı. İşte bu dünya sûretinde de bâtın âleminin mevcudiyetini aynı ölçüler ile anlayabiliriz. Hazreti Niyazî'nin dediği gibi: *"Hak'tan ayan bir nesne yok / Gözsüzlere pinhan imiş."*[56]

- Resûl (a.s), Hak'tan anlatım yoluyla buyurur ki: Bütün taayyünlerin fânî olduğu kıyâmet gününde sizin nefsinize ve zâtlarınıza olan bağlantınızı sizden alıp, zâtınızın Allah'ın zâtı ve sıfatlarınızın Allah'ın sıfatları ve fiillerinizin Allah'ın fiili olması için, sizi Bana bağlı kılarım. Bundan dolayı siz Hak'ta fânî ve onunla bâkî olursunuz. İşte bugün,

56 Ken'an Rifâî, *Sohbetler*, s. 248-249.

yâni büyük kıyâmet günü, Hak'ta "fenâ" hâlinden ibârettir. Çünkü nefse bağlılık, taayyün mevcûd iken mümkün idi. Buz gibi donmuş olan bu taayyün etmiş vücûd, zât güneşinin tecellîsiyle eridiği zaman "ben" tâbirinin bağlanacağı bir dayanak noktası kalmaz. Bir buz kütlesi, nasıl ki eriyip suya dönüşür ve ondan fânî olarak sıfâtı suyun sıfâtı olursa, bu taayyünler de öylece Hak'ta fânî olurlar. Nitekim, Hak Teâlâ Kur'ân-ı Kerîm'de, îman eden Firavun'un sihirbazlarından hikâye yoluyla beyân buyurur: *"Kâlû lâ dayra innâ ilâ rabbinâ munkalibûn"* yâni *"Önemli değil, muhakkak biz Rabb'ımıza dönücüleriz."* dediler (Şu'arâ, 50). Sonuç olarak kıyâmet gününde Hak Teâlâ bizim nefsimize olan bağıntılarımızı alıp bizi kendisine bağlı kılar. Nitekim âyet-i kerîmede buyurur: *"Fe izâ nufiha fi's-sûri fe lâ ensâbe beynehum yevme'-izin ve lâ yetesâelûn"* yâni *"İzin günü sûr'a üfürüldüğü zaman, artık onların aralarında bir bağıntı yoktur. Ve sormazlar."* (Mü'minûn, 101).[57]

- ***Mısrî Niyâzî Hazretleri ise büyük kıyâmetin alâmetlerini şöyle yorumluyor:***

Büyük kıyâmetin alâmetleri hakkındadır. Bil ki: Büyük âlemde bulunan her şey, küçük âlem olan insanda da vardır. Zira âlem, büyük olmakla beraber insanî hakîkat üzerine yaratılmıştır. Bunların mânevî büyüklük ve küçüklüklerindeki farkları, sûretteki farklarının tersinedir. Allah'ın Resûlü (s.a.s), büyük âlemin (dünyanın) kıyâmet alâmetlerini söylediğine göre elbette insan fertlerinde de melekût, ceberut ve lâhût âlemine sülûk edenler için kıyâmet alâmetleri olacaktır. İnsanın ilmen ve zevken bilmesi lâzım gelen alâmetler vardır ki, sâlik bunların hepsinden geçmedikçe büyük kıyâmete eremez, cennete giremez, Hakk'ı göremez. Böyle olursa ne yazık.

Bunu bildinse bil ki: Asfaroğullarının hurûcu, hayvanî sıfatların çıkmasından ibarettir. Çünkü insan âleminde sâlikin ilk defa yolunu kesen eşkiyâlar, bunlardır. Ye'cuc-Me'cuc'un hurûcu, eziyet veren yedi (kötü) sıfatların belirmesinden ibarettir. Deccal'in hurûcu (çıkması), dev ve şeytan sıfatlarının çıkmasından ibarettir ki bunlar riyaset, rubûbiyyet (sahiplik, büyüklenmek), hile hud'adır. Bunlar, dünya sevgisinden ileri gelir. Bundan dolayı insanın, sağ gözü şaşı olur, âhireti hiç görmez.

57 A. Avni Konuk, *Fusûsu'l-Hikem Tercüme ve Şerhi*, Hûdiyye Fassı, s. 540.

Dâbbetu'l-arz (yer hayvanının) çıkması, kalpte nefs-i levvâme'nin zuhurundan ibarettir. Yani kalbin kabrinde cennetlere bir pencere açılır ve kendisinde Allah Teâlâ'ya bir meyil belirir. Îsâ Aleyhisselâm'ın inmesi, akl-i maâd'ın (âhiret aklının), yakîn nuruyla meydana çıkması, insanın dünyaya meyletmekten vazgeçerek âhirete yönelmesinden ibarettir. O çıkınca Deccal öldürülür. Çünkü yakîn nurunun zuhuruyla cehâlet karanlığı gider. Mehdinin çıkması, tam fenâ ile akl-i küll'ün ve Büyük Ruh'un çıkmasından ibarettir. Onun hükümranlık çağında mezhepler birleşir ve onun zamanında yeryüzünde asla kâfir kalmaz. Güneşin batıdan doğması, hakîkat güneşinin ârifin hafî sırrının matla'ından (tan yerinden) doğmasıdır. Bundan dolayı âriflerin hayvanlarının nalları ters çakılmıştır denilir. Rivayet edilmiştir ki: Allah'ın Resûlü (s.a.s) âhirette Rahmân Sûresi'ni tefsir ettiği zaman âlimler tefsirlerinden utanacaklardır. Bir görüşe göre de güneşin battığı yerden doğması, ruhun bedenden ayrılması demektir. Çünkü insandaki hayvanî ruh, dünyadaki güneş durumundadır. Bedene girince orada batmıştır. Bedenen ayrılınca battığı yerden doğmuş olur. Tövbe kapısının kapanması, insanın ömrünün sonu geldiğine işarettir. Bu kapının genişliğinin yetmiş senelik mesafe olmasına gelince: Bu kapı, güneş battığı yerden doğuncaya kadar kapanmaz. Yani bu kapı insan ömrü kadar geniştir. Ömür bitip, güneş (ruh) battığı yerden doğunca (bedenden ayrılınca) bu kapı kapanmış olur. Bu hususa Hz. Peygamber'in şu hadîsinde de işaret vardır: *"Ümmetimin ömürlerinin çoğu, altmış ile yetmiş arasındadır."* ve *"Allah Teâlâ, kulunun tövbesini can boğaza gelmemiş oldukça kabul eder."* Tövbe kapısının genişliğinin zikredilip, uzunluğunun söylenmemesi de şu sebepten dolayıdır: Genişlik, daima uzunluktan azdır.

Allah Teâlâ'nın haber verdiği üzere insanın iki eceli vardır. Biri sonlu eceldir ki, dünyadaki ömür süresidir. Diğeri de sonsuz eceldir ki, bu da uhrevî ömürdür. Bil ki: Sen, bu alâmetleri geçip büyük kıyâmette durmadıkça cennete girip açıkça Hakk'ı görmedikçe önce dediğimiz gibi bin kere de dünyaya gelsen ve her gelişinde bin sene yaşasan, yine cennete girip Hakk'ı şifahen göremezsin. Allahu Teâlâ bizi ve sizi Kıyâmet-i Kübrâ'ya (Büyük Kıyâmet'e) ve Büyük Müşâhade'ye ve yakınlığa erişenlerden eylesin âmin![58]

58 Niyâzî-i Mısrî, *İrfan Sofraları*, s. 128-130.

ÂYET 3

"Ve insan, 'Ne oluyor buna!' dediği vakit."

- O sarsıntı ve çıkarma olduğu *"ve insan, 'buna ne oluyor?' dediği zaman."* Böyle denilmesi, korkunun büyüklüğünü tasvir içindir. Yani o zelzele ve çıkarmayı her gören insan, dehşetinin büyüklüğünden şaşırarak, "Bu yere ne oluyor?", "Nedir bu hal?" diye şaşkınlık ve telaşa düştüğü o belâlı zaman. Bazıları demişlerdir ki, onu gören kâfirler öyle söyleyecek. *"Vah bize, bizi yattığımız yerden kim kaldırdı?"* (Yâsîn, 52) diyecekler. Müminler ise *"İşte Rahmân'ın vadettiği şey budur. Demek peygamberler doğru söylemiş."* (Yâsîn, 52) diyecekler. Fakat bu fark, ikinci sûra üfleme ile dirilmededir. İlk zelzelede ise mümin ve kâfir her insana umumu açıktır. *"(Birinci defa) Sûr'a üflendi, göklerde ve yerde olanlar (korkudan) düşüp bayıldılar. Ancak Allah'ın dilediği kaldı."* (Zümer, 68).[59]

- *"İnsan:"* Herkes, kendisini kaplayan korkulardan, kapıldıkları aşırı dehşet ve hayretten dolayı: *"Buna ne oluyor?"* yani gördüğü korkunç şeyleri çok büyük bularak, kulakların duymadığı, dillerin söylemediği hayret verici şeylere şaşırarak, bu yere ne oldu ki, bu seferki şiddetli sarsıntı ile sallanıyor *"dediği zaman."*[60]

59 Elmalılı Hamdi Yazır, *Hak Dini Kur'an Dili*, c. 9, s. 403-404.

60 İsmail Hakkı Bursevî, *Rûhu'l-Beyân Tefsîri*, c. 10, s. 140.

- *"Ve insan, 'Ne oluyor buna!' dediği vakit."* Bu sözü her insan söyleyecektir. Çünkü yerin şiddetli sarsıntısı herkesi kaplayacaktır. İnsanlar yeryüzünün şiddetli sarsıntısını ve içindeki ölüleri dışarı fırlattığını, dağların yürütülüp toz duman edildiğini görünce, seyrettiği bu korkunç haller karşısında "Buna ne oluyor!" diye hayretini dile getirecektir. Bunu herkes söyleyecektir. Müminler olayın büyüklüğünü ifade için, kâfirlerse hayret ve şaşkınlıklarından böyle diyeceklerdir.[61]

Hem kulun değişimi hem de arzın değişimi müminlerin îmanını artırırken, kâfirlerin de hayret ve şaşkınlığını artırır.[62]

- *"Ve insan 'ne oluyor buna!' dediği vakit."* Ne oluyor buna! Niçin sarsılıyor, sallanıyor! Bunun derdi nedir? Hastalığı nedir? Mizacı mı bozuldu? Yoksa karışımlar mı galip geldi? diye sormaya başlar...[63]

---

61 İbn Acîbe el-Hasenî, *Bahrü'l-Medîd*, c. 11, s. 102.

62 *Derleyenin Notu.*

63 Muhyiddin İbn Arabî, *Tefsîr-i Kebîr Te'vilât*, c. 2, s. 1477.

ÂYET 4-5

"İşte o gün (yer) üzerinde olup bitenleri anlatır."

"Rabb'inin ona bildirmesiyle (bunu yapar)."

- Yani o olaylar olduğu gün o yer bütün haberlerini bildirir, havadislerini hâl ile ve sözlü olarak haber verip anlatır. Çünkü Rabbin ona, (yani yere) vahyetmiştir. Haber vermesini süratle emir ve telkin etmiştir de o sebeple yer o haberleri söyler, anlatır. *Keşşaf*'ta der ki: Yerin haber vermesi ve söylemesi mecazdır. Yani Allah Teâlâ yerde öyle durumlar meydana getirir ki, onlar dil ile konuşma yerine geçerler. Hatta "ne oluyor buna?" diyenler, o hâllere bakarlar da, onun ne için zelzeleye tutulduğunu ve ne için o ölüleri dışarıya attığını bilir. Ve bu olaylar, peygamberlerin korkutup ve çekindirip durdukları olay olduğunu anlarlar. Bu mânâca vahiy *"kün feyekün"* (Ol! dedi, hemen oldu) gibi tekvinî olmuş olur. Bununla beraber bir de denilmiştir ki, Allah Teâlâ yeri, o zaman gerçekten konuşturacaktır da, o üzerinde işlenmiş olan hayır ve şerri haber verecektir. Peygamberimiz'den de rivayet olunmuştur ki, herkese karşı üzerinde ne amel yaptığına şâhitlik edecektir. Yere vahyetmek, onun yaşaması mümkün olan kısımlarına vahiy olarak düşünülürse, bu söyleme ve vahyin gerçekten konuşma veya yazma halinde haber vermek ve bildirme mânâsına olarak anlaşılmasında zorluk çekilmez. Hâsılı onun ne olduğu o zaman gerçek göz önüne döküldüğü zaman anlaşılacaktır.[64]

64 Elmalılı Hamdi Yazır, *Hak Dini Kur'an Dili*, c. 9, s. 373.

- *"O gün yer, Rabbinin ona vahyetmesi sebebiyle bütün haberlerini anlatır."* Bu cümle, daha önceki üç âyetteki şartın cevabıdır. Yani yaratıklar, ya lisân-ı hâlleriyle veya gerçek dille -ki bu cumhurun görüşüdür- haberlerini anlatırlar. Allah onu konuşturur. O da üzerinde işlenen iyi kötü tüm amelleri haber verir. Öyle ki, kâfir hissettiği utançtan dolayı bir an önce cehenneme götürülmeyi ister.

Rivayet edilmiştir ki, Abdurrahman b. Sa'saa, Ebû Saîd el-Hudrî'nin himayesinde yetim bir çocuktu. Ebû Saîd: "Oğulcuğum, sen çöllerde olduğun zaman ezan okurken sesini yükselt. Çünkü ben Resûlullah'ın: *'Onu dinleyen; cin, insan, taş ve ağaç mutlaka ona şâhitlik eder.'* buyurduğunu duydum." dedi.

Anlatıldığına göre Ebû Ümeyye, Mescid-i Haram'da farz namazı kıldı. Sonra ilerleyip mescidin değişik yerlerinde namaz kılmaya başladı. Namazı bitirince: "Ey Ebû Ümeyye! Bu yaptığın ne?" denildi. *"O gün (yer) bütün haberlerini anlatacaktır."* mealindeki âyeti okudu. "Kıyâmet günü bana şâhitlik etmesini istedim." dedi. Kendisi için bir yerin zikir, tilâvet, namaz ve benzeri şeylerle şâhitlik ettiği kişiye ne mutlu! Zinâ, içki, hırsızlık ve kötülüklerle şâhitlik ettiği kimsenin de vay haline!

Denilir ki: "Ey Âdemoğlu! Allah'ın senin hakkında şâhitlik edecek yedi şâhidi var. Bunlar:

1. Mekân (yer): *"O gün yer... bütün haberlerini anlatır."* âyetinde bu belirtilmektedir.

2. Zaman: Şu hadis bunu ifade ediyor: *"Her gün, ben yeni bir günüm ve bende yapacaklarına şâhidim."* diye seslenir.

3. Dil: *"O gün dilleri, elleri ve ayakları yapmış olduklarına karşılık aleyhlerine şâhitlik edecektir."* (Nûr, 24) mealindeki âyet buna delildir.

4. Eller ve ayaklar: *"...Kazandıklarını bize elleri anlatır, ayakları da şâhitlik eder."* (Yâsîn, 65) âyeti buna işarettir.

5. İki tane melek ***(hafıza melekleri)***[65]: *"Oysa yaptıklarınızı bilen, değerli yazıcılar sizi gözetlemektedirler."* (İnfitâr, 10-12) âyetleri bunu ifade ediyor.

65 *Derleyenin Notu.*

6. Divan: Şu âyet-i kerîme bunun ifadesidir: *"Bu, size karşı gerçeği söyleyen kitabımızdır. Çünkü Biz yaptıklarınızı kaydediyorduk."* (Câsiye, 29).

7. Rahmân: Bunu da Allah Teâlâ şöyle bildiriyor: *"Ne durumda olursan ol, Kur'an'dan ne okursan oku, siz ne yaparsanız yapın, onu yapmaya giriştiğinizde Biz ona mutlaka şâhit oluruz..."* (Yûnus, 61).

Ey isyankâr! Bu şâhitler senin aleyhine şâhitlik ettikten sonra hâlin ne olur?[66]

Kıyâmette insanlar iki gruba ayrılır: Müminin îmanı, şakînin hayreti ve korkusu ortaya çıkar. İnsanlar kendi hakîkatini görür, çünkü bütün organları yaptıklarına şehâdet eder.[67]

- *"İşte o gün (yer) üzerinde olup biteni anlatır."* Yeryüzü bu şekilde sarsıldığı ve kıyâmet koptuğu zaman, yer insanlara üzerinde olan her şeyi bildirir.

"Bunu Rabb'inin ona bildirmesi ile yapar." Allah ona konuşmasını vahyeder, yani "konuş" diye emreder, o da konuşur.

Şöyle denilmiştir: Allah Teâlâ yeri konuşturur, o da üzerine hayır şer ne yapılmışsa hepsini bir bir haber verir. Bu konuda Hz. Peygamber'in (sallallahu aleyhi vesellem) şöyle buyurduğu rivayet edilmiştir: *"Yeryüzü üzerinde kim ne yapmışsa, 'şu günde şu kimse şunu yaptı' şeklinde hepsini haber verir."*[68]

Gerek toprak gerekse vücut toprağı, kendindeki değişimi bildirir.[69]

- İşte *"O gün...bütün haberlerini anlatır."* Hâl diliyle beden arz'ı her şeyi anlatır. *"Rabb'inin ona vahyetmesiyle..."* ona işaret etmesiyle, sallanmasını, yıkılmasını ve ruhun çıkması ve ölümün gerçekleşmesi

66 İsmail Hakkı Bursevî, *Rûhu'l-Beyân Tefsîri*, c. 10, s. 140-141.

67 *Derleyenin Notu.*

68 İbn Acîbe el-Hasenî, *Bahrü'l-Medîd*, c. 11, s. 102-103.

69 *Derleyenin Notu.*

esnasında ağırlıklarını dışarı atmasını emretmesiyle birlikte hâl diliyle kendisiyle ilgili her şeyi açıklar.[70]

- O gün, nurla aydınlanmış nefisler Rabb'inin ilhamı ile içlerinde saklı bulunan sırları haber verirler, ortaya çıkarırlar.[71]

- Kıyâmet gününde âsi olan insanın eli: Sen benimle şarap kadehini tutmadın mı ve şarap testisini çekmedin mi? Senin malın olmayan mala el uzatmadın mı ve almadın mı, senin helâlin olmayan nâmahremin elini tutmadın mı ve ona hainlik etmedin mi, mazluma vurmadın mı, yetime tokat atmadın mı? Günahsıza kılıç çekmedin mi? diye o âsiye şâhitlik eder. Bunun gibi dil, ağız ve dudaklar da şâhitlik ederler. Dil der ki: Benimle böyle konuşmadın mı? Bu kadar Müslümanların aleyhinde söylemedin mi? Müslümanlığın ve dinin yolunu kesen dünyada bu kadar eğri söz söylemedin mi?" Ayak da şâhitlik eder ve der ki: "Benimle meyhaneye gitmedin mi? Ve yapılması caiz olmayan işlere ve yolsuzluğa doğru koşmadın mı?" Nitekim sudan, topraktan, ateşten, elden, ayaktan ve baştan ibaret olan bu avazların cinsleri, burada birleşmenin, çokluğun bir olmuş oldukları, sonunda ona mâlum olur. *"O gün, bunları dilleri, elleri ve ayaklar, işledikleri şeylere şehâdet eder."* (Nûr, 24).[72]

- Kıyâmette insanın eli ayağı ve diğer şeyleri gibi bütün organları birer birer konuşurlar. Felsefeciler bunu yorup derler ki: El nasıl konuşabilir? Yalnız elde bir alâmet, bir işaret hâsıl olur ve bu konuşma söz yerine geçer. Mesela bir yara veya bir çıban çıkınca el: "Sıcaklık veren bir şey yedim de böyle oldum, diye [hâl diliyle] haber verir, konuşur. Yahut el siyahlanır veya yaralanırsa: "Bana bıçak değdi; kendimi kara tencereye sürdüm." diye konuşur, haber verir. İşte elin veya diğer organların konuşması bu tarzda olmalı. Sünnîler: "Hâşâ, kat'iyyen! Bu görünen el [mahsûs] ve ayak, dil gibi söz söyler ve kıyâmet

70 Muhyiddin İbn Arabî, *Tefsîr-i Kebîr Te'vilât*, c. 2, s. 1477.

71 İbn Acîbe el-Hasenî, *Bahrü'l-Medîd*, c. 11, s. 105.

72 Sultan Veled, *Maârif*, Fasıl 20, s. 98.

gününde insan: 'Ben çalışmamıştım.' diye inkâr edince, eli açık bir dille: 'Evet sen çaldın, ben de aldım.' der. O eline, ayağına bakıp: 'Sen konuşmazdın, şimdi nasıl oldu da konuşuyorsun?' diye sorar. O da der ki: *'Her şeyi söyleten Allah bizi de söyletti.'* (Fussilet, 21). Beni, her şeyi dile getiren konuşturdu. O kapıyı ve duvarı ve keseği de söyletir. Herkese konuşma kuvveti bağışlayan, Yaratan beni de konuşturdu. Senin dilini nasıl söyletti? Senin dilin bir et parçasıdır, benim elim de öyle. Bir et parçasından ibaret olan dilin söz söylemesi sana göre akla uygun geliyor ve her zaman gördüğün için imkânsız görünmüyor, yoksa dil Tanrı'nın yanında bahanedir. Ona: 'Konuş!' diye emrettiği için konuşmuştur. Bunun gibi her neye emretse, o şey de konuşur."[73]

- Ben, ilâhî kudret karşısındaki hiçliğimi ve yokluğumu bütün varlığımla hissederek, ibâdet alnımı toprağa koyuyorum ve benim canımda velîlerin nuru yandığına bu toprak şâhit olsun istiyorum.

Hissiz toprak, senin ruh saflığına ve ermişler için duyduğun derin saygı ve sevgiye nasıl şâhitlik eder diye sorma!

Kur'ân-ı Kerîm'in Zilzâl Sûresi'nde yeryüzünün, kıyâmet gününde bizim bütün hâllerimize şahâdet edeceği bildirilir: "*Yer, dehşetle sarsıldığı, yeryüzü ağırlıklarını dışarıya çıkardığı ve insanın 'Buna ne oluyor?' dediği zaman; işte o gün, Rabbinin ona vahyetmesiyle (toprak, insanlara) kendi haberlerini anlatır.*" ... "*Kim zerre kadar iyilik yapmışsa, onu görür; (ve) kim zerre kadar kötülük yapmışsa, onu görür.*" buyurulur.

Toprak, diken, otlar, ağaçlar, taşlar ve yeryüzünde her şey o ilâhî vahye tâbi olarak dile gelir. Her sözü, her sırrı, her haberi derin bir açıklıkla söyler.

Burada kıyâmet gününün büyüklüğünü ve o gündeki dehşeti sana tarife lüzum görmüyorum. Asıl irfan odur ki, insanoğlu ölmeden evvel kendi nefsinden ölmenin yollarını bulmalı, böylece de o hesap gününe Tanrı'ya varmış olarak doğmalı. Felsefeciye sorarsan; kıyâmet alâmetlerini de, ölmeden evvel ölmeyi de kabul etmez. Taşların, ağaçların dile geleceğine inanmaz. Sen ona, git başını, hiçbir gün konuşmayacağını sandığın o taşlara vur ki aklın başına gelsin, de! Ona de ki: Suların,

73 Mevlânâ, *Fîhi Mâfîh*, Fasıl 25, s. 168-169.

toprağın, güllerin ve otların dilinden ancak gönül ehli olanlar anlar. Onlar, cematlarla nebatların, kuşların ve bütün hayvanların neler söyleyip Allah'ı nasıl andıklarını yıllar yılı, kendilerini yok etmenin neş'esiyle yükselip bütün hakîkatleri idrak edecek dereceye ulaştıkları zaman görürler. Nebîlerle velîlerin gördüklerini ve duyduklarını başkalarının görüp duymaması, onların hâlâ vücut içinde, nefsin ve maddenin emrinde kör ve sağır olmalarındandır.

Hazreti Muhammed'in, henüz minber yapılmadan önce hutbelerini okurken, mübârek vücûdunu yasladığı hurma ağacı neler duymuş, ne yüce ürperişler içinde kalmış ve bu arada nasıl derin derin inlemiştir, felsefeci bunu anlar mı? O elbette nebîlerle velîlerin yakından görüp bildikleri sırların ve mânâların hakîkatinden habersizdir. Habersiz olduğu için de kendi aklınca bu sırları ve bu mânâları çözmeye çalışır. Felsefeci der ki: İnsanlar aşk duyguları içinde birtakım vehimler ve hayaller yaratırlar. Beşerî aşkın ışıkları, halk muhayyilesinde böyle duyguların, düşüncelerin ve inanışların doğmasını hazırlar. Kurtların, kuşların, taşların ve ağaçların duyup düşünen, inanıp dile gelen varlıklar olabileceğini sanmak, işte bu aldanışların bu hayallerin neticesidir.

Hazreti Ali'nin bir gün Hazreti Muhammed'e: "Yâ Resûlallah, Mekke'den sahraya çıktığım zaman tek bir taş ve ağaç görmedim ki bana selâm vermesin." deyişindeki gerçeği felsefeci elbette anlamaz. Esasen kafasındaki îmandan uzak hallerin, fesatların ve küfürlerin akisleri onu böyle şüphelere ve zanlara düşürmektedir. Kendisi nasıl bir şeyler görüyor, gözlerinin önüne bir şeyler getiriyor ve bütün bunların birer kuruntudan ibaret olduğu neticesine varıyorsa, velîlerle nebîlerin de böyle fesatçı hayaller içinde kaldıklarını sanır. Felsefeci cinleri, devleri ve şeytanı inkâr eder. Bunların hepsini vehimlerin yarattığı hayallerdir zanneder ve böyle zannettiği anda bilemez ki kendisi, inkâr ettiği şeytanın elindedir. Onun oyuncağı, onun maskarası olmuştur.

Eğer sen, ey felsefeci! Şeytanı göremiyorsan, bir aynaya bak, kendini gör. Alnındaki morartıya dikkat et. Bu morluk, başını taştan taşa vuranların gece gündüz sefahat ve çılgınlıklar peşinde koşanların yüzünde olur. Bak ve yüzünde bu renkleri olsun gör ve mademki felsefecisin, yani bir şeyler düşünebiliyorsun, hiç olmazsa bunun sırrını ve sebebini düşün. Kalplerinde böyle bir şüphe ve karanlık olan kimseler kendilerini gizleseler ve görünüşte Müslüman olsalar da ruhlarında inkârın felsefesi çöreklenmiştir.

Ey müminler! Felsefecilerin, yollarını şaşırmış olanlarına benzemekten çekinin! Çünkü felsefeci damarı hemen her insanda vardır. Hemen her insanın bir şek ve şüphe içinde kaldığı anlar olur. Sizin de içinizde henüz bilmediğiniz nice ve ne sonsuz âlemler vardır. Eğer velîlerle, nebîlerin yollarını bırakıp, felsefe şubelerine dalar, her biri ötekinin zıddını söyleyen felsefecilerin yollarına saparsanız, saptığınız yolun neticesinde yalnız hüsranla karşılaşırsınız. Her kiminki kalbinde tam bir îman yerine bir şüphe ve bir dalâlete inanış vardır, onun kalbi, kıyâmet gününde hazan yaprağı gibi titreyici olur. Sen kendini adam sandığın ve "üstün insanlığın vasfı, görünmeyen yani senin göremediğin her şeyi inkâr etmektir" zannettiğin için devlere, şeytanlara ve cinlere gülersin. Halbuki kendi bilemediğini ve kendi göremediğini aslında da yok sanmak cehâlet ve dalâletin en açık ifadesidir.

Fakat bir gün can dediğin ruh, giydiği postun içini dışına çevirir, seni ters yüzü ederse, bir taraftan görmediğin hakîkatler güneş gibi gözlerini kamaştırır, öte yandan senin içindeki görünmeyen iblislikler aynı güneş ışığına serilirse, o zaman bak ve gör ki sen de dâhil, dünyada kendilerini iyi sanmış nice din ehlinden ne feryatlar duyulur. Kendilerini iyi sananların iç yüzlerinin berbatlığını görüp bilmekten doğacak bu feryatları elbette yürekler acısıdır.

Fakat Hazreti Muhammed'in buyurdukları gibi: *"Her kul, ne halde öldü ise, ölürken kendisinde hangi sıfat galipse, tekrar dirildiği zamanda aynı sıfatla dirilecektir."* Dünya dükkânında bütün yaldızlı eşya, göze altın gibi görünmenin şevki içinde neşeli ve handandır. Bunların satıcıları ise, her gelene, bakırı altın diye göstermenin cesareti içindedir. Bunun sebebi o dükkânda bir mihenk taşı olmayışı, daha doğrusu, mihenk taşının gözlere görünmez bir yerde gizli oluşudur. İnsanların davranışları ve inanışları da böyle ya bakırdan ya altından olur. Bu îman ve davranış altınlarının kalpını hâlisten ayırt edecek ruh ve irfan mihengi bir perde arkasında örtülü ve vazife görmez halde olursa insanlar kendi bakırlarını altın sanacak kadar aldanabilirler. Bu sebepledir ki: Ey ayıpları örten Allah! Bizim günahlarımızı gizleyen perdeyi kaldırma! Kaldıracağın bu perdenin arkasından, bütün çirkinliği ile görünecek iç yüzümüzü görme ve gösterme! Bizi onlardan kurtar, bize hâlis altından bir ruh ver. Ruhumuzu senden gayrı olanlardan temizle! Kısaca, bize acı! Bize yardım et ki senden başka sığınacak yerimiz yoktur ve olmayacaktır.

Her ne kadar gece karanlığında ve aynı dükkânda hâlis altınla yan yana duran ve onun kadar parıldayan kalp altının cakası büyükse de altının hâlisi bundan alınmaz. Onun ancak gece karanlığında gösterdiği böbürlenişe güler ve vakur bir sabırla gündüzü bekler ve yanındaki sahte madene kendi hâl diliyle şunları söyler:

"Ey zavallı yalancı! Geceler, mahşer gününe kadar sürer mi sanıyorsun? Yarın nasıl olsa sabah olacak. İkimizin de üzerine güneş ışıkları vuracak.

Ey zavallı yalancı! O zaman senin nasıl kıpkızıl olduğunu ve benim altın sarılığımı kendin göreceksin."

Bilmez misin ki Allah'ın lanetlediği Şeytan'a, yüzbinlerce yıl melekler secde etmişti. Ateşten yaratılmış olmanın verdiği gurur içinde Şeytan, çağlar boyunca ilâhî âlemdeki meleklerin hocası ve onların emîri olmuştu.

Fakat aynı gurur, naz ve kibirlilik içinde bir gün topraktan yaratılan Âdem'le müsabakaya girdi. Allah'a *"Ben ondan üstünüm."* demek cesaretinde bulundu.

Sonra bizzat meleklerin önünde Hazreti Âdem'le giriştiği imtihanı kaybedince üzerine güneş ışığı ve güneş sıcaklığı vuran kirli ve pis şeylerin bütün kokularını dışarıya vermeleri gibi onun da içindeki kirler ortaya çıktı. Kendisine secde etmiş olan meleklerin maskarası oldu.[74]

- Kardeşim! Deri ve organların aleyhinde şâhitlik edeceği günden sakınmalısın. Kendine karşı ölçülü ve insaflı ol, Allah katında sana teşekkür edecekleri şekilde organlarına ölçülü davran! Biz bu durumu içerisinde bulunduğumuz hâllerde dünya hayatında açık bir şekilde müşâhede ettik. Başka bir ifadeyle organların konuşmasını açıkça gördük. Kul, dince helâl olmayan işlerde onları kullandığında organ

74 Ken'an Rifâî, *Şerhli Mesnevî-i Şerif*, s. 479-482.

kendisine şöyle der: "Ey adam! Bunu yapma! Beni sana yasaklanmış bir işi yapmaya zorlama, kıyâmet günü senin aleyhine şâhitlik edeceğim. Beni aleyhine değil, lehine şâhitlik yapacak birisi kıl, bana iyi ve ahlâka göre davran." Adam gaflet halinde olur ve bu sözleri duymaz. Bir fiil kendinden meydana geldiğinde organ şöyle der: "Rabbim! Ben bu adamı engellemeye çalıştım, o ise beni dinlemedi. Allah'ım! Onun benim vâsıtamla işlemiş olduğu günahtan ve hatâdan sana sığınırım. Her durumda organları serbest bırakmak, kalbin yorulmasına vesiledir. Çünkü Allah seni senin için yaratmış, senden de kendine ayırdığı kısmı kalbin yapmıştır. Bir kalp îmanlı, vera'lı ve temiz iken O'nu sığdırabileceğini söylemiştir. Organlarının tasarruflarıyla kalbini meşgul ettiğinde, Hakk'ın sende kendisine ayırdığı organ hakkında gazaplandığı kişilerden olursun. Hakk'a haksızlık etmekten daha büyük bir zulüm olabilir mi?[75]

---

75 İbn Arabî, *Fütûhât-ı Mekkiyye,* c. 18, s. 255-256.

ÂYET 6

"O gün insanlar amellerini görmeleri (karşılığını almaları) için grup grup kabirlerden çıkıp hesap yerine gelirler."

- *"O gün insanlar bölük bölük, çeşitli durumda ortaya çıkacaklardır."* Sudûr, vürûdun zıddıdır. Vürûd, suya gitmek olduğu gibi, sudûr da sudan dönmektir. Diğer deyimle, "vârid" gelen, "sâdir" giden demektir. Yani varmış oldukları yerden dönüp çıkacaklar, kabirlerinden mevkıfa (durağa), mahşere doğru çeşitli şekilde fırlayacaklar. Kimisi yüz aklığıyla, kimisi yüz karasıyla, kimisi selâmet, kimisi korkular ve dehşetler içinde, kimisi binitli, kimisi yaya, kimisi serbest, kimisi zincirlerle bağlı, hâsılı kimisi mesut, kimisi bedbaht yahut İbn Abbas'tan rivayet edildiği üzere *"O gün her insan topluluğunu önderleri ile çağıracağız."* (İsrâ, 71) âyeti gereğince her din ve millet sahibi ayrı olarak kendi önderleri arkasında yahut *"Andolsun ki sizi ilk defa yarattığımız şekilde bize geldiniz."* (Kehf, 48) buyurulduğu üzere her fert ilk yaratılışı gibi tek başına olarak yahut bazılarının görüşünce bölgelere göre dağılmış olarak ortaya çıkacaklar. Yahut mahşere geldikten sonra kimisi kitabını sağından almış ashâb-ı yemînden olarak cennete gitmek üzere, kimisi de kitabını solundan veya arkasından almış ashâb-ı şimalden olarak cehenneme gitmek üzere mahşerden ayrılacaklar. *"Amelleri kendilerine gösterilmek için."* Ki hayır veya şer her ne işlemişlerse ona göre cezâsını almak üzere amellerini hakkıyla görsünler, defterleriyle, ölçüleriyle hesaplarına vâkıf olsunlar. Bu mânâ, sudûrun mahşere doğru olmasına göredir. Mahşerden sudûra göre ise hayır veya şer her ne ise amellerinin cezâsını görsünler. Yani cennet ehli cennete, cehennem ehli cehenneme girsinler demek olur.[76]

Buradan anlaşılıyor ki herkesin âyân-ı sâbitesi ile dirilip, nefsinin ise bu hakîkati gördüğü güne büyük kıyâmet diyoruz. Bu durumda bazı nefisler ruh seviyesine yükseldiği ve kendi hakîkatini ortaya çıkardığı için kitabını sağından alanlar olacaklar, bazıları ise taşıdıkları ismin hakîkatine vardıklarında şaşkınlık ve pişmanlık cehennemine girerek kitabını soldan alanlar olacaklar.[77]

- *"O gün"*, anılan şeyler olduğu gün *"insanlar,"* ister hayır olsun ister şer *"amelleri"*nin karşılığı *"kendilerine gösterilmek için..."* -Gösterilecek olan, amellerinin kendisi değildir. Çünkü ameller gözle görülmezler. Çünkü buradaki görmek, bilmek anlamında değildir. Çünkü aşağıda gelecek olan; *"Artık kim zerre ağırlığınca bir hayır işlerse..."* âyeti, *"amelleri kendilerine gösterilmek için..."* sözünü açıklamaktadır. Buradaki gösterilme fiili de sadece bir tümleç aldığı için gözle görme anlamı ifade eder. Şu kadar var ki, eğer Allah o amellere nuranî veya zulmanî şekiller verirse ya da görme işi onların yazısına bağlanırsa müstesna- *"bölük bölük"*, gruplar halinde kabirlerinden *"çıkacaklar"*, hesap yerine gidecekler. Bunlardan bazılarının yüzleri ve elbiseleri beyaz, emniyet içindedirler. Önlerinde birisi: "Bunlar Allah'ın dostlarıdır." diye seslenir. Bazılarının ise yüzleri karadır. Yalın ayak, çıplak ve korkulu haldedirler. Onların önlerinden birisi de: "Bunlar Allah'ın düşmanlarıdır." diye bağırır.[78]

Demek ki insanların amel diye anılan gayretleri onlara gösterilecek. Yani herkes gayretinin neticesi olan hakîkati ile karşılaşacak.[79]

- *"O gün insanlar amellerini görmeleri,* yani amellerinin karşılığını görüp almaları *için grup grup kabirlerinden çıkıp hesap yerine gelirler."*

76 Elmalılı Hamdi Yazır, *Hak Dini Kur'an Dili*, c. 9, s. 404-405.

77 *Derleyenin Notu.*

78 İsmail Hakkı Bursevî, *Rûhu'l-Beyân Tefsîri*, c. 10, s. 141-142.

79 *Derleyenin Notu.*

Yani yukarıda anlatılan durum meydana geldiğinde, insanlar kabirlerinden çıkarlar, tabaka ve gruplar halinde hesap yerine gelirler. Kiminin yüzü bembeyaz parlar, emniyet ve güven içinde gelir. Kiminin yüzü simsiyahtır, korku ve dehşet içinde hesap yerine varır.

İnsanların kabirden çıkması ya vücut kabrinden çıkmak ya da topraktan çıkmak anlamına gelir. Büyük kıyâmette ise ölüler kabirlerinden çıkacaklardır. İşte o gün, ister küçük, ister büyük kıyâmetle olsun, herkesin kendi hakîkatini tanıdığı gündür.[80]

Bu durum bir başka âyette şöyle anlatılır:

"Sûra üfürüldüğünde grup grup (hesaba) gelirsiniz." (Nebe', 18).

Âyete şu mânâ da verilmiştir: Onlar hesap yerinden değişik gruplar halinde ayrılırlar; amel defterini sağından alanlar cennete, amel defterini solundan veya arkasından alanlar cehenneme sevk edilirler. Herkesin hayır veya şer olarak yaptığı amelin karşılığını görmesi için böyle yapılır.[81]

Amel defterini sağdan almak, dünyada gayretini mânevî yolda sarf etmek demektir. Soldan almak, nefsanî yolda sarf edilen bir ömür demektir. Arkadan almak, ömrünce yaptıklarının neticesi demektir.[82]

- *"O gün insanlar bölük bölük çıkarlar..."* [Sehl] şöyle dedi:

[O gün] herkes itimat ettiğine tâbi olur. Her kim Allah'ın ihsanına (fazlına) itimat etmişse, O'nun ihsanına tâbi olur. Her kim ameline itimat etmişse, ameline tâbi olur. Her kim de şefaate itimat etmişse, şefaate tâbi olur.[83]

İşte itimat îmanın neticesidir; neye îman ediyorsa ona itimat eder.[84]

- O gün insanlar, değişik gruplar halinde fenâdan bekâya ulaşırlar. Onların kiminde hakîkat hâli galiptir, kiminde şerîat hâli galiptir, kimi orta hâldedir.

80 *Derleyenin Notu.*

81 İbn Acîbe el-Hasenî, *Bahrü'l-Medîd*, c. 11, s. 103.

82 *Derleyenin Notu.*

83 Sehl b. Abdullah Tüsterî, *Tüsterî Tefsiri*, s. 584.

84 *Derleyenin Notu.*

Şöyle de denebilir: Hakk'a ulaşan kulların kiminde kabz (mânevî tutukluk) ve sertlik hâli galiptir. Kiminde bast (kalp huzuru, genişlik ve mânevî neşe) hâliyle yumuşaklık galiptir. Bu kimse insanlara daha faydalıdır. En doğrusunu Allah bilir.

Böylece herkes müşâhedesinde elde ettiği mânevî nimet ve derecelerle Allah yolunda yaptığı mücâhedesinin karşılığını görmüş olur.[85]

Bu âlemde bu seviyeye erişenler, kendi hakîkatlerini idrak ederler. Buradan anlaşılıyor ki, makbul olan bast hâlidir, sertlik makbul değildir.[86]

- *"O gün insanlar ... geri dönüp gelirler."* Kabirlerinden, beden mahreçlerinden sözleşme yerlerine, hesap ve cezâ yurtlarına *"darmadağınık"* olarak, mutlular ve bedbahtlar şeklinde ayrılmış *"gruplar halinde"* olarak *"amellerini görmeleri için"* gelirler. Amellerinin nefislerinin sahifelerine işlenmiş sûret ve heyetleriyle karşılıklarını almak üzere gelirler.[87]

- Hz. Mevlânâ büyük kıyâmeti şöyle yorumluyor: Bu birbirinden ayrı ruhlardır ki, arz-ı ekber gününde yani kıyâmette, ayrı ayrı hesaplar verecek, ayrı muamele ve ayrı cezâlara tâbi tutulacaklardır.

Ruh vardır ki arz-ı ekber günü dediğimiz, can'ın kendisini en büyük sevgiliye sunduğu ve onun varlığında yokluğu seçmeye geldiği günü candan ve gönülden ister. Çünkü ruh o gün, o büyük sevgiliyle visale erecektir. Bütün ömrünce bu güne hazırlandığı, bu günü beklediği için de o ruhun derûnu iyilik ve güzellikle dolmuş, onun nuruyla taşacak kadar aydınlık hâle gelmiştir.

Böyle bir günde yüzleri Hintliler gibi siyah olan ruhlara elbette rüsvaylık düşecektir. Böyleleri gün görmek istemezler. Bütün ayıpları örten gece karanlığında, ancak böyle bir karanlıkla yarışabilecek küfürleri ve günahlarıyla gizli kalmak isterler.

85 İbn Acîbe el-Hasenî, *Bahrü'l-Medîd*, c. 11, s. 106.

86 *Derleyenin Notu.*

87 Muhyiddin İbn Arabî, *Tefsîr-i Kebîr Te'vilât*, c. 2, s. 1478.

Baştan ayağa dikenden ibaret bir ağaçta gül olmaz. Buna mukabil güller ve sûsenler gibi açılan saf ve temiz ruhlar için bahar aydınlığı, iki aydın bakış gibidir. Bahar, böyle ruhları bütün güzellikleri ve güzel renkleriyle gösterir. Böyle ruhlar için âhiret ve kıyâmet de bütün safvet ve güzelliklerini ortaya koyacak benzersiz bir bahar demektir. Görülecek gül ve sûsen güzelliğinden mahrum olan ruhlar ise, baharı değil, sonbaharı isterler. Çünkü sonbahar mevsimi, dikenlerin ve dikenler gibi çirkin dalların baharıdır. Bu mevsimde güllerde de gül açmadığı için, sonbahar, adî taşla yakut arasındaki farkı kaldıran karanlık gibi, adî dikenin ne idüğünü açığa vurmayan zamandır.

Ancak bütün bunlar, hakîkati görmeyen, göremeyen gözler için böyledir. Bahçıvana sorarsan, bu fidan gül müdür, diken midir, bunu hazanda da bahardaki kadar aşikâr bilir.

Kâinatta türlü güller, türlü çiçekler yetiştiren, diken gibi ruhlara da gül gibi gönüllere de rahmetini esirgemeyen bahçıvan ise, güldeki güzellik kadar, dikendeki çirkinliği de zamanın her ânında yakından görücüdür.

Gökte her yıldız, bir ay parçası gibi görünür. Tıpkı bunun gibi yeryüzünde her irfan sahibi, dolunay gibi olan kâmil velînin bir parçası demektir. Esasen, cihan yalnız o "bir kişi"den ibarettir ve o "bir kişi" ise bütün çirkinliklerden habersizdir, bütün kötülüklerden uzak olandır. Onun ruhunda ne çirkinlik, ne kötülük, ne karanlık yer tutar.[88]

- Kıyâmet gününde hepsinin işi Tanrı'ya düşer. Yani hepsi Tanrı ile meşgul olur ve hepsi bunda birleşir. Bunun gibi dünyada herkes bir işle uğraşır. Kimi kadın sevgisiyle, kimi mal toplamakla, kimi kazanmak, kimi de bilgi elde etmekle uğraşır; bunlardan birinden zevk alır ve hoşlanır. Hepsi de: "Benim dermanım, saadetim ve huzurum bundadır." der ve ona inanır. Bu da Tanrı'nın bir rahmetidir. Çünkü insan, o sevdiği şeye gider, onu arar, bulamayıp geri döner, bir zaman bekler ve kendi kendine: "Bu zevk ve rahmet aranılmaya değer; belki ben iyi arayamadım tekrar arayayım" diye, yeniden aramaya başlar. Fakat yine bulamaz. Böylece Tanrı'nın rahmeti ona perdesiz olarak

88 Ken'an Rifâî, *Şerhli Mesnevî-i Şerif*, s. 427.

yüz gösterinceye kadar devam eder. Rahmet yüz gösterdikten sonra, bu tuttuğu yolun, gerçek yol olmadığını anlar. Fakat Tanrı'nın öyle kulları da vardır ki, onlar kıyâmetten evvel bu gayeye ulaşmışlardır. Şimdiden sonu görürler. Ali (Tanrı ondan razı olsun): "Perde kalksa da benim yakînim artmıyor." (Kelâm-ı Kibar) buyuruyor. Yani: Bu kalıbı ortadan kaldırsalar ve kıyâmet görünse de benim yakînim artmaz [demektir]. Bu şunun gibidir: Mesela, farz edelim ki karanlık gecede bir evde herkes yüzünü bir tarafa çevirmek sûretiyle namaz kılsa, gündüz olunca yüzlerini çevirmiş oldukları yönü değiştirirler. Fakat onlar arasında gece kıbleye çevirmiş olan, bu hakîkî yönden yüzünü çevirmez. Hem niçin çevirsin? Çünkü herkes yüzünü ona doğru çevirir. [Bu dünyada] Gece yüzlerini ona dönüp, başkasından yüz çevirmiş iseler, o halde, onlar için kıyâmet görünmüş ve hazır olmuştur.[89]

- Esasen insanın kıymeti, bu dünyada gördüğü, bulunduğu ve meşgul olduğu şeylerle ölçülür ve o kimse bunlar ile haşrolur. Binâenaleyh ne ile uğraşıyorsan, gerek fikrin gerek meşgalen her ne ise, neticede karşına çıkacak da odur. Sonunda hüsrâna mı uğrayacaksın, cânâna mı kavuşacaksın bunlar ilim ve amel cihetiyle tutumuna bağlıdır. Çünkü azap ve ateşin şiddeti, Allah'tan gafletin nispeti kadardır. Dünya demek, seni Allah'tan gafil kılan her ne ise o demektir. Bu yüzden de dünyaya meyil ve muhabbet, her hatânın başı olduğu gibi ondan kaçınmak da bütün ibâdetlerden üstündür.[90]

- Allah hakkında güçlüklere atılan birisini gördüğünde, onun sâdık bir mümin olduğunu bilmelisin. Allah'ın dini hususunda olduğu kadar dinin dışındaki başka işlerde de azimet ve kararlılık sahibi olduğunu gördüğünde, öyle birinin esas itibarıyla güçlü iman sahibi değil, güçlü nefis sahibi olduğunu anlamalısın. Mümin bilhassa Allah'ın hakkında güçlüyken arzu ve hevâ hakkında zayıftır. Sâdık mümine hevâ gücü gelip bir konuda yardım istediğinde, o arzusuna yardım etmez. Bunun nedeni zayıflığı ve umutsuzluğu hakkındaki kesin kanaatidir. Müminin yardımını göremeyince hevâ kırılır, bu

89 Mevlânâ, *Fîhi Mâfih*, Fasıl 7, s. 44-45.

90 Ken'an Rifâî, *Sohbetler*, s. 404.

kez organlar hevânın kendisine çağırmış olduğu işi yerine getirmekten kurtulur. Îman vâridi geldiğinde, onda bir güç ve Allah'ın yardımını bulur. Bu yardıma hiçbir şey karşı koyamaz. Çünkü ona yardım eden Allah'tır. İnsan "insan" olması itibarıyla korkak yaratılmıştır. Mümin "mümin" olması itibarıyla cesur ve atılgandır.[91]

- Dünya bir mahşerdir; kıyâmet günüde ise kalb-i selîmden gayrı geçer akçe yoktur. Her şeyi unut. Yüzünü, seni her nefes sınayan "Sahib"in eşiğine koy. Yalnız bir ömür boyunca değil, zaman ve mekân ölçüsüne sığmaz sırların imtidadı (uzayıp gitmesi) içinde bu başı o eşikten kaldırma ki, iki cihan hayatından gaye budur![92]

- Bir gün Hz. Âişe'ye (r.a) sordular:

"Ârif olan îman sahipleri, kıyâmet günü nasıl hesaba çekileceklerdir?"

Bunun üzerine Hz. Âişe şöyle anlattı:

"Onlara hesap vermek yoktur. Yalnız itap olur; azar işitirler."[93]

Kıyâmet kendi hakîkati ile karşılaşma günü olduğundan, hakîkati kıbleye dönmüş olan, bu dünyaya gelmekten maksadının hâsıl olduğunu anlar.[94]

- Kıyâmet koptuğu ve herkes öldüğü vakitte Cenâb-ı Hak: *Bugün mülk kimindir?* diye nidâ edecek. Herkes ve her şey öldüğü için kimseden ses çıkmayınca yine kendi: *"Kahhâr ve Vâhid olan Allah'ındır."* (Mü'min, 16) diye cevap verecek.

Ama bu hâl şimdi de öyle... Bu sual ve bu nidâ her zaman için sorulmakta... gözün varsa haşrı da neşri de, cenneti ve cehennemi de burada gör. Hazreti Niyazî de: *"Haşr u neşri burada gör, İsrâfil Aleyhisselâm sûrunu üflemeden."* demiyor mu? Hazreti Ali'nin de: "Ölüm, gözümden örtüyü kaldırdığı zaman bu dünyada gördüğümden fazla bir şey

91 İbn Arabî, *Fütûhât-ı Mekkiyye*, c. 18, s. 273-274.

92 Sâmiha Ayverdi, *Mülâkatlar*, s. 15.

93 Ahmed er-Rifâî, *Onların Âlemi*, 7. Hadîs-i Şerîf, s. 103.

94 *Derleyenin Notu.*

görmeyeceğim..." demiş olması aynı mânâyı teyid etmiyor mu? Zîra cennet de buradadır, cemâl de![95]

- Varlık birdir ve Varlık Tanrı'nındır. Bu yüzden hiçbir şey var değildir. Ârif, Tanrı'da kendi hayalî varlığını yok etme makamına eriştiği zaman, o "büyük kıyâmeti tecrübe eder" ve *"Bugün (kıyâmet günü) mülk kimindir? Vâhid ve Kahhâr olan Allah'ındır."* (Mü'min, 16) âyetinin anlamını kavrar.[96]

- "Acı gerçeklerle yüz yüze geleceğimiz kıyâmeti beklemeye ne hacet? Bilelim ki her ânımız bir kıyâmet günüdür. Her an, bir kıyâmet günü sayılabilir. Ama kurunun yanında yaşın da yanacağını bir bilebilsek...

Allah, kullarına, bizzat kendi elleri ile kıyâmetlerini hazırlatmakta, herkesin tek başına hesaba çekileceği günlerden nişane olarak insanoğlunu, kıran kırana denecek savaşlarla kendi cinsinin ifnâsına (kendi cinsini yok etmeye) yöneltmek sûretiyle cezâlandırmaktadır."[97]

- "Allah'ın huzuruna çıkmak için kıyâmet gününü ne beklersiniz? Her nefes o huzurdasınız. Hareketlerinizi, sözlerinizi, bilhassa niyet ve düşüncelerinizi bu anlayışa göre düzeltin."[98]

- Hz. Mustafa (Allah'ın selâm ve salâtı O'nun üzerinde olsun) ortaya çıkınca, bir tek ümmet kalmadan birbirlerinden ayrıldılar. Çünkü O'nun vücudu bir mihenk idi. Kalpı, altından ayırdı ve sıddık, zındıktan ayrıldı. Belki Peygamber, zeval bulmaz bir güneş ve o cihanın kandili idi. Âlem, O'nun varlığı olmadan, karanlık bir gece idi. Çünkü hayvanlık âlemi karanlıktır. Peygamber olmadan hiç kimse Allah yolunda yürüyemez. Karanlıkta yol nasıl belli olur, iyi kötüden nasıl ayırt edilir, siyah beyazdan nasıl ayrılır?

95 Ken'an Rifâî, *Sohbetler,* s. 178.

96 Fahreddîn-i Irâkî, *Lemaât,* 4. Parıltı, s. 58.

97 Sâmiha Ayverdi, *Ezelî Dostlar,* s. 214.

98 Sâmiha Ayverdi, *Dost,* s. 100.

"Kiminin yüzü ağaracağı, kiminin yüzü kararacağı gün" (Âl-i İmrân, 106), ak yüzün, kara yüzden belli olması, kıyâmet alâmetidir. O halde peygamberlerin vücudu kıyâmettir. Çünkü ak ve kara yüz, onların yüzlerinin güneşi ile zâhir olur. O aklık ve karalık, peygamberlerin ve evliyânın gözünde gün gibi aşikârdır. Hakîkî ve doğru müminlerin nazarında, peygamberin vücudu kıyâmettir. Çünkü onlar yarın kıyâmette ne olacağını bugün peşinen görürler. Gaflet perdesini önceden yırttıkları için muhakkak ki onların gözünde hiçbir şey gizlenmiş değildir. O, umumun kıyâmetine, şu sebepten kıyâmet derler ki kâfirlerin makamı ve melcei olan dünya kalmadığı zaman, hiç şüphe yok ki onların gaflet perdesi de yırtılmış olur. Kendi yüz karalarını açıkça görürler. Kıyâmet, Allah ve Allah'ın şaşılacak şeyleri ortada yok değil, bilakis göz önündedir. İnsana boynundaki damarından daha yakındır. Fakat görmeye mâni olan şey, o gaflet perdesidir. Her kim bu gaflet perdesinden dışarı çıkarsa, onun kıyâmeti zâhir olur.

"Kim ölürse, onun kıyâmeti kopmuştur." (Hadis). Her kim beşerî ve hayvanî sıfatlardan ve nefs-i kâfirin tabiatından ölmüş ve yok olmuşsa onun kıyâmeti kopmuş ve aşikâr olmuştur. Kıyâmet gaflet perdesinden, benlikten kurtulmaktan ve Allah'ın kemâl güneşini müşâhede etmekten ibarettir. Peygamber'in vücudu, kıyâmettir. Her kim onun vücudu ile kıyâmet bekler veya kıyâmeti ondan ayrı bilirse şaşı olur; biri, iki görür, birlikten uzak ve bigâne kalır. O kıyâmet dahi bu aynı şekil, aynı güzellik ve aynı parlaklık olacaktır. Bundan başka bir şey olmayacaktır. Allah ve Allah'ın nuru iki değildir, iki olmaz ve olamaz da. İlk ve son, bir olur. O "bir" yegâneyi kendisine çekmek ve bigâneyi uzaklaştırmak içir her bir şekilde yüz gösterir ve gözetler.

> *Mesnevî:*
>
> *Allah, o güne, kıyâmet dedi, ki o gün, sarı ve kırmızı yüzleri meydana çıkartır.*
>
> *Hakîkatte asıl gün, o evliyânın sırrıdır ki, gün, onların güneşinin yanında gölgedir.*

Âlemin varlığı, bigânenin, yegâneden; kalpın nakitten, tortunun saftan ayrılması için çalışmakta ve kaynamaktadır. Sır gözüyle baktığın zaman, her birinin kendi aslına kavuşması için bütün âlemin bu çalışmada ve coşmada olduğunu görürsün.[99]

99 Sultan Veled, *Maârif,* Fasıl 21, s. 109.

ÂYET 7-8

"Kim zerre miktarı hayır yapmışsa onu görür."

"Kim de zerre miktarı şer işlemişse onu görür."

- *"Zira her kim bir zerre miktarı hayır işlerse onu görecektir. Her kim de bir zerre miktarı şer işlerse onu görecektir."* "Fe" (edatı) göstermenin neticesini açıklamak içindir. Zerra görülür görülmez derecede, gayet küçük karıncadır. Güneşin şuaında sezilebilen zerreciklere de denilir. İbn Abbas'tan rivayet edilmiştir ki, elini toprağa sokmuş kaldırmış, sonra üflemiş de, "işte bunlardan her biri bir miskal zerre" demiştir. İkisi de azlığa meseldir. Gerçi bizim bir zerre dediğimiz içinde bile bir âlem vardır. Fakat sorumluluğun en az derecesi beşerî hissin ilgilenebileceği en küçük ölçü ile ifade edilmiştir. Asıl maksat ise en küçük bir hayır veya şerrin bile Allah katında kaybolmayacağını açıklamaktır.[100]

- *"Artık kim zerre ağırlığınca bir hayır işlemişse onu görecek. Kim de zerre ağırlığınca bir şer işlemişse onu görecektir."* Bu âyetler, amelleri görmenin detaylandırılmasıdır. *"Zerre"*, küçük karınca veya bir delikten kapalı bir yere giren güneş ışınlarında görülen toz parçaları anlamındadır. (...)

Âyetlerde ifade buyurulan mânâ şudur: "Mutluluğa erenlerden zerre miktarı hayır işleyen onu görecek, bedbahtlardan da yine zerre ağır-

100 Elmalılı Hamdi Yazır, *Hak Dini Kur'an Dili*, c. 9, s. 405.

lığınca şer işleyen onu görecektir." Kâfirin iyilikleri, küfrü sebebiyle boşa gitmiştir. Müminin büyük günahları dışındaki kötülükleri ise affedilmiştir.

Kâfirin iyiliklerinin, cezâsını hafifletmekte müessir olacağı, bu kabilden olmak üzere cömertliğinden ötürü, Allah'ın Hâtem-i Tâî'nin, Ebû Tâlib'in ve daha başka bazılarının cezâlarını hafifleteceği tarzında görüşler vardır. Ama bu, şu âyet ve hadisle reddedilmiştir: *"Onların yaptıkları her işin önüne geçeriz ve onu saçılmış toz zerreleri haline getiririz."* (Furkân, 23).

Anlaşılıyor ki kâfir iyi bir iş yaparsa, bu dünyada onun karşılığını görse de öbür âleme örtülü (kâfir) olarak gidecektir. Yani küfrü hayrını örttüğü için kıyâmette şakî olarak dirilir.[101]

Hz. Peygamber (s.a.s) Abdullah b. Cüd'an hakkında şöyle buyurmuştur: *"Ona hiçbir faydası olmaz. Çünkü o, hiçbir gün 'Ya Rabbi! Kıyâmet gününde benim günahımı bağışla.' demedi."* Rasûlullah bu sözü, Hz. Âişe (r.a): "Ya Rasûlullah! İbn Cüd'an cahiliye döneminde akrabayı gözetir, yoksullara yedirirdi. Bunların ona bir faydası olur mu?" dediği zaman söylemiştir. Hz. Peygamber'in Ebû Tâlib hakkında söylediği: "Eğer ben olmasaydım cehennemin en dip tabakasında idi." sözü ise, sadece ona has bir şefaattir.

Kâfirler Müslüman oldukları takdirde, daha önce yapmış oldukları iyilikler fayda verir. İbn Abbas'tan şöyle dediği rivayet edilmiştir: "Mümin ve kâfirin işlediği iyi veya kötü hiçbir ameli yok ki, Allah onu kendisine göstermesin. Müminin günahları bağışlanır, iyiliklerinden dolayı ise, ona sevap verilir."[102]

Bütün bunlardan anlaşılıyor ki, îmanlı olmayan kimse hayırlı iş yapsa da Yaratan'ını tanımadığı için ya da insân-ı kâmile hürmet etmediği için öbür âlemini kurtaramıyor.[103]

- Bikâî tefsirinde de şöyle denilmektedir: "Kâfir, yaptığı hayır üzere durdurulur. Ya onun karşılığı dünyada verilir veya îmana dayanmayan

101 *Derleyenin Notu.*

102 İsmail Hakkı Bursevî, *Rûhu'l-Beyân Tefsîri*, c. 10, s. 142-143.

103 *Derleyenin Notu.*

bir temel üzerine bina ettiği için boşa çıkarılır. O, mânâsız bir şekildir. Bu yüzden onun pişmanlığı artar, hüznü ve esefi güçlenir. Mümin ise, onu, sevinci artsın diye görür. Mümin şer tarafını da görür ve bağışlandığını bilir, ferahı tamamlanır. Kâfir işlediği şerri görünce, hüznü ve üzüntüsü artar."

Demek ki, kâmil insanı tanımayan, yani devrin Âdemine secde etmeyen kimse gece gündüz iyilik bile yapsa öbür âlemde şakî olarak dirilecektir.[104]

Bilginlerden birisi bu âyetin, bir hurma, bir üzüm tanesi ve bir ekmek kırıntısı gibi az bile olsa hayır işlemeye teşvik için nâzil olduğunu söylemiştir. Şüphesiz o, hâlis bir niyette olduğu zaman çoğalır. Âyet ayrıca terazide zerre kadar bir hıyanet, bir bakış, bir adım, küçük bir yalan bile olsa günahtan sakındırmaktadır. Şüphesiz o günahın, Yüce Allah'a karşı bir cür'et olduğu için büyüyüp çoğalması beklenir.

İslâm'ın ilk günlerinde insanlar, Allah'ın küçük günahlardan dolayı kendilerini müâhaze etmeyeceğini (azarlamayacağını) zannederlerdi. Bazıları küçük bir şeyi sadaka olarak vermekten utanır, ondan dolayı bir ecrin olmadığını zannederlerdi. Bu âyet inince hakîkati öğrendiler.[105]

"Her kim zerre ağırlığınca bir hayır işlemişse onu görecek. Her kim de zerre ağırlığınca bir şer işlemişse onu görecektir." **âyetlerini Haluk Nurbaki Hoca şöyle yorumluyor:**

- *"Miskale zerretin"* demek: Atom ağırlığı kadar küçük demektir. (Zerre: Atom. Miskal: Ağırlık ölçü birimi.) Demek ki en ince ayrıntılar kaydolacak.

    a. Atomun minicik ağırlığı kadar hayır ya da şer mutlaka ilâhî kompütere yansımaktadır. Hiçbir hareket, fiil yoktur ki ilâhî kayıt ekranına yansımasın.

    b. Kıyâmete yakın günlerde, en ufak zerrelerde ne kadar hayır ve şer olduğu bilim dünyasına yansıyacak ve atom gibi, miniğin de miniği bir zerrede, hayır ve şer nice kuvvetler olduğu bilinecek.

104 *Derleyenin Notu.*

105 İsmail Hakkı Bursevî, *Rûhu'l-Beyân Tefsîri*, c. 10, s. 143.

c. Enfüsî mânâya gelince: Nefs ve gönül çok hassas bir yapıya sahiptir. Atom ağırlığındaki minicik bir hayır da şer de oraya yansır ve yerleşir. Bir hadiste, Efendimiz: *"Her günah, bir zerre de olsa kalp önüne bir leke bırakır."* buyurmuştur. Kalbimizin çok hassas şekilde korunması, hele şer sevgilerden uzak tutulması gerekir. Nefs de böyledir: En ufak ihmalde bir günah deliği açar ve o noktadan şeytan titreşimi dolmaya başlar. Bu bir vesvese ile fark edilir.[106]

- Hayrı anlatan âyetin müminler hakkında, şerri anlatan âyetin de kâfirler hakkında olduğu söylenmiştir.

İbn Abbas (r.a) der ki:

"Mümin olsun kâfir olsun kim dünyada iyi veya kötü bir amel yaparsa, âhirette onu muhakkak görür. Mümin, yapmış olduğu bütün iyilik ve kötülükleri âhirette karşısında görür; Allah onun kötülüklerini affeder, iyiliklerine sevap verir. Kâfire gelince, Allah onun iyiliklerini reddeder, kötülüklerinin cezâsını verir."

Muhammed b. Kâ'b el-Kurazî şöyle demiştir:

"Kâfir kimse, yaptığı iyi işlerin karşılığını dünyada görür. Onun karşılığı ailesinde, malında ve çocuklarında kendisine verilir. Öyle ki Allah katında hiçbir hayrı bulunmadan dünyadan çıkıp gider. Müminse, günahların cezâsını dünyada çeker. Bu cezâyı kendisinde, ailesinde ve malında karşılaşacağı imtihanlarla çeker. Öyle olur ki Allah katında (cezâsını çekmediği) hiçbir kötülüğü kalmadan dünyadan çıkar gider."

Hz. Mûsâ'ya bir gün bir adam gelir ve "Ya Mûsâ, sen diyorsun ki, Allah'ı çok anın, O'na şükredin ki nimetiniz artsın. Oysa ben O'nun adını hiç anmıyorum yine de günden güne malım, evlâdım, servetim artıyor." Hz. Mûsâ duyduklarından dolayı çok üzgündür. Ama Hz. Mûsâ'nın işittikleri Cenâb-ı Hakk'a mâlumdur ve ona der ki: "Ya Mûsâ! Söyle o kuluma, Ben Allahu Azîmü'ş-şân, onu ağzından kendi adımı anma zevkini aldım. Bir insana bundan daha büyük cezâ olmaz."[107]

106 Halûk Nurbaki, *Namaz Sureleri Yorumu*, s. 79-80.

107 *Derleyenin Notu.*

Hz. Peygamber (sallallahu aleyhi vesellem) bu konuda şöyle buyurmuştur:

"Bir kul günahından tövbe edince Allah günahlarını yazıcı meleklerine unutturur, aynı şekilde ona şâhitlik edecek âzâlarında ve yeryüzüne de o günahları unutturur. Öyle olur ki onun aleyhine şâhitlik edecek hiç kimse bulunmadan kul Allah'a kavuşur."

Müfessir İbn Cüzey der ki: *"Kim zerre miktarı şer işlemişse onu görür."* âyeti kâfirler için aynen uygulanır. Müminlere gelince, onların işledikleri günahlarından dolayı azap görmeleri ancak şu altı şartla olur:

1. Müminin işlediği günah büyük günahsa,

2. Bu günahlara tövbe etmeden ölmüşse,

3. Bu günahlardan dolayı mizanda hayır tarafı ağır gelmemişse,

4. Kendisine şefaat edilmemişse,

5. Bedir'e katılanlar gibi, günahların affedilmesini hak etmiş bir kimse değilse,

Yani hem nefsiyle hem bedeniyle hem câhilliği ile savaşmamışsa...[108]

6. Allah Teâlâ onu rahmetiyle affetmemişse, mümin (geçici olarak, günahı kadar) azap görür. Günahkâr müminin durumu Allah'a kalmıştır; O, dilerse azap eder, dilerse affeder."[109]

• 7. ve 8. âyetler, müminleri, küçük de olsa her türlü hayra teşvik etmektedir. Bir kuru üzüm tanesi, bir dilim ekmek ve benzeri bir madde ile de olsa hayır yapılmalıdır. Yine bu âyetler, en küçük bir kötülükten de insanı sakındırmaktadır. Bu kötülük çok küçük bir haksızlık, haram kazanç, aldatmak, bir kere haince bakmak, bir kere harama adım atmak gibi basit görülen işler olabilir. İnsan kusurun küçüklüğüne değil, onu kime karşı yaptığına bakmalıdır. Yüce Allah'a karşı cüret ve edepsizlikle işlenen küçük kusurlar, tövbe edilmezse birikerek çoğalır, küçük iken büyük olur; insanı yakar.

Allah Resûlü bu konuda şu önemli bir uyarı yapmaktadır:

108 *Derleyenin Notu.*

109 İbn Acîbe el- Hasenî, *Bahrü'l-Medîd,* c. 11, s. 103-104.

"Günahların küçüklerinden de sakının. Küçük günahlardan sakınmayan kimselerin hali şuna benzer: Bir grup insan yolculuk yaparken bir vadide konaklarlar. Kendilerine ateş lazımdır. Herkes bir odun parçası getirir. Bu parçalar birikince büyük bir yığın olur. Onu yakarlar, ekmeklerini pişirir ve diğer işlerini görürler. Küçük günahları çekinmeden işleyen kimse de bir gün hesaba çekildiğinde (biriken onca günah) kendisini yakar, helâk eder."[110]

- Mutlulardan *"Kim zerre miktarı hayır yapmışsa onu görür."* Bedbahtlardan *"Kim zerre miktarı şer işlemişse onu görür." "Kim...yapmışsa..."* ifadesindeki "men=kim" edatı genellik ifade etmesine karşın, her iki yerde de "eştaten=darmadağınık" ifadesi tarafından hususileştirilmiştir. Çünkü bedbahtların işledikleri hayırlar, küfür ve perdelenmişlik nedeniyle boşa gider. Mutluların kötülükleri ise, îman, tövbe, hayırların baskın gelmesi ve fıtratın bozulmaması nedeniyle affedilir.[111]

- Kim bu yolda, nefsinin hazlarından ve kötü âdetlerinden birini terk ederek zerre kadar hayır yapmışsa onu görür. Kim de nefsinin zâhirdeki arzularına uymayı artırarak zerre kadar kötülük etmişse onu görür. Çünkü zâhirde nefse ne kadar uyulursa, iç âlemde o nispette noksanlık olur. Ancak kul müşâhedesinde temkin sahibi olursa, nefsin mubah hazlarını vermek, onun mânevî haline bir noksanlık getirmez.

Sûfî müfessirlerden Necmeddin-i Dâye (r.a), *et-Te'vîlâtü'n Necmiyye* adlı tefsirinde der ki:

"Herkes eliyle kazandığı yani bizzat yaptığı amelleri görsün diye hesap yerine getirilir. Her amel kendine has bir şekilde gözükür. Allah için yapılan sâlih ameller nurlu bir vaziyette gözükürken, kötü işler karanlık olarak gözükür. Ayrıca her amelin mânevî bir şekli vardır. İnsan yaptığı işleri kendine has bir şekilde görür. Mesela sâlih ameller çok güzel bir şekil ve sûrette gözükür. Kötü ameller ise değişik hayvan sûretlerinde gözükür. Bu durum sâlih amel sahiplerini sevindirirken, kötü amel sahiplerini haddinden fazla üzer ve perişan eder.[112]

---

110 İbn Acîbe el- Hasenî, *Bahrü'l-Medîd,* c. 11, s. 106-107.

111 Muhyiddin İbn Arabî, *Tefsîr-i Kebîr Te'vilât,* c. 2, s. 1478.

112 İbn Acîbe el-Hasenî, *Bahrü'l-Medîd,* c.11, s. 105-106.

- *"Artık kim zerre ağırlığınca bir hayır işlemişse onu görecektir."*

[Sehl] şöyle dedi:

Bu âyet nâzil olunca, Allah'ın Elçisi -sallallâhu aleyhi ve sellem- hutbe verdi ve hutbesinde şöyle buyurdu: "Dikkat edin! Şüphesiz dünya, şu an [elimizin altında] (hazır) bulunan geçici bir arazdır [menfaat]; ondan iyi[si] (berr) de yer, kötü[sü] (fâcir) de. Dikkat edin! Şüphesiz âhiret, gerçek (sâdık) bir sondur (ecel); onda [her şeye] gücü yeten Melik hükmeder. Dikkat edin! Şüphesiz hayrın tümü, her şeyiyle beraber cennettedir. Dikkat edin! Şüphesiz şerrin tümü, her şeyiyle beraber cehennemdedir. Dikkat edin! Allah'tan sakınarak amelde bulunun ve bilin ki amelleriniz size gösterilecektir. *"Artık kim zerre ağırlığınca bir hayır işlemişse onu görecektir. Kim de zerre miktarı şer işlemişse onu görecektir."*

Ebü'd-Derdâ (r.a) şöyle demiştir: "Takvanın kemâli, -bir zerre ağırlığı [söz konusu] olsa bile- kulun Allah[a karşı gelmek]ten sakınmasıdır. O kadar ki [kul], -haram olması endişesiyle- helâl gördüğü bazı şeyleri de terk eder. [Böylelikle] bu [durum, kul] ile haram arasında bir perde olur."

Nitekim Hz. Ali'nin şöyle söylediği nakledilir: "Dünya beni haramından menetti, ben onun helâlinden de geçtim."[113]

Sehl şöyle dedi:

Az da olsa hiçbir günahı küçümseme. Çünkü onlar şöyle demişlerdir: "Günahın ardından gelen fakat günahtan daha ağır dört şey vardır: [Günahta] ısrar etmek, [onu] hoş bulmak, [onu] önemsiz saymak ve [onunla] övünmek."

İbn Mesud -radiyallâhu anhümâ- şöyle demiştir: "Mümin; günahlarını, üzerine yıkılmasından korktuğu bir dağın eteğindeymiş gibi görür. Kâfir ise günahlarını, burnuna konan bir sinek gibi görür." Sonra [İbn Mesud sanki burnunun üzerinde bir sinek varmış gibi] uçması için eliyle şöyle işaret yaptı.

Allah'a yakın olanlar bazan helâl olan şeyleri bile Allah'la aralarında perde gibi görüp onlardan da vazgeçerler. Örneğin; hakkı olan mala mülke, evlada aşırı değer vermek.[114]

113 *Derleyenin Notu.*

114 *Derleyenin Notu.*

Sonra Sehl şöyle dedi:

[Ey] Müslümanlar topluluğu! Dil ile ikrarı ve kalpteki yakini başardınız: Şüphesiz Allah tektir, O'nun bir benzeri yoktur. Şüphesiz sizin için öyle bir gün [gelecektir] ki [Allah] o [gün] sizi diriltilecek ve zerre ağırlığınca işlediğiniz amellerden [bile] sizi hesaba çekecektir. Şayet [ameliniz] hayır ise [Allah] sizi onun için ödüllendirecek; şer ise -dilerse- cezâlandıracaktır. O halde bunu bilfiil gerçekleştirin.

[Sehl]e "Bunu bilfiil nasıl gerçekleştirebiliriz?" diye sorulunca şöyle cevap verdi:

Sizin için gerekli şu beş şeyle: Helâl yemek, helâl giymek, uzuvları korumak, size emredildiği şekilde [başkalarının sizin üzerinizdeki] hakları[nı] yerine getirmek ve kıyâmet [günü] bir kısas olarak amellerinizi yok etmemesi için Müslümanlara zarar vermekten kaçınmak. Sonra da tüm bunlar için Allah'tan yardım isteyin ki, O, sizin için bunları tamamına erdirsin.

[Sehl]e "Peki, bu hâller kulun payına nasıl düşecek?" diye sorulunca şöyle karşılık verdi:

Beşini bırakıp, beşine yapışacağı şu on şey [kul] için kaçınılmazdır: [İlk olarak kul] düşman [olan şeytan]ın vesveselerini bırakmalı, buna karşılık alıkoyduğu şeyler konusunda akla tâbi olmalıdır. [İkinci olarak] dünya iş[ler]ine önem vermeyi bırakarak, [dünya]yı ehline terk etmeli; buna karşılık âhirete ehemmiyet verip, [âhiret] ehline yardım etmelidir. [Üçüncü olarak] hevâya uymayı terk etmeli; buna karşılık her durumda Allah[a karşı gelmek]ten sakınmalıdır. [Dördüncü olarak] isyanı bırakmalı; itaatle meşgul olmalıdır. [Beşinci olarak da kul] ameli[nin iyi mi yoksa kötü olduğu]na hükmetsin diye cehâleti ve [cehâlet]le amel etmeyi (ikâme) bırakmalı; buna karşılık ilmi talep etmeli ve [ilim]le amel etmelidir.

[Sehl]e "Bunları yerine getirmek ve bunlarla amel etmek, bizim için nasıl [mümkün] olacak?" diye sorulunca şöyle karşılık verdi:

[Bunun için] dört şey gereklidir: Varacağı yer toprak olan şey için kendini yormamalı ve ona rağbet etmemelidir. Yine, varacakları yer toprak olan kardeşler edinmemeli ve onlara rağbet etmemelidir.

[Sehl'e] "[Peki] bu nasıl [gerçekleşir]?" diye sorulunca şöyle cevap verdi:

[Kulun] şunları bil[mesiyle gerçekleş]ir: O bir kuldur. Mevlâ'sı ise onun hâlini bilir; [onun her hâline] şâhittir; onun hem sevincine (ferah) hem de üzüntüsüne (terah) kâdirdir; ona karşı çok merhametlidir (Rahîm).

Allah -sübhânehu ve teâlâ- en iyi bilendir.[115]

Demek ki bu dünyadaki vazifemiz hâlimizden memnun olma sanatını elde etmektir.[116]

- İbn Arabî buyuruyor ki:

Yaklaşma menzillerinin bilinen bir şartı vardır.
Onlar var olanlar üzerinde hükümrandır.
Kıyâmet şartı gelip o günün hâkimi tecellî ettiğinde
Varlık boyun eğer ve hizmet eder.
Heyhat! Nefisler meyvelerini devşiremez.
Sadece bedende iken bir şey yapanlar devşirir.

Yakınlaşmak, yaratıkların niteliklerinden biridir. Onlar, yaklaşma ve zıddına konu olabilir. Hak, kendisini yaklaşan olmakla nitelese de çok yakındır. Kelimenin mastarı, takrib ve takarrub (yaklaştırma, yakınlaşma) şeklindedir. Şair "bilinen bir şartı vardır" -ki o etkilenmedir- derken, şunu demek ister: İş, genel olarak ancak âhirette bilinir ve ortaya çıkar. Diğer mısrada şöyle demiştir: Nefisler ancak dünya hayatında ettikleri iyilik veya kötülüğü devşirir. Şu halde onların Hakk'a yaklaşması, amellerinden meydana gelir. *"Kim zerre kadar iyilik yaparsa, onu görür, kim zerre miktarı kötülük işlerse onu görür."*[117]

Bu durumda Hak bize yakîndir ama biz o yakîni amellerimizle idrak ederiz.[118]

- "Ey Âdemoğlu! Ölüm bütün gizlilerini ortaya çıkaracak... Kıyâmet bütün haberlerini bir bir okuyacak... Azap, bütün perdelerini yırtacak... Küçük bir günah işlediğinde onun küçüklüğüne değil, kime

115 Sehl b. Abdullah Tüsterî, *Tüsterî Tefsiri*, s. 585-587.

116 *Derleyenin Notu.*

117 İbn Arabî, *Fütûhât-ı Mekkiyye*, c. 2, s. 53-54.

118 *Derleyenin Notu.*

karşı işlediğine bakmalısın. Azıcık rızık verildiğinde, o rızkın azlığına değil, o rızkı sana verene bak.

Küçük günahı küçümseme. Çünkü sen, hangi günahla bana asi olduğunu bilemezsin.

Ey Âdemoğlu! Bir kere olsun, isyanda bulunup da sonra gazâbımı tefekkür ederek isyandan vazgeçtin mi? Emrettiğim farzı, emrettiğim gibi aynen yerine getirdin mi? Muhtaçlara ve yoksullara sana verdiğim maldan ikram edip gönüllerini aldığın vâki mi hiç? Sana kötülük edenlere iyilik ettiğin var mıdır? Seni terk edeni aradığın oldu mu? Sana hıyanet içinde olanlara insaf ettin mi? Evladını terbiye ettin mi? Komşularını hoşnut edebildin mi? Din ve dünya ilimleri için âlimlere başvurdun mu?

Âdemoğulları, ben dış görünüşlerinize, güzelliğinize, soy-sopunuza bakmam. Nazargâhım gönüllerinizdir, ancak bu hasletlerle sizden razı olurum."[119]

- Kıyâmet gününde Allah: "Ey kullarım!" diyecektir, "bana hediye olarak hangi güzel ve iyi davranışlarınızı getirdiniz? Ömrünüzü neye ve nereye harcadınız? Size nimetler verdim, ne yaptınız? Size kuvvetler verdim, nereye sarf ettiniz? Size akıl verdim ne yolda kullandınız?"

Kıyâmet günü, Hakk'ın huzuruna iletilmesi gereken, îman, amel (dinin emirlerini yerine getirmek için yapılan iş) ve muhabbet (sevgi) hediyelerinden mahrum, eli boş, îmansız bir ruhun uğrayacağı dehşet büyüktür. Her iki dünya için sayısız nimet ve devletler yaratan Allah'ın, gerçi kuldan gelecek hediyeye ihtiyacı yoktur. Fakat Allah'ın huzuruna yükselecek bir ruhun ibâdet ve îman sermayesine sahip olmaya ihtiyacı büyüktür. Hesap gününde insan olarak yaratılmış bulunmanın şükranını (teşekkür) ve karşılığını ödeyebilmek için, dağarcığı boş olmamak gerektir. Allah'ın huzuruna ilk yaratıldığımız şekilde çıplak ve eli boş dönmek olmaz. Günün birinde Hakk'ın misafiri olacaklarına inanmayanlar, onun ebed mutfağından ancak ateş, kül ve toprak alabilirler. Uykudan ve oburluktan kaçıp bir temiz gönül ve bir mânevî zahîre (mahsül, tahıl) biriktirmemiş; ibâdetten lezzet almamış, oruç

119 Ahmed er-Rifâî, *Vaazlar*, s. 105-106.

tutmaktaki feragat (fedakârlıkla vazgeçmek) ve bekleyişten nasîbedar olmamış kişi âhirete neyi armağan eder?[120]

Demek ki maddî kıyâmetlerde de, ki zelzele maddî kıyâmettir, herkes kendi hakîkatini görür; îman sahibinin îmanı artar, idraksizlerin küfrü artar. 6 Şubat 2023 tarihinde ülkemizde yaşadığımız bölgesel kıyâmette de bunu aşikâr olarak gördük. Toprak altından günler sonra huzur içinde çıkanların mânevî büyüklüğü ile sarsıldık. Onlar hakîkati görmeye meyilli isimlere sahip olduklarından, Peygamber'in mübârek yakınlığı sayesinde bu büyük sıkıntılı devreyi huzurla geçirmeyi başaranlardır. Bazıları da, hatta vücutlarına bir zarar gelmemiş olsa da, nefret ve kine bulandılar, her şeyi suçlamaya başladılar. Tabii ki yanlışlarla mücadele etmeliyiz, ama birlik ve beraberlik gününde îmanla yapacağımız zerrece hayrın âhirette bize ne kadar lazım olduğunu idrak ettiren bir sûrenin açıklamasıdır bu.[121]

- Biri: "Kadı İzzeddin sana selâm gönderiyor ve her zaman sizin iyiliğinizi, hayrınızı söylüyor, sizi övüyor!" dedi. Mevlânâ buyurdu ki: Her kim bizi hayırla yâd ediyorsa onun da dünyada yâdı hayırlı olsun! Eğer bir kimse başka biri hakkında iyi şeyler söylerse o hayır, iyilik kendisinin olur ve gerçekte kendisini övmüştür. Bunun benzeri şöyledir. Mesela, bir kimse kendi evinin etrafına güller, fesleğenler dikse, her bakışında gül ve fesleğen görür ve kendisini her zaman cennetteymiş gibi hisseder. İnsanların iyiliğini söylemeye alışmış ve onların hayrıyla meşgul olan kimse, onun sevgilisi olur ve onu hatırlayınca sevdiğini yâd etmiş olur. Bu gül ve güllüktür, ruh ve rahattır. Birinin kötülüğünü söyleyince, o kimse gözünde sevimsizleşir. Onu hatırlayıp da hayali gözünün önüne gelince sanki yılan yahut akrep veyahut çerçöp görmüş gibi olur. Bunun için, mademki gece gündüz gül ve güllük ve İrem bağları görebileceksin, o halde niçin dikenlerin ve yılanların bulunduğu bir yerde dolaşıyorsun? Bütün insanları sev ki, daima çiçekler ve gül bahçeleri içinde bulunasın. Eğer hepsini düşman bilirsen, düşmanların hayali gözünün önüne gelir ve sanki gece gündüz dikenlikler ve yılanlar arasında geziyormuş gibi olursun.

120 Ken'an Rifâî, *Şerhli Mesnevî-i Şerif*, s. 464.

121 *Derleyenin Notu.*

Şu halde herkesi seven ve her şeyi hoş gören evliyâ bunu başkaları için değil, -Allah saklasın!- gözlerine çirkin, sevimsiz ve iğrenç bir hayal görünmesin diye yaparlar. Mademki bu dünyada yapılanları tahayyül ve yâd etmek mutlaka zarurîdir ve bundan kaçınılmaz, o halde iğrenç, çirkin hayallerin yollarını karıştırmaması, bozmaması için insanları anarken hepsinin hoş ve iyi olmasına çalış. Binaenaleyh halk hakkında yaptığın her şey ve onları ister iyilikle ister kötülükle olsun anman tamamıyla sana ait olur. Bu bakımdan, Allah buyuruyor ki: *"Kim iyi bir iş yaparsa kendi nefsine ve kim kötü bir iş işlerse kendisine yapar."* (Fussilet, 46) ve onun için *"Her kim bir zerre ağırlığınca iyilik ederse onu görecek ve her kim de zerre kadar kötülük işlerse onu görecek."* (Zilzâl 7-8).[122]

- Bu dünya dâr-ı mükâfat (ödüllendirme yeri) ve âlem-i âhiret (âhiret âlemi) ise, dâr-ı mücâzattır (cezâlandırma yeri). Ammâ ekseriya kötü veya iyi fiilin cezâsı bu dünyada görülür, hayır ya da şer (iyi ya da kötü) işlediğin amel (iş/fiil) her ne ise burada zuhûra gelir. İmdi onun cezâsına müterakkıb (gözeten) ve müteyakkız (uyanık/tetikte) olsan ve hâb-ı gafleti (gaflet uykusunu) terk edip mütenebbih (uyanık) bulunsan her demde (her an) o işlediğin amelin cezâsını görürsün ve mutlak kıyâmete bırakılmaz, bazı kimselerin de amellerinin eseri ve netîcesi (sonucu) âhirette görülür ve kıyâmette zuhûra gelir. Eğer sen âkil (akıllı) ve işlediğin amelin netîcesine muntazır isen (sonucunu bekliyorsan), sana kıyâmet gününü beklemeye hâcet (gerek) kalmaz ve haşr ve neşrin zuhûruna (kıyâmetteki dirilişin ortaya çıkışına) ihtiyâcın olmaz, çünkü sen müteyakkız bulundukça işlediğin amelin eserini şüphesiz bu dünyada görürsün ve âhirette de netîcesinin ne olacağını bu eserden anlarsın. Kıyâmetin gelmesini beklemeye de ihtiyâcın kalmaz. Bu halde kıyâmet, gafil ve câhiller için olur ki, onlar her kârın (işin), her fiilin hakîkatini ve âkibetini (sonucunu) ancak orada, âhirette görürler. İşte bu dünyada her amelin mukabilinde (her yapılan işin karşılığında) gelen eser ve haber birer işaret kabîlindendir (bir tür işarettir). Bunlar meselâ hastalık, hüzün ve keder ve gama düşmek ve yahut düşmanın şerrine (kötülüğüne) uğramak, zengin iken fakir ve muhtaç olmak yahut evlât ve ahfâdı (torunları) ölmek

122 Mevlânâ, *Fîhi Mâfih*, Fasıl 54, s. 306-307.

ve sâire gibi, ki bunların aksi olan güzel şeyler de sıhhatte olmak, şâd (sevinçli), mes'ut ve ferahnâk (ferah içinde) olmak ve düşmandan necat bulmak (kurtulmak) ve zengin olmak vesâire vesâiredir.

Ey Hak'tan gafil ve bî-haber (habersiz)! Sen ne vakit bir şer (fenâlık), bir kötülük işledin de onun lâyıkı olarak akabinde (sonrasında) bir eser görmedin? Ve herhangi bir iyiliği ve fenâlığı işledin de akabinde onun cezâsını görmedin? İşlediğin her fiil gerek hayır (iyilik) gerek şer olsun, eğer hayır ise, onun güzel ecrinin (sevabının/karşılığının) eseri, başka bir iyilik sûretinde sana görünür; eğer işlediğin şer ise, onun cezâsı da derhal zuhur etmeyebilir. Bu belki imhâl-i ilâhî (Allah'ın belirli bir süre vermesi) olup bir âhir vakitte zuhûra gelir (başka bir zamanda ortaya çıkar). Buna ihmâl denilmez, mühlet (süre vermek) denilir.

Yâni Cenâb-ı Hakk o kimseye mühlet (belirli bir süre) verir ki kulları belki tövbekâr olur diye. Onun için Cenâb-ı Hakk, zâlimlere birçok vakit zaman ve mühlet verir; lâkin saati gelip de cezâ vereceği zaman da kimse onu bu azaptan halâsa (kurtarmaya) kâdir olamaz (gücü yetmez). Bir de olur ki seyyie (kötülük), o yaptığın kötülüğün cezâsı ki sana gelmek mukarrer (muhakkak) idi, lâkin tövbe ettin, istiğfâr ettin (af diledin), ağladın, niyaz ettin (duâ ettin/yalvardın) bu sebepten o işlediğin günahın af olunup onun cezâsı ne dünyada ne de âhirette zuhûra gelmez.

Yahut bir seyyieyi (kötülüğü), bir günahı işledikten sonra onun akabinde (sonrasında) bir iyilik, bir gönül almaklık işledinse işte o iyilik, o kötülüğe kefâret (affı için karşılık) olup bu sûretle o kötülüğün cezâsı dünya ve âhirette zuhûra gelmez. Fakat bir kötülüğü işlesen tövbe ve istiğfâr etmesen (af dilemesen) ve onun mukabili (karşılığı) bir hayır da (iyi iş de) işlemesen onun cezâsı dünyada zâhir olmazsa bu hâl ikiden hâlî değildir (iki sebebin dışında değildir): Yâ imhâl-i ilâhîdir (Allah'ın mühlet/süre vermesidir) ki bir başka vakte bırakılmıştır. Yahut af ve bahşâyiş-i rabbânîdir (rabbânî vergi ve bağışlardır) ki, Cenâb-ı Hakk Hazretleri'nin rahmet ve mağrifetinin (affının) zuhûru, O'nun cezâsını affedip setretmiştir (örtmüştür).[123]

- Hz. Mevlânâ'ya biri: "Ezelî hükümler ve Tanrı'nın takdir ettiği şeyler hiç değişir mi?" diye sordu. [Mevlânâ] buyurdu ki: Tanrı'nın

123 Kâzım Büyükaksoy, *Ken'an Rifâî'den Mesnevî Hatıraları*, s. 83-85.

ezelde: "Kötülüğe karşı kötülük, iyiliğe karşı iyilik olmalıdır." diye verdiği hüküm asla değişmez. Çünkü ulu Tanrı Hakîm'dir. Sen kötülük et iyilik bulursun, nasıl der? Bir kimse buğday ekip arpa biçemez ve arpa ekip buğday toplayamaz. Bu imkânsızdır. Bütün velîler ve nebîler de: "İyiliğin karşılığı iyilik, kötülüğün karşılığı kötülüktür." demişlerdir. *"Bir zerre kadar hayır işleyen kimse o hayrın ve zerre kadar kötülük yapan kimse de o kötülüğün cezâsını görür."* (Zilzâl, 7-8).

Ezelî hüküm hakkında öğrenmek istediğin şeyleri söyledik ve etrafıyla anlattık. Bu asla değişmez. Yani bazen iyilik yaparsan karşılığında çok iyilik göremezsin veya ne kadar kötülük yaparsan o kadar kötülük göremezsin. Fakat mutlaka yaptığın iyiliğin veya kötülüğün cezâsını görürsün. Bu böyle olur ama asıl hüküm değişmez. Gevezenin biri: "Biz Tanrı'nın saadetinden mahrum olan şakînin (haydutun) âhiret saadetine kavuşmuş bulunan said (kutlu) ve saidin (kutlunun) de şakî olduğunu görüyoruz." dedi. (Mevlânâ) buyurdu ki: Eh! Olabilir. O şakî iyilik yaptığından said, o said de kötülük işlediğinden yahut kötü şeyler düşündüğünden dolayı şakî olmuştur. Mesela İblis: *"Beni ateşten yarattın da onu çamurdan yarattın."* (Sâd, 76) diye, Âdem'in yaratılışı hakkında itirazda bulunduğundan, meleklerin hocası iken, ebedî olarak Tanrı'nın lânetine uğradı ve bizim huzurumuzdan kovuldu. Biz de diyoruz ki: Evet, iyiliğin karşılığı iyilik, kötülüğün cezâsı kötülüktür.[124]

Şakî ve said anasının karnında şakî ve saiddir. Ama dünyada geçici olarak bazan şakîler said, saidler şakî olabilir. Sonuçta herkes ezelî hakîkatine dönecektir.[125]

- Çok fena işler yaptın, fakat ya boş bulunduğundan veya bilgisizliğinden bunun kötü olduğunu bilmiyorsun, ya da dinsiz bir arkadaş sana bunu önemsiz gibi göstermiştir. Hatta sen bunun günah olduğunun farkında bile değilsin. Şimdi bunların karşılığına bak bakalım, ne kadar sıkıntın var, ne kadar fenalık duyacaksın? Sıkıntı mutlaka bir günahın cezâsı, ferahlık ise ibâdetin karşılığıdır.[126]

---

124 Mevlânâ, *Fîhi Mâfih*, Fasıl 15, s. 105-106

125 *Derleyenin Notu.*

126 Mevlânâ, *Fîhi Mâfih*, Fasıl 15, s. 103-104.

• Hz. Mevlânâ'ya biri "Tatarlar da kıyâmete inanıyorlar ve: 'Elbette bir sorgu sual günü olacak!' diyorlar." dedi. [Mevlânâ] buyurdu ki: Yalan söylüyorlar; kendilerini Müslümanlarla bir göstermek istiyorlar. Yani biz de biliyoruz, inanıyoruz demek istiyorlar. Deveye "Nereden geliyorsun" diye sormuşlar. "Hamamdan geliyorum." karşılığını vermiş. "Ökçenden belli!" demişler. Bunun için eğer onlar kıyâmet gününe inanıyorlarsa bunun delili hani? Bu günahlar, bu zulümler, bu kötülükler, üst üste birikmiş karlar gibi kat kat yığılmıştır. Güneşin karları ve buzları erittiği gibi, günahları bırakıp Hakk'a dönme (inâbet) ve pişmanlık duyma güneşi, Tanrı'nın korkusu ortaya çıkıp o dünyanın ahvali gerçekleştiği zaman, bu isyan karlarının hepsi erir. Eğer bir kar veya buz, bu şekilde bulunurken: "Ben güneşi gördüm, Temmuz güneşi üzerime ışıklarını saldı." der ve hâlâ kar, buz halinde olursa akıllı insan buna inanır mı? Temmuz güneşi parlasın da karı buzu yerinde bıraksın! Bu imkânsız bir şeydir. Her ne kadar Ulu Tanrı, iyi ve kötü cüzlerin cezâsı kıyâmette verilecektir, diye vadetse de biz onun örneklerini dünyada her an, her lahza görmekteyiz. Mesela bir insanın yüreği ferahsa bu onun, bir insanı sevindirmiş olmasının karşılığıdır. Bunun gibi üzülürse bu da başkasını üzmüş olmasındandır. İşte bunlar o dünyanın armağanları, cezâ gününün örnekleridir.[127]

• Allah'ın karşılığında cezâlandıracağını söylediği bir günahı işleyip korkan bir müminin kendisinden meydana gelen davranış nedeniyle içinde pişmanlık duymaması mümkün değildir. Hz. Peygamber şöyle buyurmuştur: "Pişmanlık tövbedir." O halde günahkâr müminde pişmanlık vardır ve o pişmandır. Bu durumda pişmanlığın gerçekleşmesi nedeniyle tehdidin hükmü de ortadan kalkar. Çünkü müminin günahı nahoş bulması ve ondan memnun olmaması zorunludur. Bu esnada ise (günah olan) amelini yapmaktadır. Öyleyse mümin, günahı nahoş bulması ve onun günah olduğuna inanması yönünden sâlih amel sahibi iken, günahı işlemesi bakımından ise günah sahibidir. Öyleyse bu kişinin sonu, sâlih amel ile günahları katıştıranlardan olmaktır. Allah Teâlâ bu sözün ardından şöyle buyurur: *"Umulur ki Allah onların tövbesini kabul eder."* (Tevbe, 102). Allah için "umulur ki" ifadesi, zorunluluk bildirir. Allah'ın söz konusu kullarına dönmesi

127 Mevlânâ, *Fîhi Mâfih*, Fasıl 15, s. 102-103.

ise, onların tövbe etmesiyle gerçekleşir ve onlara mağfireti kazandıran ise pişmanlıklarıdır. Pişmanlık tövbe demektir. Günahkârlar pişman olduklarında, Allah'ın onlara dönmesi gerçekleşmiştir. Böyle biri, üç yönden sâlih amel sahibidir: Davranışın günah olduğuna inanması, onu yapmayı nahoş bulması ve yaptığına pişmanlık duyması. Buna karşılık, tek bir yönden de günahkârdır. O da, söz konusu günahı işlemesidir.

Bu pişmanlıkla birlikte ister söylediğimizi bilsin ister bilmesin, yine de korku kendisine hâkimdir. Çünkü o, bu tövbe üzerindeyken ölse bile, başka nahoş bir fiilin kendisinden çıkmasından korkar. Çünkü korku kendisinden ayrılmaz ve bu kez korkunun konusu tehdidin gerçekleşmesinden Hakk'ın azarlamasına ve sorgu esnasında kendisinden meydana gelen günahı itiraf etmeye intikal eder. Öyleyse sürekli korkuyu hisseder. Bu da tehdit türlerinden birisidir. Nitekim Allah şöyle buyurur: *"Kim zerre miktarı iyilik yaparsa onu görür. Kim zerre miktarı kötülük yaparsa onu görür."* (Zilzâl, 7-8). Öyleyse yaptığına vâkıf olması kaçınılmazdır ve kişi o çirkin amelini görmek -ki görmesi zorunludur- nedeniyle azarlanmaktan korkmaktadır. Allah bu âyette o amel nedeniyle cezâlandırılmaya değinmemiştir. Öyleyse zorunlu olan görmektir (cezâ değil). Bağışlanan kimselerden ise, yaptığı suçun büyüklüğünü ve bunun karşılığında kendisini bağışlamakla Allah'ın nimetinin büyüklüğünü görür. Doğru sözlünün haberinin bildirdiği budur, yalan o söze giremez, çünkü böyle bir şey ilâhî mertebe hakkında imkânsızdır.[128]

O halde günah Allah'tan uzak olmak, tövbe Allah'a dönmektir. Günahından pişman olana, önce Tevvâb olan Allah döner, kul da bunu hissederse Allah'a yakınlaşır. Hz. Âdem'in günahı gibi tövbeden sevap hâsıl olur.[129]

Hz. Ahmed er-Rifâî buyuruyor ki:

- Ey kardeş!

İçinde bulunduğun durum helâl olan bir durumsa sevabı yoktur, mubah ise mes'ûliyeti mûcibdir, haram olan bir hâl içinde isen,

128 İbn Arabî, *Fütûhât-ı Mekkiyye*, c. 9, s. 342-343.

129 *Derleyenin Notu.*

Rabb'ine mülâkî olduğun zaman: *"Zerre mikdârı şerr işleyen onun mücâzâtını görecektir."* (Zilzâl, 8) hitâb-ı ilâhîsine muhâtab olacaksın.

Size "Yollar kapandı, sele kapılıp gidiyorsunuz, Hakk'ın kerem kapısından kovuldunuz." diyemem doğrusu. Belki yarın kıyâmet gününde öyle bir lütf u ihsan, kerem ve fazilet kapısı açılır ki, iblis ile azılı kâfirler bile merhamet ümidine kapılırlar. Yalnız şu kadarını söyleyeyim, Hak Teâlâ Kur'ân-ı Kerîm'inde kendisinin *"Günahı bağışlayan, tövbeyi kabul eden ve azâbı çetin olan."* (Mü'min, 3) olduğunu haber veriyor. Öyleyse siz tövbe ile ve onun hoşnut olacağı amellerle mağfiret kapısına yakınlaşmaya çalışın, günahları terk ederek de cezâ kapısından uzaklaşmaya bakın. O'nun azamet ve kudretine aşinâ âlimlerin ondan korktuğu gibi, siz de O'ndan korkun. O'nun kerem ve ihsanına güvenerek O'ndan ümitvar olun. Çünkü müminin ümidi, korkusu kadar olmalıdır. Hatta, korku ile ümit tartılsa biri diğerinden eksik ya da fazla olmamalıdır.

En son, Hakk'ın huzuruna varılacak ve O'na dönülecektir. Her şey ecelini tamamlayacak ve aslına dönecektir. Durum böylece devam edip gider. Nitekim Hak Teâlâ Hazretleri de şöyle buyurur: *"Sizi topraktan yarattık, yine oraya döndüreceğiz ve bir kez daha ondan çıkaracağız."* (Tâ-Hâ, 55).[130]

- "Resûlullah sallellahu aleyhi ve sellem şöyle buyurdular:

Allah kıyâmet gününde sizleri yalın ayak, başı açık diriltecek, kendisi Arşı üzerinden durup uzak ve aklında olan herkesin duyabileceği yüksek bir sesle şöyle nidâ edecek:

Ben Deyyan'ım! Katımda zulüm yoktur! İzzetim ve Celâlim hakkı için bir fiske, bir elin bir ele vurması kadar basit bir haksızlık olsa dahi haberim vardır. İlâhim'den kayıp olmaz! Boynuzsuz koyunun hakkını mutlaka boynuzludan alacağım; taşa, niçin çarptığını, çomağa neden saplandığını mutlaka soracağım! Peygamber devam ederek şöyle buyurdu: İşte bana: *"Biz kıyâmet gününe mahsus adâlet terazileri koyacağız. Artık hiçbir kimse hiçbir şeyle haksızlığa uğramayacaktır."* (Enbiyâ, 47) âyeti bunun için nâzil olmuştur.[131]

130 Ahmed er-Rifâî, *Mârifet Yolu*, s. 126-127.

131 Ahmed er-Rifâî, *Vaazlar*, s. 79.

- Ehl-i sünnetin inancı odur ki: Kıyâmet günü mümin kulunu zâtına yaklaştırır ve onunla hesaplaşır. Onu bir yanına alır, insanların görmemesi için saklar.

Abdullah b. Ömer'den rivayet edildiğine göre; Resûlullah (s.a.s) Efendimiz şöyle buyurmuştur:

"Mümin kul, kıyâmet günü getirilir, Yüce Hakk'a yaklaştırılır. Onu, insanlardan gizlemek için bir yanına alır, sonra şöyle buyurur: 'Kulum, şu günahını biliyor musun?'

Bunu iki kere sorar. Kul da şöyle der: 'Evet, Yâ Rabbi biliyorum.' Böylece, bütün günahlarını ona söyletir. Bu durumda, kul, kendisinin helâke gittiğini anlar. Yüce Hak şöyle buyurur: 'Kulum, günahların bunlardır, ama ben onları dünyada iken gizledim. Bugün dahi, o günahlardan ötürü seni bağışlıyorum.'"

Burada hesaplaşmanın mânâsı şudur: Allahu Teâlâ'nın, kuluna iyi amelleri ve kötü amellerini okumak sûreti ile amellerine karşılık sevabını ve azâbını anlatmasıdır. Keza, kulun iyiliğine ve kötülüğüne olan şeyleri dahi böylelikle bildirmesidir.

Ne var ki, Muattıla zümresi, bu hesaplaşma işini inkâr etmişlerdir. Allahu Teâlâ ise, onların yalanlarını şu şekilde yüzlerine vurmaktadır:

"Onların dönüşleri ancak bizedir; keza onlarla hesaplaşmak dahi bize düşer." (Gâşiye, 25-26).

Ehl-i sünnet ulemâsının itikadına göre: Allahu Teâlâ'nın terazisi vardır. Bununla kıyâmet günü, iyilikleri ye kötülükleri tartacaktır.

Bu terazinin iki gözü, bir de ölçüyü gösteren dili vardır.

Mutezile, Murcie ve Haricîlerle birlikte bu teraziyi inkâr etti, şöyle dedi: Terazinin mânâsı adâlettir. Amellerin tartılması değildir.

Ne var ki, Allah'ın kitabında, Resûlullah'ın hadîs-i şerifinde onların yalana çıktıkları görülmektedir.

Allahu Teâlâ şöyle buyurdu:

"Kıyâmet günü için adâlet terazileri kuracağız; hiç kimseye zulüm olunmayacak. Bir tohum ağırlığında olsa dahi onu getireceğiz. Hesapçılar nâmına biz yeteriz." (Enbiyâ, 47).

Bir başka âyet-i kerîmede ise, Allahu Teâlâ şöyle buyurdu:

"O gün, kimin terazide iyilik tartısı ağır gelirse; hoşnut olacağı bir yaşantıya kavuşur.

Her kimin de iyilikleri terazide hafif gelir ise, onun anası Hâviye cehennemidir. O Hâviye'nin ne olduğunu sana ne anlatabilir? O, zorlu harareti olan bir ateştir." (Kâri'a, 6-11).

Halbuki adâlet, ağırlıkla, hafiflikle bir sıfat alamaz. Terazi, şanı Yüce Rahmân'ın elinde olacaktır. Zira, bizzat kulların hesabını o görecektir.

Bu mânâda, Nevvas b. Sem'an Kilâbî'nin (r.a) şöyle dediği anlatılmıştır:

Resûlullah (s.a.s) Efendimiz'in şöyle buyurduğunu dinledim:

"Terazi, Azîz ve Celîl olan Rahmân'ın elinde olacaktır. Kıyâmet günü, bu terazi yolu ile birtakım kimseleri yükseltirken, birtakım kimseleri de düşürecektir."

Bir başka rivayete göre de bu terazi, Cebrâil aleyhisselâmın elinde olacaktır. Bu rivayet, Huzeyfe'den (r.a) gelmiştir. Demiştir ki: Teraziye bakacak olan Cebrâil'dir. Rabbi ona şöyle buyuracaktır:

"Tart, ey Cebrâil, kullarım arasında amellerini tartıcı ol."

Ameller tartılmaya başlanır; bazısı bazısından daha ağır gelir.

Abdullah b. Ömer'den (r.a) gelen bir rivayete göre; Resûlullah (s.a.s) Efendimiz şöyle buyurmuştur:

"Kıyâmet günü terazi kurulur. Bir adam da getirilir terazinin bir gözüne konur, sayılı ameli dahi diğer gözüne konur. Ama amelleri onu çekemez. Allahu Teâlâ, onu cehenneme doğru yollar. Tam cehenneme yollanacağı sırada, Rahmân tarafından şöyle bir ses gelir: 'Acele etmeyiniz, acele etmeyiniz; onun kalan bir ameli vardır denilir.'

Bundan sonra, üzerinde 'Lâ ilâhe illallah' (Allah'tan başka ilâh yoktur) kelime-i tevhidi yazılan bir şey getirilir; teraziye konur. O getirilen şey, o iyilikleri bulunan göze konur ve terazi ağır gelir. Bunun üzerine, onun cennete götürülmesi için emir verilir."[132]

132 Abdülkâdir Geylânî, *Gunyetü't-Tâlibîn,* Fasıl 15, s. 210-212.

Kenan Rifâî Hazretleri Sohbetler kitabında şöyle diyor:

- "Dün Ekrem'e (Mimar Ekrem Hakkı Ayverdi) dedim ki: Mimarım diye niçin böbürleniyorsun? Biz de mimarız. Herkes hayatı binasının mimarıdır.

Farazâ sen, yaptığın bir yapıyı, fena malzeme kullanır, çürük ve hesapsız yaparsan, yaptığın bina yıkılır, neticede seni mes'ûl ederler. İnsanların buldukları, ferah, keder, cennet, cehennem, iyilik ve fenalık da hayatları binasını iyi veya fena kurmuş olmalarındandır. Erdiğimiz neticenin mes'ûliyeti başkalarının değil, kendimizindir.

Eğer biz de vücûdumuz binasını çürük ahlâklar ve kötülükler ile yaparsak, günün birinde kendi kendine çöküverir. Nihayet Cenâb-ı Hakk'ın huzuruna çıkarılıp: Ben sana bu vücûdu emânet vermiştim. Onu niçin çürük ve kötü malzeme ile bina ettin? diye muhakeme edilir ve neticede de mahkûm oluruz."[133]

- Dikkat et senin her sözün, düşüncen ve hareketinle gene senin nasibin bina edilmektedir. Yalnız seninki değil, beşerin nasibi de beraber. İyi yapmak kudreti sensin, kötü yapmak kudreti de sensin. Sen, dışarı ile mukayyet değilsin. Dışarı seninle mukayyettir, yani tabiat, sana bakarak tabiat olur. Kavme olsun, ferde olsun, her elem ve keder, kendi hevâ-yı nefislerinin hârice çıkıp kendilerine çarpmasından ileri gelmiştir. Âd kavmini helâk eden sarsar rüzgârı, o kavmin içinden taşan hevâ-yı nefisti. Sen tabiat mahsûlü değilsin, tabiat senin mâkesindir. Lütuf istersen eğer, lütfu evvela kendinde halket, lütuf güneşi gibi ışıklarını eksiksiz her tarafa yay. Yok eğer kahır çeşmelerini açarsan, bil ki kendi destine de kahır dolacaktır. Hilkate ait her şey senden çıkar, sana gelir. Mesut mu oldun, kendin yapmışsındır. Bedbaht mı oldun, nâfile sebep sorma, gene kendin yapmışsındır."[134]

- Bu dünyadaki siyasetler, darplar, zilletler, işte hep hevâ-yı nefsin semereleridir. Demek oluyor ki gerek bir kavme gerek bir ferde karşı zuhur eden elemler, kederler, siyasetler, belâlar hep o kavmin veya ferdin,

133 Ken'an Rifâî, *Sohbetler*, s. 426.

134 Sâmiha Ayverdi vd., *Yirminci Asrın Işığında Müslümanlık*, s. 289.

içlerinde gömülü olan hevâ-yı nefislerinin ve müştehâ-yı tabiatlarının (tabiatlarının arzularının) hârice çıkıp kendilerine karşı gelmesidir."[135]

• Tarihin kaydettiği ve en eski dediği Sokrat, Eflatun, Fisagor gibi büyük kimselerin anlayışlarıyla, Mûsâ, Îsâ ve bütün dinleri ihata eden Muhammed dininde gösterildiği gibi, asıl bu sözleri söylememize sebep olan: Allah insanı iyi gördüğünden ayırmasın temennisine karşı, işte bu zatlar diyorlar ki: Hayat, kederleri, elemleri, sürur ve neşâtı ile, hep geçmişte kazanılan şeylerin semeresidir.

Mesela Sokrat der ki: İnsan, kendi felâketini kendi hazırladığı gibi, saadetini de yine kendi hazırlar.

Resûlullah Efendimiz de buyuruyor ki: *"Öldükten sonra başınıza neler geleceğini bilseniz, iştihâ ile yemek yemez, istirâhatle uyuyamaz, başınızı alıp dağdan dağa kaçardınız."*

Cenâb-ı Hak da Kur'ân-ı Kerîm'de: *"Zerre kadar hayır işleyen hayır bulur, zerre kadar şer işleyen şer bulur. Ve yine: İyilik yaptığınız vakit kendiniz için yapıyorsunuz, kötülük yaptığınız vakit yine kendiniz için yapıyorsunuz."* buyurur.

İşte, bütün bunlar ve buna benzer nice sözleri insan görüp işitiyor da yine kuru kafalar bunlardan ders almıyor. Gelişi güzel, ulu orta yapmadığımız kalmıyor. Evet ama sonu çok acı! Hâsılı şunda ve bunda ve kendimizde gördüğümüz vakalar, felâket veya saadet, hâdiselerin hükme bağlandığı ilâhî mahkemede verilen kararların icra ve infazından başka bir şey değildir.

Allah'ımıza sığınalım da lûtf-ı hafîsiyle muamele etmesini niyaz edelim. Yoksa Hazreti Âdem'in dediği gibi: *"Yâ Rabbî, biz nefsimize zulmeyledik, eğer sen merhamet etmez ve bizi affetmezsen hüsranda kalanlardan oluruz."* (A'râf, 23).

Meliha Hanımefendi: "O ilâhî mahkemenin verdiği hükmü Cenâb-ı Hak sevgilileri yüzü suyu hürmetine hayırlara çevirir inşallah."

"Onun çevrilmesi güç Meliha! Ateş düştüğü yeri yakar. İtfaiyenin vazifesi, ateşin genişlemesine mâni olmak olduğu gibi, ehlullâhın

135 Sâmiha Ayverdi vd., *a.g.e.*, s. 437.

himmeti de o cürüm ve isyan ateşlerinin yayılıp îmanı yakmaması içindir. Yoksa, çıkan ok tene vurur. Evliyânın himmeti, onun cana geçmesine mâni olur."[136]

Hocamız Kenan Rifâî Hazretleri, üzüntülü bir hâdise sonucunda kendisine aniden gelen şeker hastalığının sebebini soran müridine şöyle cevap veriyor: "Oğlum bizler mânen hâdiselerden etkilenmeyiz. Ama mâlumâlinizdir ki, kabuklar devamlı baskıdan aşınırlar ama içindeki inciye bir şey olmaz. Biz hastalansak bile içimizdeki huzur bozulmaz, bilakis Allah'la irtibatımız aşikâr olur.[137]

• Kenan Rifâî'nin yakınlardan birinin yarın mahkemeye gideceğinden bahsedilirken, etraftan biri: Kim bilir bu davanın neticesini düşünerek ne heyecan geçiriyordur, dedi:

"Bundan, bizim de mahşer gününde olacak mahkememiz için heyecan geçirip geçirmediğimizi düşündüm de hatırıma, Kur'ân-ı Kerîm'de Cenâb-ı Hakk'ın buyurdukları geldi: *'Herkes yarın buradaki ameliyle cezâlanacaktır. Allah'ın emri yolunda gitmeyenler cehenneme sevk olunacaklardır ve orada cehennem zebanileri (zebun olduğumuz şeyler): Size Cenâb-ı Hakk'ın emirlerini söyleyen ve sizi mahşer günü ile tehdit eden resûller gelmedi mi? Niçin onları dinleyip yolunuzu düzeltmediniz de dünyanın yalancı ve geçici olan zevklerine dalıp Allah'ınızı unuttunuz? Şimdi cehenneme giriniz ve orada dâim kalınız. Bu cehennem, kibirliler için ne çirkin bir yerdir.'* (Zümer, 71-72) diyeceklerdir.

Allah'ın emirlerini memurlarından dinleyip, Hakk'ın razı olduğu yolda giderek Allah'a bağlı olan ikinci kısma ise Cenâb-ı Hakk'ın hazinedarları: *'Hoş geldiniz, Allah'ın selâmı üzerinize olsun, buyurun... Cennetlere girin ve orada dâim olarak kalın.'* (Zümer, 73) diyecekler.

İşte, Allah'ın bu sözlerinden haberimiz yok, bilmiyoruz, duymadık okumadık... diyenlere de ben dilimin döndüğü kadar söylüyorum. İster bunları can evinize kabul ediniz, isterseniz baş çeviriniz."[138]

---

136 Ken'an Rifâî, *Sohbetler*, s. 357.

137 *Derleyenin Notu.*

138 Ken'an Rifâî, *Sohbetler*, s. 455.

• Sâmiha Hanım: "Kayınvalidem, dinin bütün emirlerine harfiyen riâyet eden fakat yaptıklarını bir sevap ve ecir mukabilinde yapan bir hanım. Kocam ise dinî vazifelerine kayıtsız olmakla beraber iyi kalpli ve etrafına karşı hayırhah bir adam. Bu ikisini mukayese ettikçe, kocamın Allah indinde daha makbul olacağını zannediyorum."

"Mademki danışıyorsun, danıştığın kimse, doğruyu söylemek mecburiyetindedir. Şunu bil ki Allah, kullarından irfân-ı Muhammedî istiyor. Kendini bilmek istiyor. Dinî emirlere riâyet, senin menfaatin icâbıdır. Ve bunu yapmakla, insanlıktan maksut olanı hâsıl etmiş olmazsın. Keza, iyilik yapmak da yine insanlığın icâbıdır. Tabiî buna mukabil, Allah senin dünyalığını artırır ve karşılığını dünyada verir. Fakat yine matlûp hâsıl olmuş olmaz. Maksat kalb-i selîmdir. Ya bizzat kendin bu kalb-i selîme mâlik olacaksın yahut bir kalb-i selîm sahibi bulup onun gönlüne gireceksin.

Ben, çocukluğumda koca Dolmabahçe Sarayı'nı emektarımız olan bir bahçıvan çırağının sayesinde görmüştüm. İşte, ya saraylı, yani saraya mensup olacaksın yahut da o saraya mensup olanın kılavuzluğundan faydalanacaksın.

Âlim ol, allâme ol, ne olursan ol, elinde pasaport, yani geçiş tezkeresi olmadan seni bir memleketten bir memlekete sokmazlar. Hatta resmî veya husussî büyük bir ziyafete, davetiye tezkeresi olmadan girebilir misin? Ancak kapıda, o davet sahibinin bir dostunu bir yakınını görürsen seni içeri alırlar. İşte şefaatin mânâsı budur."[139]

• Kıyâmet gününde şefaat edecek üç sınıf insan vardır: Âlim, hâdim, yani insanlara hizmet eden kişi ve hâline sabreden fakir.[140]

• İşlerinizi güçlü kuvvetli, cesur, cömert birine tevdi ettik. Ona, size aslan payını vermesini ve en cüretli okla sizi korumasını söyledik. Ne söylediyse, onu biz söylemişiz. Ne yaptıysa onu biz yaptık. Bizim dilimizle konuşuyor. Bizim vicdanımızdaki düşünceleri tercüme etmektedir. Ona ölülerinizi diriltme, bölük pörçük halinizi derleme,

139 Ken'an Rifâî, *Sohbetler*, s. 418-419.

140 Cemâlnur Sargut, *Âyetü'l-Kürsî*, s. 114.

kızlarınızı güvende kılma, bitkilerinizi yetiştirme, bilmediklerinizi size öğretme, zaman uzasa da sayılarınız gün be gün artsa da eninde sonunda bize döneceğinizi size bildirme gücünü verdik. O halde: *"İşittik ve itaat ettik."* deyin. Sizden önce, işittik, ama isyan ettik diyenler gibi olmayın. Bunu söyledikleri için biz onları kasıp kavuran sabâ yelleriyle darmadağın ettik. Durmadan artan yağmurlarla öldürdük. Onları helâk ederek köklerini kuruttuk. Onlar hakkında verilen azap sözü gerçekleşmiş oldu. Onları kırıp geçirdik. Öyle ki yurtlarında bir tek canlı kalmadı. Onların başına gelen bu felaket Tubba ve İrem'i de kapladı.

O halde bizim dehşet verici egemenliğimize karşı çıkmaya yeltenmeyin. Azâbımızın elçisine saldırdığınızda azâbın size geç geleceğini düşünmeyin. Sizden önce nice örnekler gelip geçti. Bize karşı çıktığınız zaman başınıza geleceğini vadettiğimiz azap mutlaka gelecektir. Sizden sadır olan tavırlarınızdan ötürü, onun baş göstermesini beklemekteyiz. Sizden muhalefet tavrı sadır olduğunda bizden size bu azap intikâl edecektir. Olan olduğunda azâbın yönü size doğru çevrilecektir. Aslında yalnızca yapıp ettikleriniz size dönmekte olan. Eğer hayır işlerseniz hayırla karşılaşırsınız (*"Kim zerre ağırlığınca hayır işlerse onu görür. Kim zerre ağırlığınca şer işlerse onu görür."*).[141]

- Sâlih Peygamber hikâyesine bakarsak:

Mesnevî'ye göre Sâlih Peygamber'in devesi sâlihlerin, velîlerin ve nebîlerin bir timsaliydi. Böyle Allah'a yakınlık kazanmış kimselere fenâlık etmek çok tehlikelidir, iki cihanda hüsrana sebeptir. Cenâb-ı Hak kendi sâlihlerini korur, hatta böylelerine kötülük edenleri şiddetle cezâlandırmak için sebep halkeder. Allah'ın yarattığı deve kendi payına düşen suyu içsin diye, Sâlih Peygamber, Semûd kavmine seslenmiş, onları kötülükten uyandırmak istemişti. Bu, Kur'ân-ı Kerîm'in Şems Sûresi'nde şu âyetlerle beyan olunmuştur: *"Semûd milleti, içlerinden en kötüleri ayaklanınca, kendilerine gönderilen peygamberi yalanladı. Allah'ın peygamberi onlara devesini göstermiş ve: 'Allah'ın bu devesine ve onun su hissesine dokunmayın! demişti. Fakat onu yalancı sandılar ve devesini kestiler. Allah da günahları yüzünden onları kırıp yerle bir etti."*

141 Muhyiddin İbn Arabî, *Risaleler*, c. 2, s. 59-60.

(Şems, 11-15). Bu deve bir nâka, yani bir dişi deve idi. (...) Korkunç bir zelzele oldu. (...) Bütün bir şehir, bütün canlılarla birden yerle bir oldu.[142]

Aşağıda anlatılacağı gibi bu yok oluşta, mânevî güzelliklere sahip olanlar zarar görmez. Zarar görenler, Peygamber'in emirlerine uymayıp bölünenler Allah sevgililerini reddedenlerdir.[143]

- Bilmezler mi ki Allah dostlarının ruhlarını incitmeye gelmez. Çünkü onların ruhu, Sâlih Peygamber gibidir. Ve Tanrı ile devamlı vuslat halindedirler. Vücut ise deve gibidir. Birtakım ihtiyaçlar içindedir. Şu demek ki: Allah'la vuslata erişmiş, sâlih bir ruh için beden üzerine indirilen darbeleri duymaya takat yoktur. Böyle ruhlar, o büyük vuslatın şevki içinde, maddî acıları hissetmezler. Böylelerinin vücutlarına her ne türlü eziyet yapılsa, ruhları bundan zarar görmez. Bir ruh, bir kere Allah'ta dirilmek rütbesine ermiş olmasın, bu ruhun duyduğu zevki ve şevki, eziyet şöyle dursun, bizzat vücûdunun ölümü bile, hatta bir an için gölgeleyemez. Kaldı ki, bedende ruh, sedef içinde inci gibidir. Kötülüğün vuracağı darbeler olsa olsa sedefleri incitir. İçlerindeki inciyi değil. Şüphesiz Sâlih'in ruhundan murat; velîlerin, nebîlerin ruhudur. Yahut velîlere, nebîlere uymuş ve nefislerini yenmeye muvaffak olmuş, saf ve temiz müminlerin ruhudur. Hak yolunda yürüyenlerin ruhudur ki, böyle ruhlar esasen dış âfetlerin ve kötülerin mağlûbu olmaz. Çünkü bir velînin vücûdu kabında saklı ruh suyu, aslında, ilâhî ırmakla alışveriş halinde olup o ırmakla beslenmektedir. Bu yüzden bir velînin sûretinde görünen nur, böyle parlak bir ırmaktan akseder. Bunun içindir ki bir hadîs-i kudsîde Allah: *"Bir velîme kötü muamele eden kişi, hakîkatte bana karşı savaş açmış demektir."* buyurur. Bir hadîs-i şerifte ise *"Beni inciten, Hakk'ı incitir."* deniyor. Velîler ve nebîler, yani ruhları Hak'la alışverişte olanlar, yeryüzünde ne arıyorlar sualinin cevabı şudur ki, Hakk'a ulaşmak isteyen insan, velîlerde tecellî eden Hak nurunu görsün, onunla aydınlansın, onu kendine rehber ve örnek sayıp dünya kirlerinden temizlensin, îmana, hakîkat nuruna, bir kelime ile Allah'ına ulaşsın. İşte bunun içindir ki zâlimlerin ve kâfirlerin hiçbir darbesi, velîlerin ruhunu bulmaz. Olsa olsa vücûdunu incitir. Velîlerin vücutları devesine, aklın varsa kul köle

142 Ken'an Rifâî, *Şerhli Mesnevî-i Şerif*, s. 367-368.

143 *Derleyenin Notu.*

ol, ki bu sayede Sâlih Peygamber'le yoldaş olasın! Ruhun Sâlih'in ruhu gibi ilâhî ırmağa akan su olsun.[144]

Zelzelenin hakîkatine bakarsak, Mesnevî'nin aşağıdaki bölümü bize bazı hakîkatleri açıklamaktadır:[145]

- "Bu âlem, bu kâinat ve bütün yaratılmışlar bir âlem-i kevn ü fesâd içindedirler. Şu demek ki kâinatta her şey, bir taraftan yaratılmak bir taraftan bozulup, çürüyüp yok olmak şeklinde değişmez bir kanuna tâbidir. Bu kanun, yalnız insan için, yalnız diğer canlılar ve nebatlar için değil, bizim cemâdat dediğimiz, ölü, cansız ve donmuş sandığımız uzak ve yakın, bütün varlıklar için de kanundur. Bir münâcâtında, Fuzûlî,

Gehî toprağa eyler hikmetin bin mehlika pinhan
Gehî sun'un kılur toprâğdan bin mehlika peydâ.

diye düşünür. "(Yâ Rabbî) senin yüce hikmetin dem olur, binlerce ay yüzlü güzeli toprağa gizler, fakat senin büyük san'atın aynı demde ve aynı topraktan binlerce ay yüzlü güzel yaratır." der.

Dünya, böyledir. Bize bazen kahır, bazen lütuf yüzüyle bakar; bizi bazen sabır, bazen şükür duygularıyla doldurur. Aynı toprak, gün olur yeşil yapraklı ağaçlar ve güzel yemişlerle gülümser. Sonra sonbahar olur, Allah'ın kahır ve celâl sıfatlarını hatırlatırcasına bu ağaçlarda ne meyve ne yaprak kalır. Bütün bunlar, bize varlık ve yokluk mevzuunda düşünme imkânı verir. Varlıktan ve yokluktan bize rüzgâr getirir. Âlemleri aydınlatan güneş bile öyledir. Doğar, göklere yükselir sonra zevale yüz tutar, baş aşağı düşüp batıcı olur. Yıldızlar da öyle... Gece gökleri süsleyen bu varlıklar, gün olur, birbirlerine fazla yaklaşmaktan doğan bir çarpışma içinde yanar ve yok olurlar. Bize Güneş'ten daha güzel görünen Ay'ın, zamanla bir veremli gibi incelip hilâl ve sonra büsbütün hayal olması da böyledir. Demek ki kâinatta her şey zevale yüz tutucu, yokluğa boyun eğicidir. Düzgün duran yeryüzünün bir zelzele ile tanınmayacak hale gelmesi, nice yüce dağların zamanla toz gibi dağılması, bize nefes ve hayat veren havanın bir gün zehirli gazlarla dolup öldürücü olması, hayat kaynağı olan suyun, aynı kapta

144 Ken'an Rifâî, *Şerhli Mesnevî-i Şerif*, s. 368-369.

145 *Derleyenin Notu.*

havuzda veya gölde uzun müddet kalınca bozulup, bulanıp kokması ve kirlenmesi; dehşet saçan ateşin bir rüzgârla parlayıp yok olması ve mesela ortalığı aydınlatmakla mağrur bir mum ateşinin bir üf demekle sönmesi, bütün bunlar hep aynı varlık ve yokluk mefhumlarının akla gelen örnekleridir."[146]

- Nimetullah-i Nahcuvânî (rahmetullahu aleyh), bu sûrenin tefsirini şu nasihatle bitirmiştir: "Ey Cenâb-ı Hakk'a yönelmiş mümin! Sâlih amellere sarıl, ihlâs ve huşû ile güzel amellerini artır. Bütün bozuk ve kötü işlerinden elini çek; çek ki âhirette en güzel karşılığı göresin. Bütün iş, hâl ve amellerinde bu âyetleri göz önünde tut. Böyle yaparsan sürekli zikir halinde olursun ve yaptığın amellerin ne sonuç vereceğini çok iyi anlarsın. Allah Teâlâ, bizi lütuf ve keremiyle, sürekli zikreden, her uyarıdan öğüt alan ve âyetlerin gereğince amel eden kullarından eylesin." (Nahcuvânî, *el-Fevâtihu'l-İlâhiye*, 2/525).[147]

146 Ken'an Rifâî, *Şerhli Mesnevî-i Şerif*, s. 177-178.

147 İbn Acîbe el-Hasenî, *Bahrü'l-Medîd*, c. 11, s. 107 dipnot.

KAYNAKÇA

Abdülkâdir Geylânî, *Cilâü'l-Hâtır*, ter. Dilaver Gürer, yay. haz. Ercan Alkan, İstanbul, 2004.

Abdülkâdir Geylânî, *Gunyetü't-Tâlibîn,* çev. Doç. Dr. Abdülvehhab Öztürk, Saadet Yayınevi, İstanbul, 2008.

Ahmed Avni Konuk, *Fusûsu'l-Hikem Tercüme ve Şerhi*, 2013.

https://islamvetasavvuf13.wordpress.com/category/tasavvuf-kitaplari/fusu-sul-hikem-tercume-ve-serhi-a-avni-konuk/

Ahmed er-Rifâî, *Mârifet Yolu el- Burhânü'l Müeyyed*, ter. Prof. Dr. H. Kâmil Yılmaz, Erkam Yayınları, İstanbul, 2004.

Ahmed er-Rifâî, *Onların Âlemi,* ter. Abdülkadir Akçiçek, Alperen Yayınları, Ankara, 2005, 1. Basım.

Ahmed er-Rifâî, *Vaazlar*, sad. Naim Erdoğan, ed. Arif Pamuk, Pamuk Yayıncılık, İstanbul, 2005.

Ahmed er-Rifâî, *Sohbet Meclisleri*, ter. Dr. Ali Can Tatlı, Erkam Yayınları, İstanbul, 2003.

Bekir Topaloğlu, Zilzal Suresi, *DİA*, 2013, c. 44.

Cemâlnur Sargut, *Âyetü'l-Kürsî*, Nefes Yayınları, İstanbul, 2013, 1. Baskı.

Elmalılı Hamdi Yazır, *Hak Dini Kur'an Dili*, sad. İ. Karaçam-E. Işık-N. Bolelli-A Yücel, yay. Zehraveyn, Azim Dağıtım, İstanbul, 2011, c. 9.

Fahreddîn-i Irâkî, *Lemaât -Aşk Metafiziği-*, ter. Ercan Alkan, Hayy Kitap, İstanbul, 2012.

Halûk Nurbaki, *Namaz Sureleri Yorumu,* Damla Yayınevi, İstanbul, 2003, 7. Baskı.

İbn Acîbe el-Hasenî, *Bahrü'l-Medîd*, ter. Doç Dr. Dilaver Selvi, Semerkand, İstanbul, 2015, 4. Baskı, c. 1, 11.

İbn Arabî, *Fütûhât-ı Mekkiyye*, çev. Ekrem Demirli, Litera Yayıncılık, İstanbul, 2006, c. 2.

İbn Arabî, *Fütûhât-ı Mekkiyye*, çev. Ekrem Demirli, Litera Yayıncılık, İstanbul, c. 9.

İbn Arabî, *Fütûhât-ı Mekkiyye*, çev. Ekrem Demirli, Litera Yayıncılık, İstanbul, c. 13.

İbn Arabî, *Fütûhât-ı Mekkiyye*, çev. Ekrem Demirli, Litera Yayıncılık, İstanbul, 2012, c. 18.

İsmail Hakkı Bursevî, *Kenz-i Mahfi*, çev. Abdülkâdir Akçiçek, Bahar Yayınları, İstanbul, 2000, 5. Basım.

İsmail Hakkı Bursevî, *Rûhu'l-Beyân Tefsîri*, Damla Yayınevi, İstanbul, 2010, 7. Baskı, c. 10.

Kâzım Büyükaksoy, *Ken'an Rifâî'den Mesnevî Hatıraları*, ed. A. Eylül Yalçınkaya, Nefes Yayınları, İstanbul,

Ken'an Rifâî, *Sohbetler*, Kubbealtı Neşriyat, İstanbul, 2000, 2. Baskı.

Ken'an Rifâî, *Sohbetler*, Kubbealtı Neşriyâtı, İstanbul, 2010, 2. Baskı.

Ken'an Rifâî, *Şerhli Mesnevî-i Şerif*, Kubbealtı Neşriyâtı, İstanbul, 2000, 2. Baskı.

Metinlerle Tasavvuf Terimleri Sözlüğü, ed. Zafer Erginli, Kalem Yayınevi, İstanbul, 2006.

Mevlânâ, *Fîhi Mâfih*, çev. M. Ülker Tarıkâhya, Milli Eğitim Basımevi, İstanbul, 1985.

Muhyiddin İbn Arabî, *Risaleler*, ter. Vahdettin İnce, Kitsan, İstanbul, tarihsiz, c. 2.

Muhyiddin İbn Arabî, *Tefsîr-i Kebîr Te'vilât*, çev. Vahdettin İnce, Kitsan Yayınları, İstanbul, tarihsiz, c. 2. (Bu tefsir yanlışlıkla İbn Arabî'ye nispetle *Tefsir-i Kebir Te'vilât* ismiyle basılmış olup, aslında Kâşânî'ye aittir. Kâşâniyyü's-Semerkandî, Kemalüddin Abdürrezzak, *Te'vilât-ı Kâşâniyye*, çev. Ali Rıza Doksanyedi, haz. Vehbi Güloğlu, Ankara, Kadıoğlu Matbaası, 1987.)

Niyazî-i Mısrî, *İrfan Sofraları*, çev. Prof. Dr. Süleyman Ateş, Yeni Ufuklar Neşriyat, İstanbul, tarihsiz.

Sâmiha Ayverdi, *Dost*, Kubbealtı Neşriyâtı, İstanbul, 2010, 5. Baskı.

Sâmiha Ayverdi, *Ezelî Dostlar*, Kubbealtı Neşriyâtı, İstanbul, 2009, 2. Baskı.

Sâmiha Ayverdi, *Mülâkatlar*, Kubbealtı Neşriyâtı, İstanbul, 2005.

Sâmiha Ayverdi, *Yaşayan Ölü*, Kubbealtı Neşriyâtı, İstanbul, 2009, 4. Baskı.

Sâmiha Ayverdi-Safiye Erol-Nezihe Araz-Sofi Huri, *Yirminci Asrın Işığında Müslümanlık,* Kubbealtı Neşriyâtı, İstanbul, 2003, 5. Baskı.

Sehl b. Abdullah Tüsterî, *Tüsterî Tefsiri,* çev. Ömer Güngören, Mahmud Ulucan, Nefes Yayınları, İstanbul, 2022, 1. Baskı.

Suad el-Hakîm, *İbnü'l-Arabî Sözlüğü*, çev. Ekrem Demirli, Kabalcı Yayınevi, İstanbul, 2005, 1. Baskı.

Sultan Veled, *İbtidâ-nâme*, çev. Abdülbâkî Gölpınarlı, Konya ve Mülhakatı Eski Eserleri Sevenler Derneği, Konya, 2001.

Sultan Veled, *Maârif*, çev. Meliha Anbarcıoğlu, Konya ve Mülhakatı Eski Eserleri Sevenler Derneği, Konya, 2002.

Şefik Can, *Mesnevî Tercümesi*, Ötüken Neşriyat, İstanbul, c. 2.

GENEL DİZİN